Internationalization and Employability in Higher Education

Providing an analysis of the relationship between *Internationalization and Employability in Higher Education*, this book considers the perspectives of both students and employers to illustrate how to reach positive employment outcomes for all stakeholders.

Through a wide range of international case studies, this book delivers some key messages, including:

- The articulation of the link between internationalization and employability;
- The need for higher education institutions to communicate the benefits of an internationalized higher education beyond the academy;
- The need to ensure equity of graduate outcomes through enhanced internationalization at home;
- The impact of immigration policy on national benefits of internationalization of higher education;
- International study as a route to employability for migration purposes and building knowledge-based economies.

Considering the skills developed by students through mobility experiences, while exploring the need for enhanced internationalization of the curriculum at home, *Internationalization and Employability in Higher Education* will be a key resource for any higher education policy makers or university staff associated with careers, employment, and integrated learning. It contains important messages for employers and recruiters.

Robert Coelen is Professor of Internationalisation of Higher Education at NHL Stenden University of Applied Sciences, Leeuwarden, the Netherlands.

Cate Gribble is Senior Policy Analyst in the Office of Research Strategy at the University of Auckland, New Zealand.

Internationalization in Higher Education
Series editor: Elspeth Jones
Emerita Professor, Leeds Beckett University, UK

This series addresses key themes in the development of internationalisation within Higher Education. Up to the minute and international in both appeal and scope, books in the series focus on delivering contributions from a wide range of contexts and provide both theoretical perspectives and practical examples. Written by some of the leading experts in the field, they are vital guides that discuss and build upon evidence-based practice and provide a clear evaluation of outcomes.

The Globalization of Internationalization
Emerging Voice and Perspectives
Hans de Wit, Jocelyne Gacel-Ávila, Elspeth Jones and Nico Jooste

Intercultural Competence in Higher Education
International Approaches, Assessment and Application
Darla K. Deardorff and Lily A. Arasaratnam-Smith

Intercultural Interventions in Study Abroad
Jane Jackson and Susan Oguro

The Future Agenda for Internationalization in Higher Education
Next Generation Insights into Research, Policy, and Practice
Douglas Proctor and Laura E. Rumbley

Online Intercultural Education and Study Abroad
Theory into Practice
Jane Jackson

Internationalization and Employability in Higher Education
Robert Coelen and Cate Gribble

For more information about this series, please visit: https://www.routledge.com/ Internationalization-in-Higher-Education-Series/book-series/INTHE

Internationalization and Employability in Higher Education

Edited by
Robert Coelen and Cate Gribble

Routledge
Taylor & Francis Group

LONDON AND NEW YORK

First published 2020
by Routledge
2 Park Square, Milton Park, Abingdon, Oxon, OX14 4RN

and by Routledge
52 Vanderbilt Avenue, New York, NY 10017

Routledge is an imprint of the Taylor & Francis Group, an informa business

British Library Cataloguing-in-Publication Data
A catalogue record for this book is available from the British Library

Library of Congress Cataloging-in-Publication Data
Names: Coelen, Robert, editor. | Gribble, Cate, editor.
Title: Internationalization and employability in higher education / edited by Robert Coelen and Cate Gribble.
Description: Abingdon, Oxon ; New York, NY : Routledge, 2019. | Includes bibliographical references and index.
Identifiers: LCCN 2018061183 | ISBN 9780815368335 (hbk) | ISBN 9780815368342 (pbk) | ISBN 9781351254885 (ebk)
Subjects: LCSH: International education—Case studies. | Foreign study—Case studies. | Employability—Case studies. | Education and globalization—Case studies. | Education, Higher—Aims and objectives—Case studies.
Classification: LCC LC1090 .I5794 2019 | DDC 370.116—dc23
LC record available at https://lccn.loc.gov/2018061183

ISBN: 978-0-8153-6833-5 (hbk)
ISBN: 978-0-8153-6834-2 (pbk)
ISBN: 978-1-351-25488-5 (ebk)

Typeset in Minion Pro
by Cenveo® Publisher Services

 Printed in the United Kingdom
by Henry Ling Limited

Contents

Figures

Tables

Contributors

Christine Anderson, University of Minnesota, USA

Jos Beelen, The Hague University of Applied Sciences, the Netherlands

Brett Berquist, University of Auckland, New Zealand

Christine Bilsland, Macquarie University, Australia

Mien Wee Cheng, Monash University, Australia

Glenda Crosling, Sunway University, Malaysia

Darla K. Deardorff, Association of International Education Administrators

John Lawrence Dennis, University of Perugia, Italy

Jessica Gallagher, The University of Queensland, Australia

Wendy Green, University of Tasmania, Australia

Saskia Jensen, Goldsmiths, University of London, UK

Martha Johnson, University of Minnesota, USA

Elspeth Jones, Leeds Beckett University, UK

Eva King, The University of Queensland, Australia

Juha Leppänen, Demos Helsinki, Finland

Fion Choon Boey Lim, Victoria University, Australia

Amira El Masri, York University, Canada

Cheryl Matherly, Lehigh University, USA

Ainslie Moore, University of Auckland, New Zealand

Aleksi Neuvonen, Demos Helsinki, Finland

Tran Le Huu Nghia, Ton Duc Thang University, Vietnam

Hiroshi Ota, Hitotsubashi University, Japan

Dolly Predovic, Career Paths, Italy

Vo Phuong Quyen, Can Tho University, Vietnam

Nannette Ripmeester, Expertise in Labour Mobility

Jon Rubin, COIL Consulting

Mika Saarinen, EDUFI, Finland

Yukiko Shimmi, Tohoku University, Japan

Greeja Hemalata De Silva, Sunway College, Malaysia

Wondwosen Tamrat, St Mary's University, Ethiopia

Damtew Teferra, International Network for Higher Education in Africa

Kelly Thomson, York University, Canada

Martin Tillman, Global Career Compass

Roopa Desai Trilokekar, York University, Canada

Editors

 **Robert Coelen,** PhD, is Professor of Internationalisation of Higher Education at NHL Stenden University of Applied Sciences, Leeuwarden, the Netherlands. He holds an appointment as Visiting Professor at the Higher Education Research Institute of Tongji University, Shanghai, China, and is Director of the Centre for Internationalisation of Education, University of Groningen, Campus Fryslân. This centre has a PhD program and hosts candidates from around the world. He is a Research Associate at the Unit for Higher Education Internationalisation in the Developing World at the Nelson Mandela Metropolitan University (NMMU), Port Elizabeth, South Africa. He was formerly Interim Executive Dean at Stenden University, Qatar, Vice-President International at Stenden University of Applied Sciences, and Vice-President International at Leiden University in the Netherlands. He was Director International at The University of Queensland and at James Cook University in Australia. Before taking up these executive roles, he was a molecular biologist for about 25 years, variously at the Peter McCallum Hospital, the University of Western Australia, and James Cook University.

Robert is on the Editorial Board of the *Journal of Studies in International Education* and reviews papers for the *Journal of Applied Research in Higher Education*. He was the Founding Director of Euroscholars, an initiative of the League of European Research Universities and Chair of the Leiden University Global University Ranking Symposia. Robert publishes articles on internationalisation of higher education and co-edits books on the same topic. He has undertaken consultancies and regularly gives workshops, seminars, and keynote addresses. He has moved from being an executive practitioner in the field to being mainly involved in research. His research interests relate to the transforming powers of internationalisation activities on the development of individuals and organisations.

 **Cate Gribble,** PhD, is a Senior Policy Analyst in the Office of Research Strategy at the University of Auckland. Prior to moving to New Zealand, Cate held academic positions at both RMIT University and Deakin University, and remains an Adjunct Principal Fellow in the Science Engineering and Health Education Research (SHEER) Centre, RMIT University.

Cate's research focuses on international student mobility, migration, and employability. She has worked extensively with international students, employers, professional organisations, governments, and universities. Many of her projects have had considerable national and international significance, informing government policy, curriculum design, and university strategy. Between 2010 and 2014, Cate was co-investigator on an Australian Research Council Linkage Project, Investigating stakeholder responses to changing skilled migration policies for Australian international graduates. This national project identified the critical issue of international students and post-study employment and led to multiple projects and government consultancies on the topic. In recognition of her expertise in graduate employability, Cate was invited to give evidence to the 2016 House of Representatives Standing Committee on Education and Employment inquiry into innovation and creativity: a workforce for the future economy.

Authors

Christine Anderson, PhD, is the Academic Director at the University of Minnesota's Learning Abroad Center. Her research on mobility includes gender and cultural mores, intercultural learning on short-term programs, career competency development, and resilience. She teaches/mentors students' intercultural learning while abroad through an online course titled Global Identity: Connecting Your International Experience to Your Future. She has a PhD in comparative international development education.

Jos Beelen, PhD, is Professor of Global Learning at The Hague University of Applied Sciences as well as Visiting Professor at Coventry University. He is a senior trainer for the European Association for International Education. In addition, he conducts workshops with academics and international officers at universities across Europe, in Latin America, and in South Africa. From 2007 onward, he has also published a range of articles on internationalisation at home, some co-authored with scholars in the field from Australia and the United Kingdom.

Brett Berquist is Director International at the University of Auckland. Berquist transitioned from chairing applied languages to international education (IE) administration during the early Erasmus years, where he led a French business school from 10% to 98% IE participation, including internships. He has worked in France, the UK, United States, South Korea, and New Zealand leading internationalisation strategies. He has spoken frequently on the role of internationalisation in employability and co-chairs the content committee for the Global Internship Conference. His most recent publication is Berquist, B., Moore, K., & Milano, J. (Eds.). (2018). *International internships: Mission, methods & models, a collection of papers from the Global Internship Conference*, Boston, MA: Academic Internship Council.

Christine Bilsland is a lecturer, Professional and Community Engagement in the Faculty of Business and Economics, at Macquarie University, Australia. She worked at RMIT Vietnam's Hanoi campus for more than five years and has developed and delivered a range of education and training programs for international audiences. From a tourism industry background, her interest in transnational education began in Singapore, where she coordinated training for work integrated learning at a polytechnic and lectured at the Singapore campus of a UK university. Her research interests include transnational and international education, work integrated learning, and flexible assessment.

Mien Wee Cheng is a Malaysian educator with more than 30 years' experience working in Malaysia's public and private education sectors. Her research addresses contexts and meanings in higher education and curriculum with particular focus on cross-border higher education and educational reforms in Southeast Asia in globalising times. Mien is currently pursuing PhD studies at Monash University, Australia, and has presented her research at international conferences and published in a peer reviewed journal.

Glenda Crosling is Professor and Head, the Centre for Higher Education Research at Sunway University in Malaysia. She has international experience in the development of quality in higher education, including curriculum, teaching and learning, and quality assurance. She has been Expert Panel Chair and Member for the Malaysian Qualifications Agency, producing national educational guidelines and policy development. As well as positions in universities in Australia and Malaysia, Glenda has been Visiting Academic at universities in Thailand, China, Singapore, and Hong Kong; conference advisor for Michigan State University in Dubai; and quality panel member in Oman. She has published books, chapters, and journal articles on quality educational approaches and innovation, and regularly reviews articles for international journals.

Darla K. Deardorff, PhD, is currently executive director of the Association of International Education Administrators, a national professional organisation based in the United States. Darla holds academic positions at several different universities, including Research Fellow at Duke University and at Nelson Mandela University. Darla's expertise is international education and intercultural competence and she is regularly invited to speak on these topics around the world. She has published extensively in these areas, with seven books and more than sixty book chapters and articles, and is a leading international leader and scholar in the field.

John Lawrence Dennis, PhD, is an affiliated professor at Università Cattolica del Sacro Cuore at the Centre for Higher Education Internationalisation, Visiting Professor at the University of Alberta, and Adjunct Professor at the University of Perugia. His research, funded by the European Union, and the Italian Minister of Interior, focuses on how people intentionally influence their lives. Within international education, he is interested, primarily, in student experiences and takes an evidence-based approach to understand how theories, models, research and data are related to those student experiences. In his spare time, he runs his own company that measures student experiences within international settings, is a Cognitive Behavior Therapy practitioner, and is writing his first book, *The Importance of Feeling Uncomfortable.*

Jessica Gallagher, PhD, is the Director of Global Engagement and Entrepreneurship at The University of Queensland (UQ) where she is responsible for the continued development and implementation of the university's global strategy. She leads a number of UQ's international partnership activities and strategic engagement events and a wide range of global scholarship and mobility programs. Jessica is also a research affiliate and sessional lecturer in the School of Languages and Cultures at UQ and is a non-executive director of Scope Global, a specialist project management company delivering international development and international education programs throughout Australia, Asia, and the Pacific.

Wendy Green, PhD, is a senior lecturer (adjunct) in the School of Education at the University of Tasmania, Australia. She is an Australian Learning and Teaching Fellow, Executive Editor of the journal *Higher Education Research & Development*, Guest Editor for the *Journal of Studies in International Education*, and past Convenor of the International Education Association, Australia's National Internationalisation of the Curriculum Network. In her research and teaching practice, Wendy is particularly interested in the impact of increasing globalisation on higher education and its implications for learning, at home and abroad.

Saskia Jensen is Market Intelligence Manager at Goldsmiths, University of London, and responsible for the development and implementation of market research plans and for the coordination of student feedback surveys. Prior to her role at Goldsmiths, Saskia was a Senior Researcher at i-graduate and a regular contributor to the work of the Observatory on Borderless Higher Education. She holds a bachelor's degree in social sciences and a master's degree in international migration and intercultural studies. Saskia is a PhD student at the Centre of Internationalisation of Education, and her research explores migration patterns and trajectories in higher education, mainly focusing on China and the UK.

Martha Johnson, PhD, is the Assistant Dean for Learning Abroad at the University of Minnesota and oversees one of the largest education abroad offices in the United States, which sends over 4000 students abroad annually. She has worked in international education since 1991 for organisations and institutions in the United States, Ireland, Australia, and the United Kingdom. Her experience includes on-site program management, program development and marketing, management of a large university education abroad office, and teaching of short-term programs. She holds a PhD in American studies with an emphasis in drama and the performance of gender, race, and cultural identity from the University of East Anglia, Norwich, UK.

Elspeth Jones is Emerita Professor of the Internationalisation of Higher Education, Leeds Beckett University, and Honorary Visiting Fellow, Centre for Higher Education Internationalisation (CHEI), Università Cattolica del Sacro Cuore, Milan. She has undertaken work for universities around the world and for organisations including the European Commission, European Parliament, British Council, European Association for International Education (EAIE), and

IEAA Australia. Her specialisms include personal, professional, and employability outcomes from international mobility and internationalisation of curriculum at home. She has published widely and is series editor of Internationalisation in Higher Education (Routledge) and winner of the EAIE Award for Excellence in Research.

Eva King, BVSc, is a PhD student in the School of Veterinary Science at The University of Queensland. Formerly in private clinical practice and a clinical communication skills coach, she is currently developing a grounded theory of work integrated learning in undergraduate clinical education, which accounts for high levels of student cultural and linguistic diversity. Eva's other research interests include graduate employability, international student education, and the metacognitive scaffolding of learners and educators in relation to clinical workplace learning practices.

Juha Leppänen (M.Soc.Sc.) is the Chief Executive at Demos Helsinki, a leading independent Nordic think tank that focuses on ensuring that societies and organisations can succeed in current and future demands, both in the Nordics and globally. He is an experienced author and speaker, and has worked with topics such as future of work and learning for the past ten years. He is an active advisor on strategy and policy and serves as a Royal Society of Arts Fellow.

Fion Choon Boey Lim, PhD, is an expert in transnational education, and currently works as the Educational Quality Coordinator (Transnational Education and External Delivery) at Victoria University (VU). Fion has extensive experience in transnational education that ranges from managing commercial profitability and stakeholder engagement to curriculum development, teaching, research, and managing the academic quality and delivery of transnational delivery. She is a member of the Academic Board at VU and a member of International Committee of VCAA (Victorian Curriculum and Assessment Authority). Fion has published journal articles in various areas relating to transnational education and is a regular presenter at conferences.

Amira El Masri is a doctoral candidate at the Faculty of Education, York University. Her areas of research are internationalisation of higher education from a policy perspective and international students' experiences. She participated in studies examining the policy discourses of international students as "ideal immigrants," internationalisation of K–12 teacher education, and world-class universities' discourse. Her doctoral research investigates the construction of international education as policy in Ontario, the actors contributing to this construction, and the power dynamics between them. On a professional level, she has worked at different post-secondary education institutions in Canada and abroad.

Cheryl Matherly is the Vice-President and Vice Provost for International Affairs at Lehigh University. Prior to Lehigh, Matherly was Vice Provost for Global Education at the University of Tulsa and taught in the School for

Urban Education. She has served as Assistant Dean of Students for Career and International Education at Rice University. Dr. Matherly has written extensively on topics related to international education and employability. She has received four National Science Foundation grants for projects related to the preparation of science and engineering graduates for the global workforce. She holds a doctorate in education from the University of Houston.

Ainslie Moore is Deputy Director, International Operations, at the University of Auckland. Moore leads the international programs and partnerships team. She brings 15 years of higher education experience in organisations such as IDP Education Australia, the Australian National University (ANU), and the Australian Vice-Chancellors' Committee, and has served as Policy Director, International, at Universities Australia for over a decade. In this role, she worked closely with a wide range of international education policies, including work integrated learning. During this period, she completed a secondment with Austrade in Washington, D.C., leading their North American Education desk. Ainslie holds a bachelor's degree in communications (Canberra) and master's degree in public policy (ANU).

Aleksi Neuvonen is the co-founder of the Nordic think tank Demos Helsinki. He is a futures researcher and an expert on urban development and societal transformation, with a twenty-year career in multi-disciplinary social research. Currently, Aleksi is in charge of Demos Helsinki's research activities. He holds an MA (philosophy) from University of Helsinki and is currently preparing his PhD in planning theory in Tampere University of Technology and Radboud University, Nijmegen. He has taught futures studies and scenario methods in number of European universities.

Tran Le Huu Nghia is a Research Fellow at Informetrics Research Group and with the Faculty of Social Sciences and Humanities, Ton Duc Thang University, Ho Chi Minh City, Vietnam. He completed his PhD at the University of Melbourne, Australia, as an awardee of the Australian Government's Endeavour Postgraduate Award. His research interests include teaching and learning in higher education, graduate employability, international education, teacher education, and TESOL. He can be contacted at tranlehuunghia@tdtu.edu.vn.

Hiroshi Ota, PhD, is Professor at the Center for General Education at Hitotsubashi University (HU), where he serves as Director of the Hitotsubashi University Global Education Program. Before his current position, he worked for the Office for the Promotion of International Relations at HU, the School of Commerce and Management at HU as international student advisor, the Office of International Education at SUNY-Buffalo, and Toyo University. His research focuses on higher education policies and practices related to internationalisation and international student mobility from a comparative perspective. From SUNY-Buffalo, Ota received his Ed.M. and Ph.D. in comparative and global studies in education.

Dolly Predovic founded Career Paths, a consulting company in the field of higher education. For over 20 years, Dolly was Professor of Corporate Finance at SDA Bocconi, where she concluded her academic career as director of the corporate finance master's degree program. In 1990, she participated in the planning and realisation of the first international program at Bocconi University, Master in International Economics and Management (MIEM). She was director of the International Executive Education division and Professor of Corporate Finance and Valuation in the MBA program. Dolly is a candidate for a PhD in higher education internationalisation at Centre for Higher Education Internationalisation.

Vo Phuong Quyen is a Senior Lecturer at School of Foreign Languages, Can Tho University, Vietnam. She completed her master's degree at Unitec Institution of Technology, Auckland, New Zealand, as an awardee of NZAID scholarship of New Zealand Government. Her research interests include internationalisation of higher education, learner-centred approaches, intercultural communicative competence, teacher professional development, and TESOL. She can be contacted at vpquyen@ctu.edu.vn

Nannette Ripmeester is Director of Expertise in Labour Mobility, Client Services Director Europe for i-graduate, and founder of the educational gamification app, CareerProfessor.works. Nannette is part of the NAFSA Trainer Corps and Advisory Board Member of Codarts University. She frequently presents on employability, graduate outcomes, and cultural differences across the globe. With over 25 years of experience working for large corporate clients and higher education institutions around the world, she understands what makes people internationally employable.

Jon Rubin was Founder and Director of the SUNY COIL (Collaborative Online International Learning) Center from 2006 to 2017. He directed the COIL Institute for Globally Networked Learning in the Humanities (2010–13), funded by the National Endowment for the Humanities, which engaged 47 U.S. and international universities in COIL course development. He also led the COIL Center's award program with the American Council for Education (2013–14), directed the COIL Center's Stevens Initiative project in the MENA region (2015–17) and launched the State Department–funded U.S.-Mexico Multistate COIL project, which linked 18 Mexican higher education institutions to U.S. campuses. He is Director of COIL Consulting (coilconsult.com) which supports university COIL initiatives.

Mika Saarinen is Counsellor of Education and Head of Section at the Finnish National Agency for Education (EDUFI), the national development body of education and training in Finland. He has worked for the past twenty years with both higher education and VET education policy and EU-issues, conducting studies and writing and lecturing widely within these fields. He sits on number of national and international committees related to the VET and EU-cooperation. He holds an MA within theoretical philosophy from the University of Helsinki and he also has done further studies in international politics and adult education.

Yukiko Shimmi, PhD, is Senior Assistant Professor at Tohoku University, Miyagi, Japan. Shimmi received her doctorate in higher education at Boston College where she worked as a research assistant at the Center for International Higher Education. She earned her master's degree in educational psychology at the University of Minnesota as a Fulbright scholar. She also holds a bachelor's degree in human relations from Keio University in Japan. Shimmi's research focuses on the impact of study abroad experiences on students from the perspectives of personal and career development.

Greeja Hemalata De Silva currently holds the position of Director, Victoria University (Melbourne), Undergraduate Programme at Sunway College, a position she was offered in 2009. She graduated in 1997 with a Master in Business Administration degree from Universiti Malaya, the pioneer university in Malaysia. It was from this same university that she was awarded a Bachelor of Economics degree in 1987. Prior to her appointment as director of programme, she was the Principal Lecturer of Management and Organisation Behaviour for 10 years for the programme. She has conducted joint research with her VU counterparts during her teaching years and was a winner in the 2007 Carrick Australian Awards for University Teaching. She has also worked in the corporate sector for about 10 years prior to her entry into the academic arena.

Wondwosen Tamrat is an Associate Professor and Founding President of St Mary's University, Addis Ababa, Ethiopia. He is a collaborating scholar of the Program for Research on Private Higher Education (PROPHE) at the State University of New York at Albany, united States, and coordinator of the private higher education sub-cluster of the Continental Education Strategy of Africa (CESA-AU). He regularly writes on Ethiopian higher education and is a frequent contributor to *University World News*, *International Higher Education*, and *Inside Higher Education*. He may be reached at wondwosentamrat@gmail.com.

Damtew Teferra is Professor of Higher Education and Founding Director of the International Network for Higher Education in Africa, earlier at the Center for International Higher Education (CIHE), Boston College, and now at the University of Kwazulu-Natal, South Africa. Teferra, the former Director for Africa and the Middle East of the Ford Foundation International Fellowships Program, is Founding Editor of *International Journal of African Higher Education*. He is the author/co-editor of a dozen books, including the award-winning books *African Higher Education: An International Reference Handbook* (Indiana University Press, 2003), *Funding Higher Education in Sub-Saharan Africa* (Palgrave Macmillan, 2013) and Flagship Universities in Africa (Palgrave Macmillan, 2017).

Kelly Thomson is Assistant Professor (tenured) in the School of Administrative Studies, Faculty of Liberal Arts & Professional Studies, York University, Canada. She uses interactionist and postcolonial perspectives to study how actors negotiate their social worlds. Her current work focuses on change initiatives in health care, transitions of migrant accounting professionals, and international students. Her work has been published in the *Journal of Business Ethics, Academic Medicine, Critical Perspectives on Accounting,* and *Journal of Management,* among others.

Martin Tillman is a nationally recognised expert, author, and thought leader. He is President of Global Career Compass, an international consulting practice focused on the impact of education abroad experiences on student career development and employability. Formerly, he served as Associate Director of Career Services at the Johns Hopkins University School of Advanced International Studies in Washington, D.C. He holds a bachelor's degree in political science from the State University of New York at Stony Brook, master's degree from Colgate University in student personnel administration in higher education, and a master's degree in intercultural management from the SIT Graduate Institute.

Roopa Desai Trilokekar is an Associate Professor, Post-secondary Education at the Faculty of Education, York University. Her research interests include government policy on higher education and the internationalisation of Canadian higher education. She is a co-editor of *International Education as Public Policy in Canada* (forthcoming), Montreal: McGill-Queen's University Press; *Making Policy in Turbulent Times; Challenge and Prospects for Higher Education* (2013) Montreal: McGill-Queens University Press; and *Canada's Universities Go Global* (2009) Toronto: James Lorimer and Company (CAUT Series). Her comparative research work spans several countries, including Canada, Germany, Australia, India, and the United States.

Foreword to the series, Internationalization in Higher Education

This series addresses the rapidly changing and highly topical field of internationalisation in higher education. Increasingly visible in institutional strategies as well as national and international agendas since the latter part of the twentieth century, internationalisation has been informed by diverse disciplines but continues to be subject to variation in interpretation. In part, its rise can be seen as a response to globalisation and growing competition among higher education institutions. Indeed, use of the term "internationalisation" itself is not uncontested, particularly in those countries with a colonial heritage or where economic rationales for international education play a minor role.

There are compelling drivers for university leaders to adopt an integrated rather than a uni-dimensional approach to internationalisation. Intensifying competition for talent, changes in global student flows, international branch campuses and growing complexity in cross-border activity, along with the rising influence of institutional rankings, all provide economic impetus and reputational consequences of success or failure.

However, there is also recognition of the need to prepare students for changing local and global environments in both personal and professional life. Intensifying employer and student demand reflects growing interest in international and intercultural experiences and competencies. University leadership, academics, and support staff must respond accordingly, with programs and activities which are appropriate to a changing global landscape, and informed by internationally relevant research and collaborative partnerships. Added incentive is provided by the awareness that the intercultural competence required for global contexts is equally important for living and working in diverse multi-cultural societies. Internationalisation thus has both global and more local intercultural interests at its heart.

Internationalisation as a powerful force for change and the enhancement of quality is an underlying theme of this series. It addresses the complex and varied topics arising as internationalisation continues to develop and grow. The series aims to reflect current concerns, with volumes written or edited by leading thinkers and authors from around the world, while giving a voice to emerging researchers. It examines some of the critical contemporary issues in the field of internationalisation, and offers theoretical perspectives with practical applications for higher education leaders, academics, and practitioners alike.

This volume in the series addresses various aspects of the interface between internationalisation and employability. The views of employers are crucial to this topic, so the extent to which they understand and value the experiences of potential employees is an important factor.

The book considers the skills developed by students through mobility experiences, while also reflecting on internationalisation of the curriculum at home, and transnational education. The experience of international study as a route to employability for migration purposes is another important theme, and insights into the experience of both students and employers come under scrutiny. Collaborative online learning can offer authentic engagement with people from different cultural backgrounds and the book explores how developing virtual teamwork by this means presents students with valuable skills for use in contemporary professional environments.

Authors in this timely volume address these topics from several global vantage points. They illustrate what is needed to turn good intentions into positive outcomes for all stakeholders and the book will prove valuable for readers both in a range of institutional roles and in different countries around the world.

Elspeth Jones, Series editor
Emerita Professor of the Internationalization
of Higher Education Leeds Beckett University, UK

Introduction

Cate Gribble and Robert Coelen

Increased international student mobility, growth in transnational education, and the emergence of internationalisation-at-home initiatives are now features of the higher education environment in many contexts. The internationalisation of higher education is, in part, a response to work environments which are increasingly globally integrated. As higher education institutions face pressure to equip graduates with skills, knowledge, and attributes for the global labour market, there is now growing awareness of the link between the internationalisation of higher education and the development of transversal skills valued by employers.

However, despite wider recognition of the links between internationalisation and employability, important challenges remain. A major theme of this volume is the disconnect between the contribution international education makes to the development of key employability skills and the views of employers. Studies of employer attitudes in a range of national contexts, including Canada, Australia, China, Finland, Malaysia, and Japan, reveal a disturbing lack of understanding of the critical transversal skills acquired via international education and how they stand to benefit employers. Employers are increasingly seeking "globally minded graduates" with strong communications skills and interpersonal skills, and a capacity to adapt to a range of workplace scenarios. However, there is poor understanding of how international education can contribute to the development of these skills, competencies, and attributes. In many cases, this lack of awareness is preventing nations from harnessing the potential of globally educated graduates. This finding highlights the importance of educating employers on the benefits of international education and ensuring students are trained in articulating the career-related benefits they have accrued to a broad audience.

Equity or spreading the employability benefits of internationalisation across the whole student population is also a major theme. How can we ensure the benefits of internationalisation are available to the majority of students rather than a privileged elite? The growth in transnational education (TNE) has opened up international education opportunities to growing numbers of students in emerging economies. However, these students are equally concerned with how their international education experience will position them in increasingly competitive labour markets. Consequently, providing programs and experiences that will best equip TNE graduates for the labour market has emerged as a significant challenge for TNE programs in emerging economies, such as those of Vietnam and Malaysia.

Importantly, internationalisation at home (IaH) offers the potential for all students to benefit from internationalisation without leaving their home campus and to reach all students, not simply those involved in mobility programmes. Technology and the internet offer enormous scope to expand the way students engage beyond their home institution and to develop critical transversal skills, including intercultural awareness and working in teams, even when they are virtual. Co-curricular activities also offer opportunities for students to further engage within and beyond the institution, including in the local community, in order to develop critical skills. However, misconceptions about IaH, limited skills among academics, and lack of institutional strategy are some of the major challenges.

The overarching aim of this volume is to deepen our understanding of the main issues and challenges associated with a complex phenomenon. The aim is to fully investigate how, and to what extent, various modes of internationalisation in higher education impact on employability. Our focus is on employability, rather than on employment which is about getting a job. We adopt Knight and Yorke's (2003) definition, which interprets employability as "achievements, understandings and personal attributes that make individuals more likely to gain employment and to be successful in their chosen occupations." Nevertheless, we accept that other authors may have chosen to use different definitions and we have gathered the various conceptualisations via footnotes[1] throughout this volume.

Central to this volume are the two distinct modes of student mobility (intra-degree mobility, or learning abroad, and full degree mobility) along with non-mobile students, either through IaH or TNE. The distinction between the two types of mobility is considered critical as the motivation and experiences of students who carry out a mobility experience as part of their domestically delivered degree can differ significantly from those of a student who completes a full degree in another country, often with a broader migration goal. Moreover, attitudes of employers towards these two types of mobility experiences can also vary considerably. Given the central importance of employers to any investigation of the topic, the extent to which employers understand, value, and shape internationalisation in higher education is an important consideration throughout the book.

Part I: Learning abroad and employability

The focus of Part 1 is intra-degree student mobility or learning abroad, where students include an international learning experience as part of their domestically delivered degree. The current emphasis on learning abroad is closely linked to employability as governments, institutions, and students themselves are looking for ways to boost graduate employability, and learning mobility is increasingly considered a way to develop graduate attributes.

Cheryl Matherly and Martin Tillman set the scene for this section of the book by providing an overview of national policy on learning abroad and the growing trend to purposefully link learning abroad programs to employability. Increasingly, learning abroad is viewed as a "high impact practice" for helping students develop critical employability skills, including intercultural skills, self-efficacy, the ability to work with people of diverse backgrounds, and a global outlook.

A consistent theme across this section of the book is the critical importance of articulating the employability benefits of learning abroad. Juha Leppänen, Aleksi Neuvonen, and Mika Saarinen highlight the value of raising awareness of the "hidden competencies" developed via international experiences and ensuring that employers and government recognise how learning abroad contributes to the development of cognitive skills highly valued in labour markets. Wendy Green, Eva King, and Jessica Gallagher reveal a tendency among Australian employers to underestimate the benefits of new graduates and emphasise the importance of "re-storying" personal experiences into career-relevant stories. In a similar vein, Martha Johnson and Christine Anderson report on the Career Integration Initiative at the University of Minnesota that resulted in new methods for guiding students towards deeper competency gains, along with understanding and articulation of skill transference from abroad to workplace. Dolly Predovic and John Dennis examine the potential for game-based analytics to provide insights into the hidden behaviours associated with the higher order skills that employers value the most, and offer us an opportunity to think more creatively about employability skills development through internationalisation.

The role played by mobility in determining both individual and national prosperity is perhaps best illustrated in the case of Japan. Shifting demographics, greater domestic tertiary opportunities, and a weak Japanese economy have contributed to a decline in outbound mobility. However, there is now a major push by the Japanese government to reverse this trend as the government recognises that the survival of the Japanese economy hinges on greater regional and global engagement, which requires graduates with a global mind-set. Hiroshi Ota and Yukiko Shimmi explore the challenges facing Japan, including the need to counter current scepticism among employers about the effect of short-term study abroad programs.

Part II: International student migration and employability

In many instances, international education is linked to migration, with the decision to study abroad part of an overall migration plan. In part, the trend for international students to seek post-study employment has been driven by host nation policy, with a growing number of countries viewing international students as both an important source of revenue and a supply of skilled labour. Finding the right balance between providing post-study work opportunities without displacing local graduates in competitive graduate labour markets has proved challenging for governments, particularly in the climate of anti-immigration populism in many countries. International students who do remain have mixed experiences of the host country labour markets.

The relationship between the internationalisation of higher education and employability is complex and multi-faceted and often characterised by a disjuncture between the kind of messages and policy promoted at a national level and institutional and workplace practices. Roopa Desai Trilokekar, Kelly Thomson, and Amira El Masri provide important insights into attitudes of employers towards international education and the extent to which employers understand, value, and shape internationalisation in higher education. The finding that international students who are able to demonstrate their "Canadianness" have better chances of being recruited than those who do not, is in stark contrast to the international education rhetoric of success in an era of globalisation, requiring international experience and the cross-cultural skills. The findings of this chapter highlight important issues facing other major host nations, such as Australia, the UK, and New Zealand, who are tackling similar challenges as international graduates seek to include post-study work experience as part of their overall international education experience.

New Zealand (NZ) provides an interesting case study of how a small nation built on migration is attempting to manage the flows of students and skilled migrants via policy and immigration settings. Like other host nations, NZ has been very successful in attracting international students, acknowledging the role played by international graduates in bringing the skills and professional and vocational qualifications NZ needs. At the same time, the country experiences high levels of outbound mobility, with NZ university graduates having among the highest mobility rates in the world. Brett Berquist and Ainslie Moore highlight the importance of New Zealand's strong data sets and comprehensive analysis in providing a clearer understanding of the factors influencing domestic and international student choices for study and employment, whether in NZ or offshore. The result is a vibrant and mobile labour market for both domestic and international graduates in NZ offering important insights relevant to other national contexts.

In China, a booming economy, improvement of employment opportunities, and a more liberal lifestyle have resulted in an increase of returnees in recent years. However, Saskia Jensen argues that despite a general understanding of the positive impact an international education has on the individual, a Western degree does not necessarily result in a successful study-to-work transition and does not guarantee a desirable job upon graduation. While an internationally educated workforce is expected to make positive contributions in the changing context of China's position in a global market and is increasingly in demand, there is a pressing need to align programs with student expectations and to effectively communicate and deliver on these expectations. Importantly, returning students must complement the knowledge and skills acquired overseas with an understanding of local practices. By adopting this approach, they are positioning themselves as bridges between China and the world, highlighting the often-complex set of skills, knowledge, and behaviour required by international graduates transitioning into the labour market.

This notion of international graduates needing to straddle two worlds in order to succeed professionally is reinforced in the TNE section of this book. Increasingly, institutions will be required to ensure international graduates are able to adapt to a range of professional cultural contexts.

Part III: Transnational education and employability

Transnational education (TNE) comprises students completing a foreign degree "offshore" either with a partner institution, through international branch campuses, via distance learning, or through a combination of these. While migration is not typically the principal motivation, enhanced employability and improved career options are often important drivers of TNE students. The employability of TNE students has until recently been largely overlooked, with the assumption that TNE students acquire automatic employability benefits from their overseas qualification, transitioning seamlessly into the home country labour market. However, as the authors in this section explain, the TNE landscape is complex and diverse, requiring a range of models and approaches in order to ensure students develop the employability skills they will need to succeed in a range of professional settings.

Elspeth Jones's chapter provides a valuable and timely overview of the TNE landscape in the context of employability, emphasising the significant opportunity that TNE settings offer to develop employability skills that can advantage TNE graduates in local labour markets. As noted by Jensen, there is growing awareness among employers of the need for employees who can straddle two cultures. Jones argues that an effective model of developing employability in TNE settings will support students to interpret their new-found knowledge and skills in the local labour market while also interpreting employability within the local paradigm. However, the complex TNE landscape along with a lack of research into outcomes for students, and in particular the development of employability skills in a range of TNE contexts, suggest that the potential for TNE to make a real difference in the professional lives of graduates is yet to be realised.

Despite the focus on incorporating work integrated learning (WIL) into higher education curricula, there has been little research on WIL in TNE settings. In her study of WIL from the perspectives of three local external stakeholder groups of an Australian university operating in Vietnam, Christine Bilsland provides insights into the role of WIL in supporting equitable employability outcomes for TNE students. In addition, the boundary-spanning relationships that transpire from WIL partnerships are another important benefit of WIL in TNE locations.

The importance of WIL in TNE is also highlighted by Tran Le Huu Nghia and Vo Phuong Quyen who investigate how imported programs offered by a Vietnamese university contribute to the development of graduate employability and career advancement prospects. The authors argue that including greater WIL opportunities in TNE settings will result in better employment outcomes. WIL experiences will allow TNE students to apply their knowledge and skills to authentic work situations, connect with more industry-based professionals, and develop their sense of belonging to the industry by fostering their professional identity. Fion Choon Boey Lim, Glenda Crosling, Greeja Hemalata De Silva, and Mien Wee Cheng's study of TNE in Malaysia reinforces the importance of developing the employability of TNE students in order to ensure optimum graduate employment outcomes. The authors argue that institutions should reconsider their curriculum design for the needs of transnational students, with a particular focus on the soft skills valued by employers.

These case studies, along with the current and predicted expansion of TNE programs globally, present a compelling argument for more studies on the types and extent of employability skills embedded in TNE curricula, and the level to which graduates are trained or prepared to successfully transition into graduate employment.

Part IV: Internationalisation at home and employability

Increasingly, there is growing awareness that the majority of students will not engage in an overseas mobility experience, resulting in greater investment in internationalisation at home (IaH) and "internationalising of the curriculum" (IoC) at the home campus. Equity remains a major concern and socioeconomic background continues to be the strongest predictor of mobility. Higher education is being challenged to bring the benefits of a period of study abroad to the non-mobile student. Institutions are seeking to create opportunities for students to develop global perspectives and global citizenship in the home campus environment.

While the benefits of IaH are well recognised, the practicalities of converting good intentions into practice and achieving meaningful outcomes is the challenge facing institutions. Jos Beelen proposes that by explicitly linking employability skills with internationalisation, universities can overcome institutional barriers, including misconceptions around IaH, the absence of strategies, limited skills of academics, and the need for greater connection between stakeholders. The importance of overtly linking employability skills and attributes to internationalisation is echoed by Darla Deardoff and Nannette Ripmeester. The authors argue that higher education institutions need to be more intentional and explicit about how they are addressing the value of employability skills, particularly intercultural skills, and their importance for success in the workplace.

In an attempt to deliver meaningful international experiences at scale, a number of universities are tapping into global networks in order to provide their students with international exposure. Many initiatives are designed to mimic global workplaces, with students required to tackle language issues, time zones, and other challenges associated with working in global teams. COIL (Collaborative Online International Learning) is one such initiative. In his chapter, Jon Rubin, Founder and Director of the SUNY COIL Centre, explains that COIL takes advantage of internet technology to authentically engage other cultures from within the local classroom, providing a valuable introduction to working in virtual teams and a unique approach to internationalising the curriculum. This type of initiative presents an exciting opportunity to deliver the benefits of internationalisation at scale.

In the past decade, interest in internationalisation of higher education has grown dramatically, largely in response to increased student mobility, growth in TNE, and widespread recognition of the importance of providing all students with exposure to an internationalised higher education experience via internationalisation-at-home initiatives. Moreover, concerns around graduate employability in a rapidly shifting global labour market have led many universities to prioritise internationalisation initiatives. The chapters in this book examine the complex relationship between higher education and the labour market in an increasingly globalised environment, offering important insights, and perspectives from a range of national contexts and professional domains.

Note

1. These other definitions and conceptualisations can be found on pages 12, 25, 25, 60, 62, 92, 117, 164.

Part I

Learning abroad
and employability

Chapter 1

Linking learning abroad and employability

Cheryl Matherly and Martin Tillman

Universities around the world have increasingly embraced learning abroad as a "high-impact practice" for helping students develop intercultural skills, self-efficacy, the ability to work with people of diverse backgrounds, and a global outlook (Kuh, O'Donnell, & Reed, 2013; Farrugia & Sanger, 2017). Numerous surveys and research reports affirm that international experience in the form of work, study, service, or volunteering are highly desired forms of off-campus learning for developing skills and competencies valued by employers.

This chapter explores the following questions: Why is employability an expected outcome for higher education? What are factors that have influenced the coupling of learning abroad with national strategies for promoting employability as an outcome for higher education? What are the skills, knowledge, and attitudes required for employability that students develop as outcomes of a learning abroad experience? How can campuses align their internationalisation policies and practices with expectations of the global marketplace? What is the role of business and industry in contributing to the applied knowledge and skill development of students?

This chapter uses the term "learning abroad" to describe the diversity of international experience in which students engage while in college or university. In addition to traditional study abroad, higher education systems are increasingly looking to alternative pedagogies to link students' academics with workplace preparation. Work integrated learning (WIL) describes mechanisms through which practical experiences are used to teach theoretical concepts. It encompasses internships, sandwich programs, field work, and cooperative education (Rowe, 2017; Smith et al., 2009). We use the term "learning abroad" as a general term for all abroad experiences, and "WIL" is used interchangeably with the terms "internships," "service learning," and "field work," depending upon the national context and choice of language in specific research studies.

Employability as an outcome for higher education

Employability is a widely expected outcome for higher education and, increasingly, learning abroad programs are evaluated by how well they prepare students for success in entering the workforce (Matherly & Tillman, 2015; British

Council, 2017; Farrugia & Sanger, 2017).[1] Hillage & Pollard (1998) define employability[2] as the "capability to gain initial employment, maintain employment and obtain new employment if required. It is also, ideally, about the quality of such work or employment" (p. 1). In this context, education is expected to provide marketable skills and abilities relevant to job performance, so that the more highly educated people are the more productive they will be, and more successful in terms of both incomes and work opportunities (Cai, 2013).

The reason that most higher education systems have adopted an "employability agenda" is instrumental purposes. Employment rates are highest among higher education graduates, and graduates tend to earn relatively high salaries and enjoy stable employment conditions. These are conditions influenced by the growth of occupations requiring higher-level skills and the shrinking number of occupations associated with lower levels of education (OECD, 2013). A "knowledge-based economy" in which economic success is based upon the utilisation of intangible assets, such as knowledge, skills, and innovative potential, is understood as a key component affecting national economic competitive advantage (OECD, 1996; Kok, 2004).

Concerns regarding preparing graduates for entering the knowledge economy and understanding economic globalisation have impacted how higher education institutions educate students and align their curricula to the needs of their local, national, and regional workplaces. Campus decision makers, increasingly, have reacted to these forces by developing a new transnational academic narrative linking learning abroad programs to employability, and to contributing to more purposeful and integrated academic and career development outcomes (Murrell & Schulz, 2017; Crossman & Clarke, 2010). The benefits from traditional study abroad and experiential education experiences are increasingly described in terms of the ways in which they prepare global citizens, educate career-ready graduates, build essential (sometimes industry-specific) professional skills and cross-cultural competencies, and foster a better understanding of critical world issues.

The expectation that higher education institutions should be held accountable for student employability became a priority for academic institutions around the world following the global recession in 2008. As a result, the past decade has seen a wide body of both qualitative and quantitative research linking learning outcomes of education abroad to student employability (Farrugia & Sanger, 2017; Yokota, 2016; Potts, 2015; European Commission, 2014; DiPietro, 2013; Jones, 2013a; Tillman, 2012; Archer & Davison, 2008). This sample of studies and surveys, from the United States, Japan, Australia, the EU, and the UK, reach a similar conclusion: learning abroad may correlate with an increased likelihood of employability (with a concomitant high impact on long-term career development and professional advancement) after graduation.

It is in this context that governments and national policy organisations promote learning abroad as a strategy to increase the employability of its workforce, to encourage stronger trade relationships, and to develop soft diplomacy as a tool of foreign policy (Gribble & Tran, 2016; Farrugia & Sanger, 2017). What follows are examples of regional and national policies in European, Asian, South American, and North American contexts that promote employability as a desired outcome for learning abroad programs.

Regional and national policies to encourage learning abroad

Europe

Teichler (2015) describes the Erasmus program, established in 1987, as a "breakthrough" in moving learning abroad from "an exceptional choice to a normal option" (p. 17). The Bologna Declaration of 1999, which called for the creation of a common structure of higher education across Europe to facilitate student mobility, set 2020 as a target date by which 20% of all students should have a period of mobility, which could include study or internships (Teichler, 2015; Gribble & Tran, 2016). Since it was created, Erasmus programs, including Erasmus Mundus established in 2003 and Erasmus+ established in 2014, have given nine million people the chance to study, train, volunteer, or gain professional experience abroad (European Commission, 2017).

The Erasmus Impact Study (European Commission, 2014) affirmed the effectiveness of the mobility programs in increasing the employability of college graduates. The study found that Erasmus alums were half as likely to experience long-term unemployment as compared with their counterparts who did not go abroad. Five years after graduation, Erasmus students had an unemployment rate 23% lower than their non-mobile peers. Almost 1 in 10 Erasmus alums who had interned abroad started his or her own company (European Commission, 2014). Androulla Vassiliou, European Commissioner for Education, Culture, Multilingualism and Youth, noted the significance of these findings, "given the context of unacceptably high levels of youth unemployment in the EU... The message is clear: if you study or train abroad, you are more likely to increase your job prospects" (in "New study makes the link", 2014).

Case study: The Erasmus for Young Entrepreneurs program

Erasmus for Young Entrepreneurs was established in 2009 as an exchange program that prepares new or aspiring entrepreneurs by matching them with experienced mentors in another EU country. It was created within the frameworks of the Small Business Act for Europe and the Entrepreneurship 2020 Action Plan, and seeks to address unemployment in Europe by boosting growth and creating new jobs. Assessments of the program suggest that it has been very successful: 36.5% of the participating entrepreneurs have created their own businesses, 65% of host entrepreneurs have extended operations to new national markets, and participants' business growth has been stronger than average for European small enterprises. Since the program was established, nearly 4520 exchanges, involving 9040 new and experienced entrepreneurs, across the 28 EU member states and 9 additional participating countries, have successfully taken place (Apolitical group, n.d.; Erasmus for Young Entrepreneurs, 2017).

UK

In comparison to other European countries, the number of students in the UK participating in learning abroad programs remains low. The 27,405 UK students who went abroad in 2015–16 represent only 1.6% of all UK students. Most participated in traditional study abroad, but 23% completed a work or internship placement (Go International, 2018). Brexit, the UK decision to exit the European Union, will mean that UK students will lose their ability to enrol in Erasmus. Given that Erasmus exchanges accounted for 40% of the mobile graduates, there is growing concern that the UK will be challenged to maintain, much less grow, its current rates of student mobility (Dingley, 2016).

The British Council's Generation UK, which predated the Brexit vote, aims to shift the focus for student mobility away from Europe to India and China, countries that represent important investment and trade regions. Funded by the Department for Business, Innovation and Skills, the Department for Employment and Learning, of the governments of Northern Ireland and Wales, it represents an effort to link mobility with national priorities, including employability (Gribble & Tran, 2016). Generation UK–China, for example, has set a goal that 80,000 UK students will study or work in China by 2020 in order to boost their employability and gain a global mind-set (British Council, n.d.). Generation UK–India, launched in 2014 with support from the Indian Ministry of Human Resource Development, has a goal to send 25,000 UK students to India between 2015 and 2020 to complete internships and teaching assistantships, or participate in study abroad programs. Like its China counterpart, the goals for the program were deeply rooted in UK–India trade priorities and a need to prepare graduates who were ready to lead business operations (Alphin, Chan, & Lavine, 2017).

Individual countries in the UK have developed their own mobility strategies. Scotland adopted the Developing Scotland's Global Citizens project and funded the National Union of Students to develop Scotland Goes Global learning abroad programs. Northern Ireland promoted mobility through its Graduating to Success initiative, and the Welsh government adopted the 2013 Policy Statement on Higher Education in order to expand outward mobility as part of its employability strategy (Gribble & Tran, 2016).

Asia

Inter-regional student mobility is central to the Association of Southeast Asian Nations (ASEAN) vision to create a "politically cohesive, economically integrated, socially responsible and truly rules-based, people-oriented, people centred ASEAN" (Djajadikerta & Zheng, 2015). Gribble (2016) notes that the aim is economic; mobile students are more likely to become mobile workers, taking advantage of the economic opportunities in the region that could benefit their home countries. Associations such as the University Mobility in Asia and the Pacific (UMAP), an association of government and NGOs focused on student mobility, and Campus Asia (Collective Action for Mobility Program of University Students in Asia), which currently consists of Japanese, Chinese, and Korean universities but may expand to other ASEAN countries, share the goal of increasing competitiveness of the region and developing students who can compete globally (Gribble & Tran, 2016; Matross Helms et al., 2015).

The challenges to this strategy, however, are great. The ASEAN community is extremely heterogeneous and includes countries with very different economies, such as Singapore, one of the world's most competitive economies, and Myanmar, where over a quarter of the population lives below the poverty threshold . Singaporean institutions participate in learning abroad programs at a very high rate, as compared to member countries such as Myanmar, Cambodia, and Laos where such opportunities remain a luxury. Further, many of the students who are most prepared to study abroad prefer "exotic" locations, which students frequently consider to be in Europe or the United States but not in Asia (Gribble, 2016).

Several Asian countries have adopted their own national policies to encourage short-term mobility within Asia. In 2010, the Chinese Central Government issued the Guidelines of the National Program for Medium and Long-term Educational Reform and Development, which laid out a plan to raise the international status of Chinese higher education and its graduates by supporting students for study abroad at top-tier universities and research institutes (China National Congress, 2010). The Chinese Ministry of Education should be authorized the China Scholarship Council to launch its CSC PhD Scholarship, which funds students to study at foreign universities, and a similar scheme to support undergraduate students for academic, research, and industrial internship experiences (Gribble & Tran, 2016).

In Japan,[3] the 2013 Japan Revitalisation Strategy, part of Prime Minister Shinzo's Abe's Abeducation Initiative, set a national goal to double the number of students studying abroad to 120,000 by 2020 (McCrostie, 2017; Ota & Watabe, 2018). As one strategy to meet this goal, the Ministry of Education, Culture, Sports, Science and Technology (MEXT) launched Tobitate! (Leap for Tomorrow), an initiative that includes government and industry funded scholarships for university and high school students, and promotional events involving prominent Japanese business people, sports stars, and artists advocating for the personal and professional benefits of study abroad (McCrostie, 2017; Gribble & Tran, 2016). The results of this initiative have been mixed. OECD figures indicate that Japanese students' participation in study abroad fell from 60,138 in 2012 to 53,197 in 2014, down from a 2004 peak of 82,945. In response, many Japanese universities encourage shorter study abroad trips, assuming that students were reluctant to study abroad because they were too busy with their studies. Between 2009 and 2015, the percentage of Japanese students studying abroad for less than a month increased from 46 to 61%. Fewer than 2000 students study abroad for more than a year. These trends have given rise to national debates as to whether short-term programs can accomplish the goals for preparing graduates to be globally competitive and competent speakers of English (McCrostie, 2017; Ota & Watabe, 2018).

Case study: TOMODACHI Initiative

The TOMODACHI Initiative is a public–private partnership that began out of efforts to support Japan's recovery from the 2011 earthquake and tsunami in Tohoku. Tomodachi, which means "a friend," now seeks to prepare American and Japanese leaders to strengthen global relations between their two countries and to develop global skills and mind-sets through education, cultural, and leadership exchanges. It is led by the United States Embassy in Tokyo and the U.S.–Japan Council, and is supported by the Japanese government, private industry, and individuals in the United States and Japan. As an example of the programs supported by this fund, the TOMODACHI-STEM@Rice Program is a five-week research internship program for 10 female undergraduates attending Japanese universities and majoring in science or engineering. Students work in research labs at Rice University in Houston, Texas, and complete training in communications, presentations, and intercultural team work. The TOMODACHI Youth Exchange is a five-week seminar that focuses on civic engagement and social entrepreneurship. The TOMODACHI Generation Morgan Stanley Ambassadors Program is a two-week seminar that focuses on leadership development and social entrepreneurship skills. Between 2011 and 2016, the TOMODACHI Initiative funded 216 programs and involved 5700 participants (TOMODACHI Initiative 2016 Annual Report, 2016; TOMODACHI, n.d.)

Latin America

A signature program of the Obama administration, the 100,000 Strong in the Americas program helped catalyse mobility between the United States and Latin America. The initiative's goal is to grow the number of U.S. students studying in the Americas to 100,000 by 2020 to strengthen bi-national relations and prepare students for a global workforce (100,000 Strong in the Americas, n.d.). The program leverages industry partners to provide resources for individual institutions to develop new learning abroad programs. Following its launch, Mexico announced Proyecta 100,000, which aims to send 100,000 Mexican students to study in the United States by 2018, and to expand joint research and innovation centres in order to increase the economic competitiveness of both countries (Proyecta 100,000, n.d.). In 2015, the Institute of International Education (IIE) reported a 17% increase in the number of Mexican students studying in the United States, a result largely attributed to initiatives of the 100,000 Strong program. The United States was the top choice for Mexican students to go abroad, that country becoming the 10th most popular source country of international students (Institute for International Education, 2016). Although this represents significant growth, Mexico, like all of Latin America, still reports some of the lowest rates of outbound student mobility, and current political tensions between the United States and Mexico may contribute to a short-term dip in Mexican students' interest in studying in the United States (Trines, 2017; Gacel-Avila, 2018).

The most common strategy among Latin American governments to encourage outbound mobility has been to provide scholarship money for learning abroad programs, especially those in the science, technology, energy and math fields. The best known of these is the Brazil Scientific Mobility Program (BSMP), which had a goal to send 100,000 students for short-term study over five years (Institute for International Education, n.d., c). When the program launched in 2011, Brazil had already seen a large growth in the number of students studying abroad. The Brazilian Educational and Language Travel Association (BELTA) estimated that the number of Brazilians studying abroad grew by nearly 600% between 2003 and 2014, many for short-term foreign language study (Gribble & Tran, 2016). BSMP had a specific goal to develop Brazil's future research capacity by investing in international training of university students and sending them for a year of study abroad and internships in the United States, Canada, UK, France, and Germany (Institute for International Education, n.d., c). A recession in Brazil led to the suspension of the program in 2015. Concerns about the Brazilian economy and the eroding value of its currency have made study abroad less attractive to many students, and outbound student mobility from Brazil is expected to continue to decline (ICEF Monitor, 2015).

United States

In the United States, flagship scholarship programs, such as Fulbright and the Benjamin Gilman International Scholarship Program for low income students, have comprised most of the government's strategy to promote learning abroad (Gribble & Tran, 2016). While goals for these programs are to contribute to economic competitiveness and public diplomacy, the call to grow participation in study abroad as an employability strategy has largely come from outside government. The Institute for International Education (IIE) launched Generation Study Abroad in 2014, with an ambitious goal to have 600,000 students participate in learning abroad programs by 2019, the 100th anniversary of its founding. IIE has attracted over 700 partners, including universities, industry, Non-governmental organizations (NGOS), and government (Institute for

International Education, n.d., a). The IIE has made it a key goal to expand the diversity of students participating in learning abroad by reducing financial barriers and creating scholarships for underrepresented students (Gribble & Tran, 2016).

Despite the investment in Generation Study Abroad, participation in study abroad by U.S. students still lags behind the program's goals. For 2015–16, the most recent year for which data is available, 325,339 students studied abroad, a 4% increase from the previous year, but still far short of the 600,000 goal (Institute for International Education, 2017).

Case study: Iacocca International Internship Program

The Iacocca International Internship Program is a flagship international education program at Lehigh University in Bethlehem, PA, and central to the university's goal to provide educational access to students regardless of financial background. It is a key feature of the institution's strategy to meet its Generation Study Abroad goals. The program was established in 2011 with a gift from Lehigh alum and former CEO of Chrysler Corp Lee Iacocca, who sought to support a program that prepared students for a global workplace. The program provides fully funded 8- to 10-week internships with companies around the globe and gives priority to applicants who have never travelled abroad or who have a high level of financial need. Since the program was established, 405 students have completed internships in over 40 different countries (Iacocca International Internship Program, n.d.). An assessment of learning outcomes for 2017 participants suggested that the program impacted students' communication skills, global perspectives, teamwork, professionalism, and problem-solving skills. Students also demonstrated significant gains on measures of general self-efficacy (Grove & Ham, 2017).

Australia

Australia, widely recognised as one of the most international systems of higher education, has prioritised strategies to increase the number of students learning abroad. The government has linked international education to national prosperity, cultural understanding, and economic and cultural development (Adams, Banks, & Olsen, 2011). The government's signature international education initiative, the New Colombo Plan, makes available scholarship funds to encourage Australian students to study and complete WIL programs in Asia to increase their familiarity with the region (Australian Government Department of Foreign Affairs and Trade, 2018; Ziguras, 2018). The initiative has been effective. In 2015, 38,000 Australian students participated in a learning abroad experience, up from 7000 just 10 years earlier. One in five Australian undergraduates completed a learning abroad experience while at university, with 45% choosing to study in Asia (Ziguras, 2018; Potts, 2016, December 20).

Case study: New Colombo Internship and Mentorship Network

The New Colombo Plan (NCP), a signature initiative of the Australian government, supports Australian undergraduates to study and undertake internships in the Indo-Pacific region. Internships and mentorships are a hallmark of the NCP. An internship is defined as paid or unpaid professional, full-time or part-time, work experience for which a student has intentional learning goals relevant to their academic qualification and professional development. A mentorship is a personal development relationship, where a business professional or academic helps guide a student in her or his study or work to support learning and professional growth. The NCP Internship and Mentorship Network allows organisations to post WIL opportunities, and for students and universities to search positions (Australian Government, n.d.). Over its first five years, the NCP supported more than 30,000 Australian undergraduate students to live, work, and study in the Indo-Pacific (Ziguras, 2018). The Australian government has prioritised the continued investment in the program as key for deepening national understanding of the Pacific region (2017 Foreign Policy White Paper, 2017).

This summary of supranational, regional, and national strategies indicates that learning abroad is increasingly being adopted as a strategy to promote economic competitiveness; business, diplomatic, and trade connections; and, ultimately, student employability. The next section explores specific research that links learning abroad with competencies which improve students' employability.

Skills, knowledge, and attitudes required for employability that students develop as an outcome from learning abroad

Factors affecting employability

Multiple surveys and studies in the past 20 years by human resource managers and industry leaders in different countries have reached similar conclusions, citing comparable clusters of essential knowledge, skills, attitudes, and intercultural competencies that may contribute to a graduate's employability (Bikson & Law, 1994; Deardorff, 2006; Hunter, White, & Godbey, 2006; Spitzberg & Changnon, 2009; Playfoot & Hall, 2009). These traits have remained remarkably consistent over time and can be grouped broadly into the four categories first identified by Bikson & Law (1994):

- Domain knowledge– involves knowledge gained in specific subject areas.
- Cognitive, social, and personal skills – includes problem-solving and decision-making ability, working in groups with colleagues of different backgrounds, flexibility and adaptability, and related skills.

- Prior work experience and on-the-job training – includes internships, apprenticeships, service learning, and volunteering.
- Cross-cultural competence – involves an ability to understand differences among and ability to adapt to other cultures, most frequently considered an outcome from learning abroad.

A number of recent, large-scale transnational studies of employer perspectives have found a high degree of correlation between learning abroad and employability, especially when job applicants demonstrate that their international experience has explicitly strengthened key skills and competencies of value to employers. The QS Global Employer Survey remains the largest global opinion survey of its type undertaken to date, and it informs a better understanding of how industry recruiters worldwide value study abroad experience. The report draws on over 10,000 respondents from 116 countries on 5 continents. Its principal finding indicates that employers worldwide do value international study when recruiting talent, with a 60% affirmative response to the primary question. While the survey did not attempt to define "intercultural communications skills," a majority of responding employers said they measure this in their recruitment process (Molony, Sowter, & Potts, 2011).

An international survey of over 350 large employers in the private, public, and NGO sectors, in 9 nations (Brazil, China, India, Indonesia, Jordan, South Africa, UAE, UK, and the U.S.), found that employers desired that candidates have skills to navigate multicultural environments and that these intercultural skills are lacking in the current labour market (British Council, 2013a). The study noted that "employers are under strong pressure to find employees who are not only technically proficient, but also culturally astute and able to thrive in a global work environment" (p. 3). Employers noted that intercultural skills, specifically, the ability to understand different cultural contexts and viewpoints, demonstration of respect for others, and knowledge of a foreign language contributed to teams running efficiently, building trust with clients, and developing relationships with new clients. Of all nations surveyed, only employers in Brazil and China were likely to rate intercultural skills as not very important. More than half of the employers surveyed in other countries reported that they actively encouraged employees to develop intercultural skills.

The Erasmus Impact Study (European Commission, 2014) surveyed 55,000 students from 34 nations who studied or trained abroad, 650 employers, and 5000 academic and non-academic staff at 1000 higher education institutions in order to analyse the effects of Erasmus student mobility in relation to studies and placements on individual skills enhancement, employability, and institutional development. The study reported several significant findings:

- International experience was considered important to employability by 61% of employers.
- Unemployment five years after graduation among students who participated was 23% lower than in the cohort that did not participate in an Erasmus program.

- Graduates with international "background" were given increased professional responsibility according to 64% of employers.
- Personality traits which strengthened employability, including tolerance, confidence, problem-solving, curiosity, self-understanding of one's strengths and weaknesses, and decisiveness, were looked for by 92% of employers (European Commission, 2014).

Despite these impressive results, some employers remain equivocal about the value of learning abroad, sometimes labelling it "academic tourism," even when the experiences are linked with traits listed above. A survey of Finnish employers sheds light on this conundrum. Only 37% of employers surveyed – and only 10% of those operating internationally – indicated that an international experience made a student more employable. The researchers concluded that those who had an "extended" or broader idea of learning abroad were more likely to consider it valuable career preparation. These employers listed among student outcomes the ability to think outside one's sphere of experience, new abilities and skills developed during free time, an ability to work with diverse groups of people, and a likelihood of following global media. The researchers concluded that the competencies gained from international experiences are related to the needs of employers but are often hidden, and called for universities to work more intentionally with students and employers to make competencies, such as productivity, resilience, and curiosity, gained from their international experiences, more visible (Centre for International Mobility, 2014).[4]

Case study: AIFS electronic portfolios

AIFS, a non-profit study abroad and international exchange organisation, adopted electronic portfolios as a tool for helping prepare students to articulate outcomes from learning abroad to potential employers. E-portfolios are increasingly common in colleges and universities, and are only beginning to be used by study abroad organisations. A portfolio requires a student to assemble examples of work to demonstrate gains on specific measures. This can help students identify transferrable work skills from experiences, such as international travel, cross-cultural encounters, or involvement in student organisations. Research suggests that e-portfolios are particularly effective at helping students develop a personal learning experience, connect different areas of their learning (academics, career, and international experiences), judge their own work effectively, gain awareness of their own progress, and learn to showcase themselves to graduate schools and potential employers. AIFS developed the workbook "Marketing Your International Experience," which prompts students to reflect on their learning in three dimensions: cultural understanding, personal growth and values, and professional and career development. Students connect outcomes from their learning abroad experience with knowledge, skills, and attitudes expected by employers, and practice writing "elevator pitches" to capture salient outcomes from their international experience (Hubbard, Manginelli, Kaltved, & Durham, 2017).

Outcomes from learning abroad

Malicki and Potts (2013) found that academic research and long-term studies conducted over a span of fifty years, "unequivocally [show] that studying overseas significantly augments the 'international skills' of graduates" (p. 2). Their literature search determined that overseas study programs promoted development of the following skills and competencies:

- Understanding of the complexity of global issues;
- Applying disciplinary knowledge in a global context;
- Ability, and comfort, to work with people from other cultures;
- Intercultural awareness;
- Adaptability and tolerance;
- Cognitive skills (in those who have not travelled previously);
- Self-confidence and self-reliance;
- Open-mindedness and independence; and
- Both general and culturally specific creativity.

Their meta-analysis of the research literature found that, 10 to 15 years after graduation, a significant number of learning abroad program alumni reported that their overseas experience enhanced their overall employability. For students who had participated in programs as short as one month, there were gains in their intellectual, social, and personal development.

The Institute of International Education completed the largest and most comprehensive survey of U.S. study abroad alumni, investigating the connection between study abroad programs and development of skills that contribute to employment and career development (Farrugia & Sanger, 2017). The study surveyed over 4500 program alumni in the academic years 1999–00 and 2016–17. This was the first national survey in the United States in which researchers sought to explicitly understand the impact of study abroad in assisting students gain an "employment edge," and to assess whether there was a correlation between a student's international experience and their employability. The researchers reported these key outcomes:

- Skills gained through study abroad are perceived to have a long-term impact on career progression and promotion. More than 50% of respondents reported that their international experience contributed to a job offer at some point.
- Student intentionality and participation in highly structured programs were found to contribute to skill development. Respondents who said they had "career prospects in mind when choosing to study abroad" were better

able to articulate both the skill development and career impact they gained through the experience (pp. 18–19).

- Study abroad programs with clearly articulated career-related goals help students identify the transferable skills they expect to learn prior to studying abroad, which then helps them articulate how they learned those skills to employers.
- Importantly, students "who intentionally sought to develop work-related skills through study abroad" reported more positive employment outcomes (p. 19).

Farrugia and Sanger (2017) framed the soft skills and competencies which students reported in three categories: intrapersonal competencies, cognitive competencies, and interpersonal competencies: "A majority of respondents reported that their study abroad experience helped develop or improve intercultural skills, curiosity, flexibility and adaptability, confidence and self-awareness to a significant degree. About half of respondents reported increases in interpersonal skills, communications, problem solving, language skills, tolerance for ambiguity…to a significant degree" (p. 12).

Learning abroad, and specifically WIL programs, such as internships, research, and service learning in cross-cultural settings, are considered high-impact modalities of experiential learning (Kuh, O'Donnell, & Reed, 2013). A three-year assessment of U.S. students who participated in domestic and research work in Japan found international experiences that combine intensive language and culture instruction, hands-on cutting-edge research experience, and intentional activities that require participant reflection upon the way in which they experience the culture in research improved students' global understanding in context, thereby better preparing them for engineering global workforces (Matherly, Phillips, & Ragusa, 2015).

Given the interest of employers in closing the skills gap, these applied learning experiences provide employers with opportunities to directly impact the development of skills and competencies most applicable for their businesses. Malerich's (2009) survey of the literature highlights the critical need for the principal stakeholders – academic institutions, employers, and students – to "create new levels of partnerships to develop international internship experiences through which all stakeholders gain." This alignment of interests enhances prospects for learning outcomes which favourably impact student employability in the field or sector in which they worked, served, or volunteered (Nolting, Donohue, Matherly, & Tillman, 2013).

Conclusions

The heightened attention among international educators to focus their planning and allocation of resources in ways that purposefully link their learning abroad programs to employability outcomes has become a more common fixture within global higher education institutions.[5] All stakeholders, on campuses and within the local, national, or regional workforce, are engaged and focused on how campuses and national learning abroad program initiatives succeed in developing skills and competencies of graduates which make them employable in all sectors of the global economy.

The demands that higher education institutions commit to broadening access has brought new challenges to traditional models of learning abroad. The base of students expecting to participate in learning abroad programs has expanded and has contributed to changing expectations for these experiences. To more fully engage all students desiring the advantages that international experience adds to their prospects of employability, campus leaders have to more aggressively make the case for both short- and longer-term returns on student investment in learning abroad. Thus, there is a new, pragmatic approach necessary in the design of learning abroad programs. Making this case is easier in light of the correlation which researchers have found between learning abroad and employability. Students and their families need to be made aware of this linkage and the important ways in which learning abroad can contribute very directly to student career development and post-graduation employment.

Notes

1. See also Jensen (this volume), page 122, about rising student expectations.
2. Other discussions about the definition or concept of employability can be found on pages 25, 25, 60, 62, 92, 117, 164.
3. See also Ota & Shimmi (this volume) for a more detailed treatise, page 78.
4. See also Leppänen et al. (this volume) for a more in-depth treatise on page 39.
5. See also Beelen (this volume) for a similar approach in IaH on page 200.

Chapter 2

How can international learning experiences enhance employability?

Critical insights from new graduates
and the people who employ them

Wendy Green, Eva King, and Jessica Gallagher

Introduction

With reports of a downturn in graduate employment rates (Karmel & Carroll, 2016), universities are keen to ensure that their students develop clear and tangible career pathways (Matherly & Tillman, 2015). In this climate, the rationale for promoting "outbound mobility experiences" (OMEs)[1] has shifted from the traditional focus on the personal and cultural benefits of these programs to their benefits in terms of enhanced employability. Governments and higher education institutions, which fund outbound mobility programs, now expect OMEs to be transformative of participants' professional as well as personal lives (British Academy, 2012; DFAT, 2017).

Yet, the benefits of international experience to employers and to new graduates tend to be assumed rather than understood. Researchers have long decried the lack of empirical evidence about employers' perspectives on this topic (King, Findlay, & Aherns, 2010). Likewise, little attention has been given to the "uses" students make of their international experiences in terms of career development and employability (Potts, 2015). In preference to the term graduate "outcomes," Rizvi introduced the term "uses" of international education to signify the ongoing, agentic processes through which "students struggle to make sense of their experiences [in a foreign country]; the ways in which they assess their past and imagine their future; and the ways in which they feel positioned and actively locate themselves within dominant [political and cultural] narratives" (Rizvi, 2005, p. 81). As such, Rizvi's term is consistent with recent work by Bennett (2016), who defines employability as the ability to find, create, and sustain meaningful work across lengthening career lifespans.[2] Taking this perspective here, we consider employability to be a developmental and agentic process, which must begin long before students graduate and continue throughout their lives.

Based on a recent nationally funded Australian project, this chapter presents fresh insights on the perceived benefits of outbound mobility experiences (OMEs) to employability, from the perspectives of past participants in OMEs and the employers of new graduates. The research was conducted across three

Australian universities and included the engagement of prominent employers of new graduates in nationally and internationally oriented workplaces.

Background

During the past decade, there has been a notable increase, globally, in the development and promotion of student mobility experiences, as evidenced by the significant funding of programs such as the U.S.'s Generation Study Abroad program, the European Erasmus+ program, the Re-vitalisation Strategy of Japan, and the Brazilian initiative, Science Without Borders, among others. In Australia, the context of this study, the New Colombo Plan (NCP), launched in 2014, was developed by the Australian government to lift knowledge of the Indo-Pacific region by supporting undergraduates to study and undertake internships in the region. The program, which encompasses both a prestigious scholarship scheme as well as funding for discipline-specific mobility projects, has made available $50 million to fund approximately 10,000 students annually. Students have access to funding to undertake short- and longer-term study, internships, mentorships, practicums, and research. By the end of 2018, it is expected that more than 30,000 Australians will have been funded to study and undertake internships in the Indo-Pacific through the NCP program (DFAT, 2017).

The rationale behind these initiatives is multifaceted. Mobility programs are expected to not only benefit the individual but also to support broader institutional and national economic and social interests by creating people-to-people links and knowledge sets which benefit educational linkages, corporate relations, and international diplomacy efforts. At the core of these national funding schemes for student mobility has been the aim for students to develop global competencies and have access to a global network of peers, collaborations, and employers. Universities worldwide have been quick to leverage mobility funding schemes, recognising the wide-reaching benefits of international mobility experiences and purported links to strong employment outcomes. Indeed, student mobility experiences have now been almost inextricably linked with the employability agenda in higher education.

Literature review

OME is widely associated with the development of professionally relevant skills and dispositions (Adams, Banks, & Olsen, 2011), and universities market such programs, promising they will provide participants with a "competitive edge" in a tightening graduate job market (Potts, 2015). Such claims, however, are not well supported by research. There are few studies that have comprehensively examined the impact of OME on employability from the perspectives of new graduates (Potts, 2015) or employers (Crossman & Clarke, 2010; King et al., 2010). Of those studies which do focus on employability, few have comprehensively considered whether the nature of OME – in terms of duration, location, and professional relevance – has an impact on employability. Instead, OME research has tended to focus on areas of personal growth and transformation. While many studies find OME promotes personal growth (McNamee & Faulker, 2001; Pence & Macgillivray, 2008; Van Hoof & Verbeeten, 2005), some have argued that students' self-reported "transformation" may be a self-fulfilling prophecy (Sutton & Rubin, 2010) and suggest that transformational "epiphanies" can be "fake" or "temporary" (Mernard-Warwick & Palmer, 2012, p. 132).

Among those studies which focus specifically on OME graduates' perspectives of employability, Teichler and Janson (2007) found that former ERASMUS students did not believe that their OME advantaged them in terms of income and social status during their early career. Indeed, they felt that the professional value of OME was declining, although it remained professionally valuable for central and Eastern European students. In contrast, Franklin's (2010) American study revealed that the majority of OME alumni, 10 years after their international experience, believed that the knowledge, skills, and self-awareness gained through OME were professionally applicable, and that their international experience had positively shaped their career path, leading them to gravitate toward positions with an international or multicultural dimension.

Findings regarding the professional value of OME may be context-specific (Potts, 2015). Potts's (2015) study of Australian OME alumni provides insights into the benefits of international study in relation to employability, current job, and early career development. Participants in this study identified the development of at least four areas associated with employability: communication skills, teamwork skills, problem-solving skills, and self-management skills. Potts also found that the majority (65%) of respondents believed their OME was most helpful in obtaining their first job, but less relevant once they began work. The majority (63%) believed that their OME would have a positive impact on their longer-term career prospects, however. There is some evidence that this expectation of future value may be warranted (Crossman & Clarke, 2010; Molony, Sowter, & Potts, 2011; Prospect Marketing, 2006).

Further research is required in order to understand employers' perspectives on OME. While several studies conducted in the EU (Bracht et al., 2006; Teichler, 2012) suggest that OME is viewed positively by European employers during the recruitment process, one British report concluded that "solid evidence on employers perspectives on international student mobility is a major lacuna in research" (King et al., 2010, p. 47). When employers were asked in another British study to list the qualities and attributes they look for in graduate employees, international experience did "not come high on the list, if it is mentioned at all" (Fielden, Middlehurst, & Woodfield, 2007, p. 14). In the Australian context, one of the few large-scale studies (Prospect Marketing, 2006) found that more employers in multinational firms (70%) valued OME than did state-based or national employers (43% and 55%, respectively). Norris and Gillespie (2009) found a similar pattern in the United States. The 2006 Prospect Marketing study also found that although overseas study was viewed positively by potential employers, it was considered to be unimportant against other skills, attributes, and experiences when evaluating graduate candidates. A comparative international study (Molony et al., 2011) indicates that undervaluing of OME by Australian employers has persisted, with the finding that just 34% of Australian employers value international experience in comparison to the global average of 60%. According to Molony et al. (2011), Australian employers' low appreciation of OME may be because Australian students tend to go abroad to culturally or linguistically familiar places, few employers have studied abroad so they don't see the benefits, and graduates and universities do not articulate OME benefits in employer-relevant terms while the OME discourse emphasises personal not professional benefits.

Taken together, these studies suggest that our understanding of the professional value of OME from the perspectives of employees and employers is emergent. Broadly speaking, indications are that employers, particularly in international and globally oriented organisations, value OME. Yet, there may be significant regional differences in this respect, with employers in Anglophone countries more likely to undervalue international experience than those in the EU. Regardless of location, however, the research reviewed here suggests that OME alumni must be able to articulate the value of OME in a language relevant to their employer; international experience may have value to employers *if* graduates are able to reframe their stories in language employers understand (Gardner, Steglitz, & Gross, 2008; Jones, 2013b; Gothard, Gray, & Downey, 2012). As a corollary of this finding, some researchers are pointing to the role universities must play in formally supporting students' development of professional skills and identities through OME (Gothard et al., 2012; Potts, 2015; VandeBerg, 2007). From these tentative conclusions, new questions arise, including the following:

- What are the approaches and strategies taken by new OME graduates who successfully secure graduate positions and manage their early careers in their chosen field?
- How do these "successful" graduates develop and use these approaches and strategies?
- How and why do current employers of graduates from Australian universities value, or not value, OME?
- Are there some types of OMEs that are more professionally valuable than others; for example, in terms of duration, location, and work experience opportunities?

Methodology

To explore these questions in the Australian context, we conducted individual, semi-structured interviews with two groups of informants: 14 recent graduates who had undertaken international study/internships while at university and were subsequently employed in graduate positions, and eight employers of recent graduates. Both graduates and employers were purposefully selected in order to provide maximum diversity regarding gender, discipline, field of employment, cultural-linguistic backgrounds, and, for graduates, host countries for their OME. In addition to ensuring diversity, only those graduates who had successfully applied for graduate positions in their chosen field were selected for this study. At the time of the interviews, our graduates had been working in their first graduate positions for a period of 6 to 12 months in the following fields; journalism, law, medicine, engineering, marketing, business, and public policy. They were based in positions around Australia and overseas.

The employers invited to participate in interviews worked in the public and private sectors, and in large and medium-sized businesses or organisations. Surprisingly, to us, many employers declined our invitation, stating the following reasons: they had not thought about the value of OME and felt they had nothing of value to say, it was not important to their business, or they had negative perceptions about OME and felt they would be unhelpful to the researchers. All employers agreeing to be interviewed were based in Australia at the time of the interview, although just over half of them represented international or globally oriented workplaces, while the rest were from locally or nationally oriented businesses. They were in leadership positions in financial planning, banking, law, public service, health, education, and telecommunications.

During the interviews, graduates were asked to tell their own story about their OME, their career aspirations, current employment, and longer-term aims. They were prompted to elaborate on approaches and strategies during each phase of their OME – preparation, time abroad, and the return home – as well as the role their OME played during the recruitment phase and day-to-day work. Employers were asked about what they generally looked for in new graduates and specifically about their perceptions of OMEs in relation to graduate employability.

The interviews, lasting between 45 minutes and one hour were recorded, transcribed, and analysed thematically. Beginning with some potential themes gleaned from our literature review, we took an inductive and iterative approach to analysing the transcripts, moving recursively, back and forth between the transcripts, the literature, and emerging themes until we found the best fit (Braun & Clarke, 2006). All participants were given the opportunity to comment on the emerging findings during the analytical process, and these were incorporated into the final analysis.

All participants understood the ethical implications of their involvement in the study and signed consent forms before their interviews. To protect their privacy, we have avoided the provision of detailed personal information and have assigned numbers to employers (for example, E1), and to graduates (for example, G1).

Findings regarding recent graduate and employer perceptions of the benefits of OME to employability

Not surprisingly, analysis of the interviews mirrored previous studies regarding perceived benefits of OME and perceptions of personal growth. Following a brief summary of these findings below, we elaborate on additional findings which bring new insights to our understanding of perceptions about OMEs, specifically in terms of employability. Employers' and graduates' perceptions of OME are grouped thematically: first, in terms of its relevance to recruitment and early careers; second, in relation to the type of OME undertaken; and third, in relation to the specific strategies employed by the new graduates to realise the professional value of their OME.

Personal growth

Our graduate participants had little doubt that their OMEs propelled their personal growth. In line with previous research (Potts, 2015; Van Hoof & Verbeeten, 2005), they spoke of developing life skills (such as adaptability), resourcefulness, resilience, problem solving, patience, help-seeking behaviours, organisational skills, interpersonal skills (such as rapport building, conflict resolution, negotiation, assessing, and trustworthiness), leadership, and independence. Overall, they felt they developed more confidence in their capacity to handle challenging situations in the future. Many commented on their development of empathy and worldliness – a sense of perspective and appreciation for alternate worldviews. Some felt they had become less egocentric, self-conscious, culturally blind, and dependent as a result of their experiences overseas. Interestingly, while the graduates emphasised different aspects of personal growth from OMEs, they all believed that it enhanced their employability, and they gave specific examples of using such skills and attitudes during recruitment and while at work.

Employers, too, unanimously saw personal growth as an outcome of OME, although the degree that it was valued in relation to employability differed between employers. For example, E6, a HR manager for a corporate investment firm with national and international bases and clients, "place[d] a good degree of emphasis [on the personal growth gained from OME] because … it demonstrates courage, get up and go, resilience." E3, the foreign-born owner/manager of a locally based financial planning firm with some international clients, also saw some value in OME related to personal growth, but he placed more emphasis on work experience in the local context.

Relevance at the recruitment phase

All graduates felt that their OME helped them successfully apply for their current positions. They were thoughtful and proactive in drawing attention to experiences and in highlighting benefits in terms of relevance to their prospective employers in their resumes and interviews. They felt that their OME gave them something to talk about in their interview and helped them to impart a sense of who they were and the qualities they possessed. For example, some referred to their OME as concrete evidence of their ability to move to a new city and establish social and professional networks. Because they felt confident in their ability to meet these and other associated challenges, they generally felt the interview process was in itself less daunting than it would otherwise have been.

While all employers we interviewed recognised the personal growth benefits of OME, they stressed that in and of itself OME would not automatically make students more employable. As E4, the HR manager of a national accounting firm explains, "I don't think we would view the [OME] in itself as something that would add value to the organisation." Some felt OME contributed to the overall appeal of the candidate. E6 viewed it "very favourably," for a number of reasons, as he explains:

> Strategically, [E6's company] has a global growth agenda…. So, having people that have some outside-of-Australia experience is really beneficial for that reason. Second, I think it builds a great sense of maturity and independence and worldliness. Being away from the nest, out of your comfort zone, it makes you grow up pretty quickly. I think that is a really strong attribute … it demonstrates courage, get up and go, resilience – when you're a long way from home. The third thing, for me, is around perspective. Having worked offshore I know that Australia's just a small part of the world. Bringing a global mind-set is a very valuable thing.

In contrast to employers like E6, some had less positive views of OMEs and explained that this shaped their approach to recruitment interviews. Several employers emphasised the importance of locally derived knowledge and work experience, and feared that time spent overseas meant less time to develop locally relevant knowledge and skills. This concern was brought home to one of the graduates in our study. G7, while a civil engineering student, had spent all his university holidays on language exchange programs in Asia. He was unsuccessful in securing employment as a civil engineer in Australia, because employers preferred to recruit graduates who had spent their holidays gaining Australian industry experience. At the time of the interview, G7 was working for an Australian trade consultancy firm based in China.

Finally, new OME graduates were perceived to be "flight risks"[3] by some employers, even those who were generally positive in their views of OME. As E4 explains:

> The only risk we would see [with OME graduates is] that person could be a flight risk for us. They might not necessarily be looking to stay long term … they might have an interest in being based overseas further into their career. That's not necessarily always an issue but it might ring some alarm bells for us when we are recruiting … So that kind of more international, global focus might actually work against them.

Relevance in the workplace

Beyond recruitment, all new graduates and some employers felt graduates' OME held benefits for employability once in the workplace. Graduates spoke of many instances when they were able to draw on their international experience to enhance interactions within multicultural workplaces or to create common ground with co-workers by swapping travel stories. They also felt that it was less daunting to move to a new city and establish new social networks, they were less afraid to ask for help and own up to mistakes, and they coped better with day-to-day ups and downs, partly as a result of their OME. G9, a graduate in a marketing firm explains:

> Travelling helps to train your mind to focus on what's important in those moments when you're being bombarded by thousands of different demands and wondering what direction you need to go in, what to pay attention to.

Some employers mentioned that they capitalised on their OME graduates' experiences, for example, by pairing a graduate whose OME was in China with a client from Beijing. More often, however, graduates and employers saw OME as a long-term investment, the value of which would be most apparent later in their careers. Because they had observed that leaders in their respective industries had travelled and worked internationally, they reflected that international experience, even if not immediately useful, might be more important once they gained more experience. Only G4 already felt that the skills she developed through OME had helped her to progress her public service career more swiftly than her peers had.

As the interviews with employers progressed, we noticed the employers tended to become more reflective about previously unrecognised benefits of OME. In the reflective space of the interview, some initially less positive employers came to mention several potential advantages of an OME graduate as the interview progressed. Advantages recognised with reflection included the following: enhanced cultural awareness and the capacity to speak languages other than English, particularly Mandarin, in the multi-cultural communities that their locally based businesses served; the professional value of the graduate's development of "get up and go," tenacity, and perseverance; and international connections. Such shifts in perspective during the interview process suggest the potential value for universities in engaging employers in dialogue in a manner somewhat akin to "learning conversations" (Laurillard, 1997). This point will be taken up further in the following discussion section.

Interestingly, one employer, E5, the CEO of a firm which organises international internships for students, observed that "Australia lags behind the rest of the world" in understanding the benefits of OME to employability. Mirroring research findings (e.g., Teichler, 2012), E5 explained that, in her experience, U.S. and European employers in particular seek to recruit culturally aware graduates, given the increasingly globalised marketplace: "If you want to prepare people for the world, and for global business and global career opportunities, then they need to do that abroad. I don't believe you can get … real insight to another country and the culture until you live in that country."

How important was the nature of the OME?

Employers were also asked whether the type of OME, in terms of its duration, nature (work, study, or both), and location made a difference to its value. In contrast to some studies showing distinct preferences for specific types of OMEs among some employers (Franklin, 2010; Norris & Gillespie, 2009), our interviewees generally provided quite nuanced responses. Neither employers nor graduates believed that it mattered significantly whether the OME was part of a traditional student exchange or a work-related experience. Our employers and graduates generally felt that longer experiences – one to two semesters of study, or three- to six-month internships – offered the time, space, and opportunities students needed to gain value from OME, whereas shorter experiences seemed too close to a holiday to get students "out of their comfort zones." Nevertheless, employers understood that that the quality of OMEs differed between people, and that these differences could only be appreciated by talking to individual employees. As E7 explained:

> On face value, a longer stint or an internship abroad seems more beneficial than just going off and doing a semester. But you generally don't know until you speak to the individual to see what they've gone through, how they've grown and valued the experience … what they got out of it.

Disciplinary differences influenced whether or not the OME location was important. The engineering and medical graduates had chosen destinations that equipped them with knowledge or skills that could not be obtained through study in their home universities. For graduates of law, marketing, and journalism, however, the destination was not perceived to matter so much.

Our study concurred with Potts's (2015) Australian study in finding that graduates who had had multiple OMEs emphasised their value. Through multiple OMEs, they believed they had become more comfortable challenging themselves; for example, by spending more time with locals and local students and less time with fellow exchange students. They found each OME went more smoothly, as they adapted more quickly and were then able to turn their attention to other professional opportunities. For example, when medical student G5 went on her third international exchange, she felt confident enough to ask her supervisors if she could do a clinical audit for the surgical ward at the hospital she was placed at. On G4's third exchange, she managed to work with locals to organise a donation scheme whereby exchange students could donate unwanted furniture at the conclusion of their stay.

Capitalising on the benefits – before, during, and after OMEs

The strongest, most consistent finding in our study concerns the importance of student agency in realising the employability benefits of OME. Common to all the graduates' narratives were three themes: they had actively pursued and planned for career-enhancing opportunities before, during, and after their time abroad; they recognised the importance of documenting and reflecting on experiences; and they developed the ability to reframe their travel experiences (travel stories) in order to make them relevant in specific professional contexts (career stories).

Pursuing professional development before, during, and after being abroad

While some students experience disconnection between their time abroad and their life at home, seeing their time away as a "dream" or as "living in a bubble" (Green & Leggett, 2015), the graduates in this study understood OME as having three important interconnected phases: preparing, being there, and coming back. Before departure, they sought out connections that would help them plan where to go and how to line up internships or professional development opportunities. They continued to do this while away and after they returned home. G7 and G4, for example, both involved themselves with Australia Chamber of Commerce, embassy events, and Australia-China Youth Associations during their China-based OMEs. Journalism graduate G6 explained how at the conclusion of her study and internship in Washington, D.C., she was able to stay on in the United States to take a job with a politician leading into the U.S. mid-term elections. This afforded her access to places like the State of the Union address and the Iowa caucuses: "there were lots of things that I did that I would never have thought I would be able to do as an exchange student." Back home, the graduates continued to build on their OME by becoming more engaged in their studies and co-curricular activities. G1, who had studied in a Canadian university, made more of an effort to engage with lecturers, and joined an international student society upon her return, while G4 purposefully made an effort to work with international students on group projects, thereby continuing to develop professionally valuable skills.

The theme of networking, building upon, and extending international relationships featured strongly in the new graduates' accounts of their time before departure, while away, and upon returning home. This finding may be reflective of the relatively high socio-economic status of OME students from Australian universities and particularly from the "group of eight" highest ranked universities (Daly, 2011). Indeed, research (Green, Gannaway, Sheppard, & Jamarani, 2015) undertaken at one of the three universities involved in this study found that OME participants generally had high cultural, social, and economic capital and enjoyed "multiple dimensions of privilege [that] typically work to make study abroad imaginable, affordable and do-able" (p. 513). Such students, who have typically travelled internationally with their families, are more likely to feel confident about forging international connections at the start of their OMEs. At the same time, the new graduates in this study typically sought advice about networking from lecturers at their home and host universities, rather than drawing on their families' social capital. This suggests universities and their staff could do more to guide OME students in the development of networking skills.

Documenting and reflecting

Self-reflection was another common theme across the graduate interviews. Some graduates felt they became more self-reflective about their goals, their view of the world, and their place in it during their OME. This, in turn, helped them to refine and focus their career goals; for example, a stint volunteering on a student-run radio station while abroad led G2, a science major, to refocus his career aspirations to science communication. G6, who was already studying journalism realised that her career focus would be on political journalism. While some reflection might be expected (a brief reflective exercise being a condition of their scholarships) some of our interviewees showed considerable reflexivity. As G4 found,

> Now that I've had these overseas experiences......I can see where I've come from and how I've developed from those experiences.

In contrast, others did not readily engage in reflection until they were applying for jobs. Indeed, all interviewees (employers and graduates) could see value in a formal resource designed to support reflection on OMEs and to articulate the benefits in terms of employability attributes. As G12 speculated,

> Not everyone has the foresight and self-awareness to really actively reflect on their experience. When you're away you wouldn't necessarily be [thinking about] employment later. Making time for that [especially] after you come back is really important and a structured program where you can reflect would [be helpful].

Further emphasising the need to support a more rigorous process of reflection for OME students, our graduate interviewees contrasted their own attitude to what they believed to be a general perception amongst their peers that a semester abroad was fun, a break from studying, as it didn't count towards their GPA, and an opportunity to party and sightsee. Our interviewees felt that many OME peers did not realise how it could develop their employability. As G4 commented, "the way the exchange is promoted....is that it's fun, time to party and have the best time of your life. But no one really thinks – what if you actually focus on your career and what you can do to enhance that – as well as having fun."

"Re-storying" – from travel story to career story

The graduates also shared an ability to reframe their experiences abroad into narratives that were relevant to the specific demands of the job – an ability that is vital in job interviews. For example, G9 explained:

> I would bring up stories of what I'd done abroad to demonstrate how I've acted in a particular circumstance or how I've displayed a particular skill. In

my interview they asked me how I managed stress. I talked about when I was snowboarding in the Rockies and there was an avalanche. We needed to get out of it. We needed to stay focussed and work as a team.

Discussion

Through extended individual interviews, we engaged deeply with employers of graduates and new graduates who had successfully applied for graduate positions in order to develop a nuanced understanding of employability development as a long and complex process involving a high degree of student agency. The views of the employers interviewed, as well as of those who declined to participate, concur with and extend previous research on employer attitudes. While those employers in globally oriented workplaces were more likely than those more locally oriented to view OME as favourable, both nationally and internationally focussed employers stressed that employees must articulate how and why their OME is professionally relevant. Generally, employers also perceived OME to be more valuable for mid-career rather than in entry-level positions. In line with previous research (Gardner, Steglitz, & Gross, 2009; Jones, 2013b; Prospect Marketing, 2006), these findings emphasise the importance of new graduates clearly explaining the value of their OME in terms relevant to each employment situation. In addition, our interviews provide new insights regarding employers' negative preconceptions of OME, such as fears of OME alumni being flight risks and having insufficient local knowledge and experience.

Thematic analysis of our graduates' accounts of their OME – from predeparture, time abroad, return to university, and into their first graduate positions – revealed how they developed specific strategies at each of these stages in order to enhance the professional benefits of their experience. These strategies included actively planning for learning experiences in the understanding that the value of OME does not stem from the fact of going but from what one learns while away, actively building career-related networks at each stage of the OME, documenting and reflecting on career-relevant experience at each stage of the OME, and re-storying personal experiences into career-relevant stories when applying for positions and beginning their graduate working lives.

Although we do not intend to generalise such findings from this small, qualitative study, a number of implications for both practice and research can be drawn when we consider our findings in the context of the current literature. Our study lends further weight to calls for formal learning programs to assist students to plan for, reflect on, identify, and articulate the value of OME in terms of employability. Informed by our findings and the current literature, we developed an online, multimedia, and co-curricular program, which supports students' development of professionalism and key employability skills at each phase of their international experience (Green et al 2016). Titled, "Putting your international experience to work", this program is divided into three modules (Preparing, Being there, and Coming back), which align with the three OME phases identified by researchers (Gothard et al., 2012) and by our OME graduate interviewees.

This program provides students with a structured approach to maximising the potential value of OME by guiding students at each stage in planning, networking, documenting, reflecting, and re-storying.

Another implication concerns the need to promote awareness about the benefits of OME to employers. If global mobility programs are to have the desired impact on employability, more attention needs to be given to understanding employers' perspectives. Interviews with employers in this study revealed a tendency to underestimate the employability benefits of OMEs. Interestingly, a Finnish study (Leppänen, Saarinen, & Airas, 2014) highlighted similar findings and concluded that the competencies acquired through OME are "hidden: we are not able to express or recognise them" (p. 5).

Observing that in the dialogic space of the semi-structured interviews employers tended to become more reflective about the possible benefits of OME as their interview progressed, our study suggests the potential value of research that engages employers in "learning conversations" (Laullilard, 1997). From this perspective, employers' perceptions – like students' perceptions – are socially constructed and open to change through dialogue. By extending the approach we took in this study, we might, for example, in the future engage with employers in participatory action research in order to open up possibilities of changes to the perceptions and practices of all parties involved (Kemmis, 2007).

Indeed, this study has revealed several other avenues for further research. Few studies to date have investigated employability-related differences between different types of OME. Of those that have, some provide contradictory findings (Franklin, 2010; Norris & Gillespie, 2009). On the other hand, our study shows that a select number of employers had no preconceived notions regarding the duration, location, and type of program; rather, they felt that it was up to individual students to find and articulate professionally valuable experiences in any type of OME. Further larger scale studies – across and between different geo-political regions – are needed before we can have clarity on this question.

Another area in need of further research concerns the longer-term employability benefits of OME. One large-scale, recent study (Farrugia & Sanger, 2017) of 4500 American students found that longer OME programs generally have a higher impact on subsequent job offers and on the development of employability skills than do short-term programs. Again, however, the current and previous studies suggest that geopolitical context may be a significant factor. Finally, now that some universities are beginning to develop and offer formal programs to support student learning through OME, such programs need to be evaluated and improved through action research cycles.

Conclusions

Based on a recent, nationally funded Australian project, this chapter has presented fresh insights into the perceived benefits of outbound mobility experiences (OMEs) to employability, from the perspectives of past participants in mobility programs and employers of new graduates. Regarding employers, our research confirmed and expanded upon previous findings that Australian employers tend to underestimate the benefits of new graduates' OME. Those employers in international organisations or businesses were more likely than those in national organisations to view OME as favourable. However, some employers expressed concerns that new OME graduates constituted flight risks and may not have locally relevant knowledge and skills.

Also, in line with previous research (e.g., Potts, 2015), our new OME graduates clearly articulated what they believed were the personal and professional benefits of their OME. Furthermore, thematic analysis of their reflections – from pre-departure, time abroad, return to university, and into their first graduate positions – provided fresh insights regarding specific strategies they had developed in order to enhance the professional benefits of their experience. In brief, these include actively planning for learning experiences, actively building career-related networks at each stage of the OME, documenting and reflecting on career-relevant experience at each stage of the OME, continuing to develop international and employability-related capabilities after returning home, and re-storying personal experiences into career-relevant stories when applying for positions.

Our approach enabled deep engagement with employers as well as a nuanced understanding of "employability" development as a long and complex process involving a high degree of student agency. Our findings interpreted in light of current research can inform the development of learning programs to support students' development of professionalism and key employability skills at each phase of their international experience – preparing, being there, and coming back.

Notes

1. Throughout this chapter, the term "outbound mobility experiences" (OME) is primarily used to signify a student's experience of undertaking an academic activity in another country while remaining formally enrolled in an institution in the home country. Such experiences may include study abroad, international internships, international study programs, outbound mobility, or student exchange.
2. Other discussions about the definition of employability can be found on pages 12, 60, 62, 92, 117, 164.
3. See also discussion on page 136.

Chapter 3

Hidden competences

Finnish employers' and students' appreciation of the effect of learning abroad on employability

Juha Leppänen, Aleksi Neuvonen, and Mika Saarinen

Introduction

Over the past one-half decade we have witnessed a remarkable shift in the discussion concerning the future of work and employment patterns. The parallel trends of digitalisation (accelerated by the emergence of cloud computing, artificial intelligence, new methods of machine learning, and advanced robotics) and globalisation of value chains in many industries have provoked a series of questions regarding which professions are likely to disappear and which will remain, and which skills are needed in the future. This development is also affecting the context in which educational policies and programmes supporting internationalisation operate; attitudes towards international learning abroad have polarised. For many, operating within a domain of international networks has become increasingly commonplace, but for others, increasing international mobility and migration, globalisation of the economy, and growing worldwide connectivity are sources of deepening anxiety. The old promise of learning abroad as being a source of special capabilities that enhance employability and overall competences seems to be in fluctuation.

As a reaction to these broad and evolving changes in our societies, employment patterns, and workplaces, a new discourse on skills, abilities, and attitudes, especially in relation to education and training, has emerged. Over the past few years, various authorities, institutions, and authors have debated the skills and competencies most likely to promote productivity in the workplace and support career choices in the turbulent digital era. (World Economic Forum, 2015; OECD, 2016) Typically, these lists of 21st-century skills reach beyond traditional content knowledge and towards competencies that would enable people to master constantly changing situations and tasks, and increasing quantities of information. However, relatively little research has been done on how employers' account for these competencies when they recruit new employees.

In 2012–13, the Centre for International Mobility (CIMO) (since 2017, merged into the Finnish National Agency for Education, or EDUFI) and the think tank Demos Helsinki examined how employers rated the knowledge, skills, and competencies acquired through learning abroad in their recruitment processes

(Leppänen, Saarinen, & Airas, 2014). The study also aimed to gain a deeper understanding of employers' views and expectations in relation to learning abroad, overall.

This article reports results from this study and connects them with recent discussions on work–life skills and competences, related changes in education policy, and current discourse on transformation towards future, post-industrial employment patterns.

International expertise: a new understanding

In 2005, CIMO conducted a study to understand the significance of learning abroad in the recruitment processes in companies, public organisations, and non-governmental organisations in Finland (Garam, 2005). It comprised an analysis of about 700 survey answers as well as 22 in-depth interviews from Finnish employers. The study found that, despite well-known trends in globalisation and increases in international activity, very few employers considered learning abroad very central when hiring new employees. Learning abroad was mainly seen as linked to language skills and cultural understanding, and relevant to only a minority of companies and positions.

These results formed the backdrop for a more comprehensive study by CIMO and Demos Helsinki, carried out in 2012–13. The new study comprised a survey asking both employers and students how important, as a part of the recruitment process, they consider an applicant's international experience. It also asked employers which attributes they value most when recruiting new employees. This survey yielded over 2000 responses: 283 responses from employers and 1770 responses from students. Responding employers included a representative variety of different industries from private, public, and non-governmental organisations. Likewise, responding students included those from both secondary, vocational, and higher education in different disciplines (Leppänen, et al., 2013). Figure 3.1 presents these results alongside the results from 2005.

The study started with qualitative research on how employers, students, and experts perceive the concept of learning abroad. Through a series of three workshops with 130 participants and over 20 individual interviews, we found that the existing conceptual framework (learning abroad) is, although important, too narrow in a 21st-century society. In the analysis derived from the empirical data collected in workshops and interviews, we understood that a more holistic framework is needed to capture various dimensions and meanings that the phenomenon relates to. The new framework should account for different areas of international interactions; not just through formal, but also every day, situations. Thus, international expertise is used as a framework to describe both learning and developing competencies from international interactions, including also learning abroad.

The new survey results confirmed the findings from CIMO's previous study from 2005. Most of the employers did not consider international expertise

How international expertise matters in recruitment, %

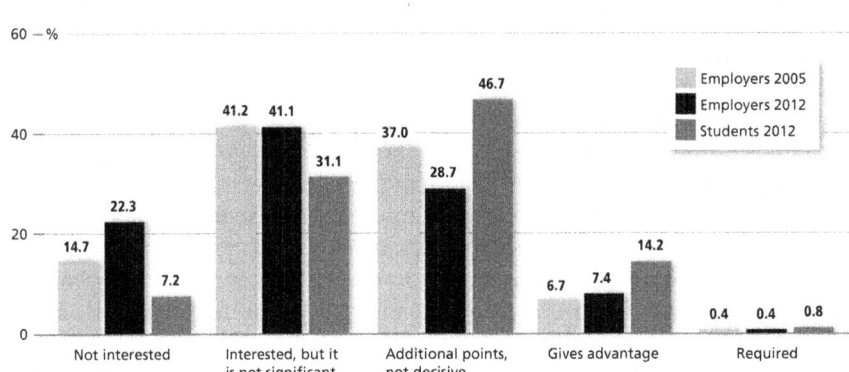

Figure 3.1 Perceptions of employers (in 2005 and 2012) and students (in 2012) about the relevance of international expertise.

important in the recruitment process, despite the fact that they might otherwise give it value (overall, 90% of employers had a generally positive view of international expertise). The percentages were even lower than in 2005. In 2012, only 36.5% of employers valued international expertise, in comparison to 44.1% in 2005. This figure was just above 50% for companies with international operations and a mere 10% for those without. The economic sectors of the companies had little impact on the result.

Recruitment criteria that employers considered highly important were reliability, the ability to access and analyse information, and problem-solving skills. Communication skills and cooperation skills were considered central in recruitment. However, employers are clearly not a homogeneous group, so it could also be seen that different recruitment criteria were considered important by different employers. As expected, employers who valued international expertise also placed greater relative value on language skills, willingness to travel for work, and experiences of studying or working abroad. Students, in contrast to employers, saw international expertise as a personal asset in their working lives, with more than half of them (61.2%) displaying this view. This indicates that students might overestimate the degree to which employers value the knowledge and skills acquired via international experiences.

Towards a deeper understanding of the effects of international expertise

The substantial difference in the value students and employers placed on international expertise called for further investigation. It was hypothesised that the difference might arise from disparities in how employers and students perceive the competences attained through international experience. In other words, the difference in views between students and employers might lie in the scope and plurality of attributes they associate with international expertise. This hypothesis led the research group to study the conceptual framework of international expertise in related competences in more detail. The attributes given to international expertise were further analysed in exploratory workshops and semi-structured interviews, where employers, students, and experts were asked to name the attributes that they associate with international expertise.

First, the traditional understanding of international expertise still appeared to be valid: international experience was seen to equip people with language skills, the willingness to travel, and the ability to work with different kinds of people. A new insight, however, was that in addition to many expected skills and competencies, participants linked many additional attributes to international expertise. These attributes comprise the second hypothesis of an *extended understanding* of international expertise.

The extended understanding of international expertise was also visible in the survey results when a further analysis of the material was carried out. Based on the survey, students and employers, in fact, associated very similar attributes to international expertise, overall. Half of the Finnish employers we surveyed associated international expertise strongly or very strongly with the following attributes: interest in new things, empathy, persistence, self-knowledge, self-confidence, and reliability. In a similar vein, a group of students perceived international expertise as an ability to think outside the box, or to perceive things outside one's own living environment and own country. To this group of students, international expertise could mean networking abilities and creativity as well as the ability to adapt, and a willingness to work with people from different backgrounds.

Interestingly, the attributes that Finnish employers associated with international expertise were also rated among the most important recruitment criteria overall, as shown in Figure 3.2. What does this overlap mean? International expertise can perhaps be a potent indicator in helping to identify qualities that employers appreciate. In other words, even if employers do not value international expertise, as such, in the recruitment setting it is still bundled together with many other skills and qualities that are valued by employers.

The new understanding of international expertise was further analysed by using factor analysis, forming groups of correlating attributes based on how employers link them to international expertise. Combining the survey results in this way with insights from workshops, we found that international expertise could be grouped under three overarching attributes: productivity, resilience, and curiosity. Productivity is understood as high efficiency and capability. In factor analysis, the linked attributes were efficiency, analytical ability, problem-solving ability, and reliability. The connection to international expertise was apparent. When coming across new cultures and situations, employees must develop their ability to efficiently come up with new solutions. In the same vein, many workshop participants made a connection between international expertise and highly capable individuals seeking global experiences.

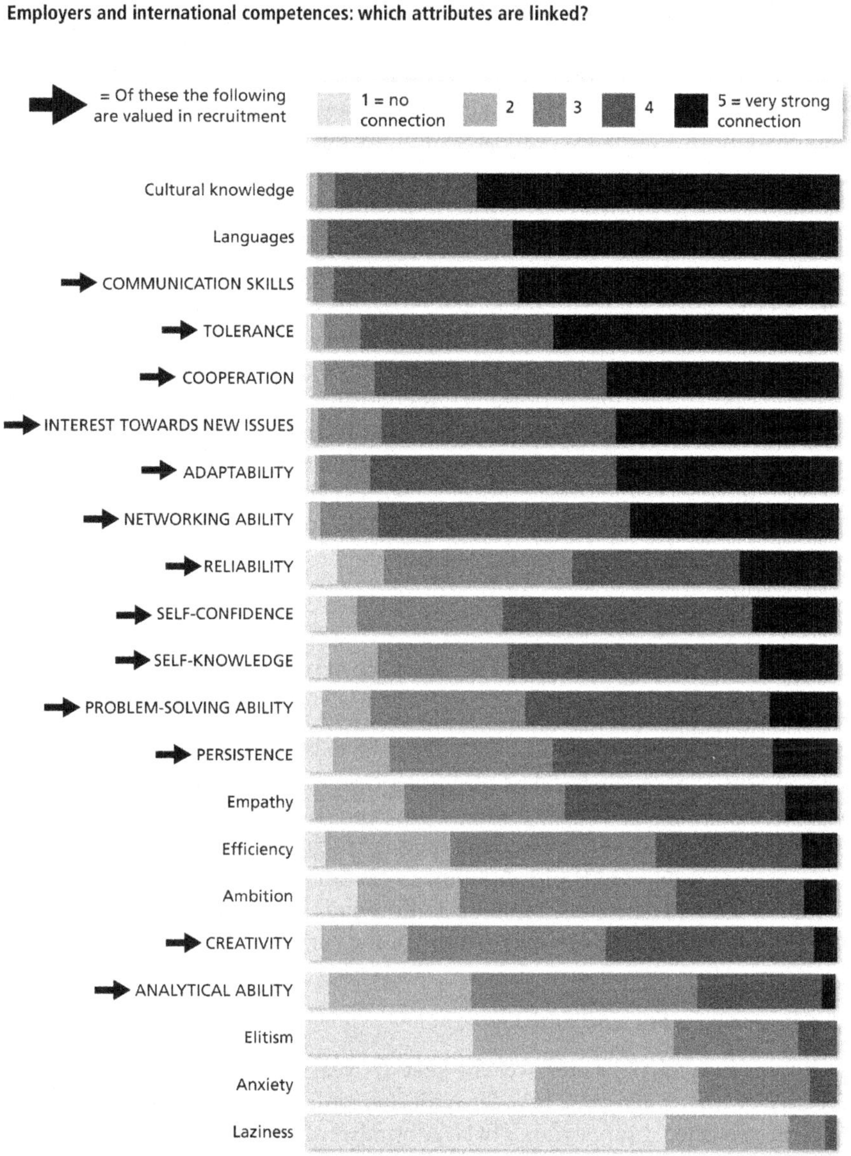

Employers and international competences: which attributes are linked?

= Of these the following are valued in recruitment	1 = no connection	2	3	4	5 = very strong connection

Cultural knowledge

Languages

➤ COMMUNICATION SKILLS

➤ TOLERANCE

➤ COOPERATION

➤ INTEREST TOWARDS NEW ISSUES

➤ ADAPTABILITY

➤ NETWORKING ABILITY

➤ RELIABILITY

➤ SELF-CONFIDENCE

➤ SELF-KNOWLEDGE

➤ PROBLEM-SOLVING ABILITY

➤ PERSISTENCE

Empathy

Efficiency

Ambition

➤ CREATIVITY

➤ ANALYTICAL ABILITY

Elitism

Anxiety

Laziness

Figure 3.2 Significant linkage. Attributes that employers and students associated with international expertise and those prized for recruitment.

Resilience captures the growth in individual ability to handle adversity through increased flexibility and persistence, which can help focus on constructive solutions. In factor analysis, the attributes grouped under resilience were self-awareness and persistence. In the workshops, resilience was often the overarching denominator for skills attained from international experience, in particular from experiencing and living through new situations.

Finally, curiosity illustrates how individuals approach new phenomena with a positive and open mind. The linked attributes were tolerance, interest in new issues, cultural knowledge, cooperation, and adaptability. In the workshops, many participants interpreted the benefits of international experiences as an interest in new phenomena, a constant drive to learn, and openness to previously unknown situations. It is a set of competences that is closely related to OECD's recently launched PISA framework for global competence (OECD and Asia Society, 2018), and with the global mindedness (Garam & Andreotti, 2015) concept of a research team associated with CIMO.

The extended approach to international expertise includes traditional language skills, communication skills, intercultural knowledge, and tolerance. However, productivity, resilience, and curiosity augment the traditional view and complete our picture of how expertise fits into today's working life. Together, the traditional view and these three new factors help us understand what today's employers perceive as the value of international expertise. They also form a concrete and coherent narrative for the necessity of international expertise in today's working life.

International expertise in the 21st century

Five years on, the results of our 2012–13 study seem even more timely and relevant than when the study was initially published. Our conclusions preceded many discussions that have taken place over the past few years around the future of work, new ways of understanding skills, and initiatives to reform education and match the needs of the emerging digital, global, and interconnected era. In particular, the projected transformation to post-industrial employment patterns cannot be ignored when talking about skills required in employment. The following sections outline how our results sit with the current debates.

The future of work and employment

One of the big global debates over the past five years, at least since publication of *The Second Machine Age* by Erik Brynjolfsson and Andrew McAfee in 2014, has been the projected disappearance of large number of jobs due to rapid advances in digital technologies, such as the emergence of artificial intelligence and advanced robotics. In the thirty years preceding, debate centred on the disappearance of blue collar and manufacturing jobs. The new discourse on employment, however, focuses on the end of routine jobs, regardless of whether those routines are built around manual or cognitive skills.

The extent of projected job losses over the coming decades varies greatly – between 10% and 60% in developed countries. While there is significant interest around which professions are likely to experience decline or increased demand, this discussion may be of secondary importance. Current industrialised economies may be entering a period very similar to the "Engels Pause" experienced between 1790 and 1850 (Hautamäki, Leppänen, Mokka, & Neuvonen, 2017). During that period, industrialising societies went through several decades of job loss and real wage stagnation before they could take advantage of the benefits of new technologies and methods of production. Productivity started to grow when the institutions supporting society and business were redesigned according to the new operating practices. These institutions included education providers. Our education systems were created to meet the employment needs of an industrial society. During the process of industrialisation, the need for educated workers soared, and states started providing education for the masses. This, in turn, benefitted industries, as educated people accelerated technological innovation. States began to invest in the public provision of infrastructure, as well as in science and technologies. This investment boosted both economic growth and social well-being (Allen, 2017).

The big question is whether this same formula of interlinked increases in education and technology will also guide us through the current transformation; will the jobs lost in manufacturing and services eventually be replaced by jobs that require more skills and provide better income? If this scenario is to transpire, traditional modes of teaching and learning are likely to require significant transformation to prepare students for the realities of the changing global labour market.

The rise of metacognitive skills: the growing demand for curiosity and resilience

Changing societies, businesses, and work life highlight the need for a new set of skills and competences. These competences are often described as metacognitive skills – skills that contribute to one's awareness of one's own thought, and one's ability to apply skills, once learned, to new situations (Lai, 2011). As fewer jobs offer long-term security, and many job descriptions change constantly, metacognitive skills, such as resilience and curiosity, serve as important tools for individuals to cope and even thrive in current and future work life.

Resilience is a quality that helps individuals avoid the stress associated with a changing work life. (Shatté, Perlman, Smith, & Lynch, 2017). Resilient workers adapt, know their limits and strengths, and are confident in what they know and persistent in their endeavours. While these are attributes traditionally linked with a good employee, they are expected to be even more valuable in rapidly changing working environments where stable careers are increasingly rare. Resilience enables employees to recover and continue working even as the context of work changes.

Curiosity, on the other hand, fosters both individual learning and a sense of meaning that give an individual the agility to thrive in the future labour market: an intrinsic interest in new phenomena and developments. For a company, curiosity leads to previously unknown possibilities and opportunities. This, in turn, can lead to creating value in new, often digital, ecosystems. For the public sector, curiosity enables the capacity to experiment and learn. It is likely that curiosity will continue to raise its status as a societal strength in the future, leading to a significant impact on the job market. This is due to the increasing complexity of societal problems requiring innovative solutions.

Curiosity, resilience, and the global discourse on skills

How do resilience and curiosity sit with the broader debate on future skills? A new discourse on skills and competences has emerged since our 2012–13 study, linked to the projected labour market trends described above. According to the OECD, "skills have become the global currency of the 21st century" (OECD, 2016). While the OECD does not define these skills in more detail, it can be implicitly understood that the concept of 21st-century skills here refers to a broad set of knowledge, skills, competences, work habits, and character traits that are considered critically important to success in today's world. There appears to be growing consensus around the idea that employees of the future require a broad set of skills. However, definitions differ of what these skills actually include. For example, some define 21st-century skills as transversal (generic) skills, others as interdisciplinary skills. According to the World Economic Forum, students require strong skills in areas such as language, arts, mathematics, and science but they must also be adept at skills such as critical thinking, problem-solving, persistence, collaboration, and curiosity (World Economic Forum, 2015).

More recently, the U.S. based Institute for International Education (IIE) Centre for Academic Mobility Research and Impact compiled an overview of studies on new types of hard, soft, and (meta)skills (Farrugia & Sanger, 2017). The study clustered them into *cognitive competencies* (cognitive processes and strategies, knowledge, and creativity), *intrapersonal competencies* (intellectual openness, work ethic, and positive self-evaluation), and *interpersonal competencies* (teamwork and leadership).

The ideas of a multiplicity of required skills and of clustering of these competences are echoed in the work carried out in our survey of 2012–13, where the extended understanding of international competences encompassed productivity, resilience, and curiosity, underscored by smaller skill sets and competences. Similar results have also been highlighted by other research in the field of psychology and behavioural sciences, especially skills related to managing and mediating complex social relationships, such as communication, team working skills, cooperation, empathy, and networking (Zimmerman & Meyer, 2013). Furthermore, both our study and those of others (Maddux et al., 2013) have identified increased multicultural engagement as a step towards a growth in integrative complexity, which can also be a key to resilience and constructive curiosity.

Implications for the field of education and working life

Based on the results of this research, it seems that more work needs to be done by authorities, educational institutions, and employers to highlight the range of skills and attributes developed via international experiences. These are, after all, the kind of skills sought after by the labour market and society.

First, educational institutions, authorities, and agencies promoting learning abroad need to engage in a more thorough dialogue with both public and private employers to make the hidden competences understood and recognised. There is a need to discuss the learning outcomes and their definitions and descriptions as well as manifestations to be able to present expertise acquired through international experience in a way that speaks to employers, and so that we can improve their relevance on the labour market. Educational institutions need to engage in defining and making visible, also, the broader learning outcomes of international experiences, those that will cover more than the traditional language skills, intercultural competences, or tolerance. This wider concept of international expertise will, in this case, encompass at least such skills as productivity, resilience, and curiosity.

Second, students and young people need tools and guidance to help them recognise their hidden expertise, and also to be able to better describe the competences gained, thereby, making them visible and relevant for future employers. And third, government policy and, particularly, education systems will need to revise their outlook on key skills, at all levels of education, to also encompass such skills and attributes as are highlighted in this research as key to facing the future challenges successfully.

Notably, since our study in 2012–13, some developments have also taken place within this arena. In, for example, Finland, in contrast to most of the world's countries, 21st-century skills have recently been considered in the design of basic education. A new national core curriculum for basic education was implemented in schools in 2016 by the Finnish National Agency for Education (EDUFI). The focus was set on transversal competences and on working across school subjects.

If, as our study suggests, international experiences give rise to competences like resilience and curiosity, the European Union's Erasmus+ programme can be seen to already have addressed students' hidden competences throughout its 30-year history. However, the issue of the broader effects of international experiences has not been widely recognised by the Erasmus+ programme until very recently. In fact, the topic of learning abroad was long seen as an insular, exceptional, and separated learning experience. The broader links and situating learning abroad within a wider framework were properly addressed for the first time only in 2014 in the Erasmus Impact Study (European Commission, 2014) and referred to more recently in the 2018 mid-term evaluation of the Erasmus+ -programme (European Commission, DG Education and Culture, 2018).

Furthermore, the newest OECD PISA assessment of 2018 (OECD PISA website) will consider what is referred to as "global competences," based on the

OECD PISA Global Competence Framework (OECD and Asia Society, 2018). The framework encompasses such skill sets as the capacity to examine local, global, and intercultural issues; to understand and appreciate the perspectives and world views of others; to engage in open, appropriate, and effective interactions with people from different cultures; and to act for collective well-being and sustainable development.

The way forward: international expertise as a route to future skills

The transitions happening in working life, within the job markets, and with regards to future skills and competences seem to be continuous. A concrete outcome of this is the growing labour market relevance of the so-called metacognitive skills. These skills highlight the ability to learn, grow, collaborate with others, and prosper in future societies. As is suggested by the previous sections, both the theoretical debate on 21st-century skills and the policy initiatives are beginning to recognise the potential of international experiences to foster such skills. This link between international experiences and sets of metacognitive skills highly valued in working life now, is something we demonstrated in our 2012–13 study.

While there is growing evidence supporting the value of learning abroad and of other international experience in developing critical employability skills and competences, the recognition of its key role is restricted by its current framing as mainly language skills, tolerance, and cultural knowledge. There is also a growing threat, the thought that this kind of framing of learning abroad cannot, at least in the long run, build societal inclusion for different groups of people as well as cohesion between these groups. Instead, international expertise could end up being highly divisive, something solely belonging to "Anywheres" (people with university education, access to international job markets, and a highly mobile, global lifestyle) with a widening divide with the "Somewheres" (those rooted to specific place, usually with conservative values and less education). The potential emergence of such a gap, already by itself, underlines the need for broader understanding of international expertise and of the ways how it can be achieved and of the benefits it can provide. An extended understanding of international expertise crystallises the connection between international experience and employability in the coming century, for both policy and practice.

Chapter 4

The impact of education abroad on competency development

Martha Johnson and Christine Anderson

International educators have, for a long time, anecdotally observed the positive impact experiences abroad can have on a student's professional development. This chapter is a case study detailing how the University of Minnesota (UofM) broadened and strengthened a curriculum integration strategy by focusing on career readiness for students while abroad and more effectively linking back to the university upon return. In order to garner more support for initiatives tied to career integration abroad with senior leadership at the UofM, UofM alumni who had experiences abroad were surveyed on their perceptions of the influence of the sojourn abroad on their career skill development and professional success. The outcomes of this research led to changes in support of students prior to departure, new program design while in the host country, and a more intentional approach for the students' re-entry back to the university. This chapter discusses the project, the shift that consequently occurred within the institution, the alumni study, and the new methods devised for guiding students towards deeper competency gains, articulation, and understanding of skill transference from abroad to workplace.

From curriculum to career integration

In 1999, the president of the University of Minnesota announced a bold goal to have 50% of the university's undergraduates undertake a substantive experience abroad by the time they completed their degrees. At the time this goal was announced, little research had been done on the long-term impacts of an experience abroad on academic, developmental, or career goals. While educators certainly understood, anecdotally, the transformation that seemed to be catalysed by study or work abroad, the practice remained marginal at the majority of U.S. universities, particularly public and state institutions. Conventional wisdom suggested that such a goal was inconceivable at a massive, public, urban university such as the University of Minnesota, with enrolments of over 50,000 students a year.

The central education abroad office at the UofM, the Learning Abroad Center, initiated and sustained a project called Curriculum Integration as a response to the university's ambitious goal. The initiative was awarded two major grants to fund collaboration between education abroad academic staff and departmental faculty to pre-identify coursework abroad for underrepresented curricular areas, primarily STEM (science, technology, engineering, and math), match equivalencies, and provide a seamless path for students to study abroad and simultaneously maintain progress towards their degree. Over a 15-year period of time, over more than one hundred academic departments successfully identified curriculum matches abroad and designated optimal semesters and modules for students to pursue study abroad, and also developed faculty-led programs or new partnerships where there were gaps.

The work on curriculum integration, including multiple environmental and climate surveys, provided insight into the perceptions of students and academic departments in general, and of learning abroad specifically, including the goals, outcomes, and skills students seek as they invest time, money, and personal capital in going abroad. The research and feedback, however, increasingly revealed that the curriculum is only *one* way to enter the conversation. Curriculum Integration proved to be particularly challenging in a few disciplines where the cohorts were harder to define. The best example of this is pre-health. Students seeking careers in various health fields that are studied at the graduate and professional level in the United States, including medicine and public health, are not in a single degree program or college. At the University of Minnesota, for instance, students can pursue a biology major in two separate colleges.

The career integration initiative

To better address the intersection of study abroad and career planning, the Learning Abroad Center (LAC) convened a cross-campus working group in 2012 to intentionally include the career perspective and to better define and support career planning in program selection and preparation. In other words, in the effort to base experience abroad in the curriculum we had neglected both the primary motivation and desired outcomes for many students seeking to study abroad. Conversations about careers and education abroad, at least in the United States, tend to morph very quickly into a discussion of internships, research, or other sorts of programs abroad that have a relatively clear connection to career plans. However, the majority of students studying abroad are not doing internships or research, and little work has historically been done to develop tools to understand and articulate the impact of other models, such as instructor-led programs or exchange study experiences.

Beginning in September 2012, the LAC leadership and committee agreed to apply the methodology of curriculum integration to a set of specific career related goals. The career integration initiative sought to build upon our proven strategies and integrate experience abroad into career and life planning. The goals identified were as follows:

- Apply the methodology of curriculum integration to a specific focus on career planning. Engage campus career and education abroad colleagues in a dialogue.
- Partner to integrate learning abroad resources into career advising structures.
- Communicate the cross cultural and global needs of industries to students.
- Integrate career-related outcomes into articulated individual program learning outcomes.
- Create program selection and advising tools designed to help students choose opportunities to explore or build skills in career interests.
- Identify student goals for careers earlier in advising and planning for going abroad.
- Assist students in maximising career reflection and opportunities on site.
- Expand resources and support for returned students in communicating and articulating the value of their specific experience abroad.

Since the inception of the initiative, the Learning Abroad Center has consulted and collaborated with more than fifty career professionals and advisors on campus. The university has hosted three highly successful career integration conferences, in 2014, 2016, and 2018. The conference papers have culminated in companion publications, and in so doing, generated some of the early and seminal scholarship on the intersection of education abroad and career development.

Additionally, the LAC has hosted site visits and on-site workshops abroad. These opportunities provided the career professionals with a better understanding of the in-country experiences of students while abroad. Career colleagues quickly identified ways to enhance career dimensions on site and to better facilitate career-focused reflection intentionally. The dialogue helped expose assumptions on the part of both the career and education abroad professionals. For instance, one career counsellor admitted that while she had always highlighted the intercultural learning potential in an internship abroad, she had not appreciated the level of the work students were doing and the tangible professional skill development she observed when visiting internships in Italy.

Simultaneously, the career component to the university's highly successful online one-credit culture class was expanded, and, in fact, the title of the class changed to Global Identity: Connecting Your International Experience with Your Future in order to make the career connection more explicit and highlight the skill development focus.

Intention, goals for alumni survey, and research context

Based on this foundation and overall commitment, the leadership of the Learning Abroad Center decided to design a survey for University of Minnesota alumni who had studied abroad, with the explicit goal of investigating what impact their time abroad had on skill development, early career choices, and opportunities, as well as the long-term influence the experience had on their professional lives.

The LAC sought to contribute to the growing body of research in this area. One unique feature of this study is that the population spans approximately forty years. As Franklin (2010) notes, "Nearly all known research lacks a longitudinal component" (p. 170). While other studies showed that education abroad may influence career skill gains (Farrigua & Sanger, 2017; Teichler & Janson, 2007), the LAC research sought to understand and document the connection for University of Minnesota alumni, specifically. Multiple goals for the study were identified, such as gaining a better understanding of whether UofM learning and development outcomes were being met. The basic study question, however, was simply, "Does an education abroad experience impact career and skill development?"

Exploring the literature, there is evidence that skill enhancement abroad can happen, and that there is a lack of acknowledgment of this connection by recruiters. This may be due to the gap in research on why time spent studying abroad would cause this increase to occur, often at a rapid pace. For example, Teichler and Janson (2007) conclude that, "Both the majority of former ERASMUS students and employers believe that internationally experienced students turn out to be superior in many professionally relevant competences than formerly nonmobile students" (p. 493). While Potts's (2015) focus was not on mapping learning abroad outcomes to employability skills, she concluded that, "one of the most important findings of this study is the potential capacity of learning abroad to contribute to the mission of the higher education sector to develop high-level employability skills in all graduates" (p. 13). Research indicates that a further benefit to competency gains from time abroad is the enduring impact (Franklin, 2010; Fry & Paige, 2008; Norris & Norris, 2005).

Yet, there remains a divide between recruiters identifying skills that have been shown to increase while abroad and those correlating studying abroad specifically as a factor in skill development. Crossman & Clark (2010) reported that agricultural companies had only begun to make the connection between hiring culturally competent employees better management of a diverse workforce. Crawford, Lang, Fink, Dalton, and Fielitz (2011) found employers, students, faculty, and alumni rank international experiences as the least important of all experiences that students undertake during their academic careers. Gardner, Gross, and Steglitz (2008) contribute this disconnect to the employers not understanding the value if they have not studied or worked abroad themselves.

We do our students a disservice by not making the connection between education abroad and career skill development more obvious for employers. Farrigua and Sanger (2017) compiled a list from American and European studies of the fifteen most desired hard and soft skills by employers. These skills included communication, confidence, flexibility or adaptability, intercultural, interpersonal, language, self-awareness, and tolerance for ambiguity (p. 7). Survey respondents reported positive skill gains from an education abroad experience in fourteen of the fifteen skills; the exception being technical or software skills. When comparing these desired skills to a definition of intercultural competence, it becomes clear why education abroad professionals should be claiming a space in the career competency development domain. Deardorff (2009) describes intercultural competence as "the ability to develop targeted knowledge, skills, and attitudes that lead to visible behaviour and communication that are both effective and appropriate in intercultural interactions."

Education abroad research has shown that properly facilitated time spent studying abroad increases students' intercultural competence (Hemming Lou & Weber Bosley, 2012; Vande Berg, Connor-Linton, & Paige, 2009). The act of increasing cultural competence is simultaneously enhancing students' ability to communicate, often in a second language; boosting their interpersonal skills; and improving their flexibility and tolerance of ambiguity. The symbiotic relationship between intercultural learning and desired career skill growth should be further leveraged and enhanced by education abroad professionals in order to close the link between what students are learning abroad and employers' perceptions of the experience.

Study design

This study aims to evaluate the impact of the study abroad experience on the career choices and trajectory of University of Minnesota alumni. The study also aims to understand how alumni perceive influence on personal growth and skill development. This is a mixed-methods study that investigates these influences on a population that was four to forty years removed from their experiences abroad. The survey included both scaled and open-ended questions. This allowed for a comparison with perceived gain in career skill, with variables such as duration, language study, and location.

Eleven randomly chosen respondents from the initial online survey were interviewed and asked to reflect more deeply on the impact of their experiences. Ten interviewees participated in a semester program between 1998 and 2012 with no internship, and one participated on a summer program with an internship. As this sample is strongly skewed towards semester programs, the data cannot be compared to the entire data set, yet some interesting patterns surfaced. Although no questions were asked about adversity, adaptation and resilience were emergent themes in all 11 interviews. The basic pattern of the interview was to discuss a challenge that was overcome, such as new language or homestay, and an increase in confidence, which facilitated skill gains in other areas.

The second round of coding was more intentional, and included the interview transcripts and a randomly chosen sub-set of the 106 open-ended responses to the question, "How did study abroad influence you as a global professional?" These responses were grouped by program durations of a month or less (N=32), two–three months (N=24), four–six months (N=31), and a year or more (N=20). The code construct was based on the Kelley and Meyers (1995) cross-cultural adaptation dimensions modified for a stronger focus on resilience (Fletcher & Sakar, 2013). The highlighted word in the definition denotes the construct name used in this article: emotional resilience (**persistence**), flexibility/openness (**behavioural**/personal interactions/new experiences), perceptual acuity (**cognitive**/understanding of others' perspectives), and personal autonomy (**independence**/maturity/growth/confidence).

Demographics

Approximately 700 University of Minnesota alumni who studied abroad responded to the survey. The gender breakdown was reflective of study abroad for the United States in general, with participants being 26% male and 73% female. Ages of participants ranged from 20 to 51+ years. It is heavily weighted towards younger alumni with 471 respondents in the 20- to 25-year-old and 26- to 30-year-old categories and 240 in the 31-year-old and above categories. The race/ethnicity breakdown is as follows: 634 White, 28 Asian, 15 Hispanic, 7 African American, 3 Native American, and 20 Unknown.

Analysis

In the descriptive statistics, the influence of education abroad on perceived skill gain is strong. The below statistics are in response to the question, "From your point of view today, to what extent do you consider your education abroad experience worthwhile in the following regards?"

Table 4.1 is a small but critical sample of this perception. The high gains in maturity and personal development as well as confidence are salient findings, as

Table 4.1 Benefit of study abroad experience for skills gains

Competency/skill	Lowest*	Middle	Highest*
Maturity and personal development	1% (9)	7% (49)	92% (647)
Confidence	2% (18)	8% (58)	89% (607)
Interpersonal and communication skills	3% (24)	12% (82)	85% (600)
New perspectives of your home country	3% (20)	8% (57)	89% (627)
Appreciate and interact with individuals different from yourself	4% (25)	8% (54)	89% (626)
Critical and analytical thinking	14% (99)	26% (186)	60% (419)
Creative and innovative thinking	11% (77)	26% (186)	63% (440)

* Lowest is the combination of those who disagree and strongly disagree. Highest is the combination of those who agree and strongly agree.

92% and 89% of the population, respectively, attributed gains in these domains to their education abroad experience. The high percentages indicate that variables such as duration or location do not appear to impact the sense that an experience studying abroad is a catalyst for personal growth. Thirty-one percent of alumni who studied abroad for a month or less coded for "independence" in response to how study abroad prepared them to be a global professional, compared to 42% in the 4 to 6-month category. An example response from the month or less group is, "foreign language skills, teamwork ability, communication, confidence."

Eighty-nine percent of total respondents strongly believed that they had new perspectives on their home country and a better appreciation of the other. This illustrates the cognitive and behavioural shift described in intercultural learning literature (Ward, 2001). The code percentages across duration contributing towards a behavioural shift to be a better global professional are similar for all durations, at 56%–58%, but in the year or category it jumps to 85%. The cognitive construct is quite even across all duration types, at between 52% and 58%. Often, these constructs are linked in responses, such as this reflection from the two- to three-month category: "The biggest impact was to learn to engage with others realising we all have different world views and experiences which impact on how we make decisions and work as a team to solve problems." We posit that the challenge of an education abroad experience leads to greater maturity and increased confidence. This, combined with a broadened practical knowledge of the world, facilitates students' ability to gain skills in other areas, such as critical or innovative thinking.

The data was analysed for statistical significance between the independent variables of gender, race/ethnicity, age, location of program, language of instruction, class standing, and duration of program, as well as for key outcomes, such as impact in first job, increase in self-confidence, broadening of worldview, and growth in many skills. There was no significant difference in gender or race/ethnicity. The population is overwhelmingly caucasian, thus no significance in this area was expected.

Location and language learning

Study abroad location impact may be best understood in conjunction with findings on taking classes in a language other than English. Alumni taking classes in a language other than English identified the connection between education abroad and skill gains in the following areas at a significantly higher rate than those who studied in English only: long-term career prospects, ability to learn new ideas quickly, and influence of skill set on career prospects.

As language learning was perceived to have a positive influence on long-term career prospects in the total population, this may explain the gap between the low perceived impact of education abroad on long-term career prospects in Australia/New Zealand (N=22) where students always take classes in English, compared to the much higher impact in Latin America (N=79) where students commonly take classes in Spanish. It is common for students to live with host families in Latin America, which could also be a factor in accelerated language learning and confidence.

The robust influence that learning in a new language has on career prospects, the ability to learn new ideas quickly, and skill set influencing a career suggests the importance of building language learning into program structures. Sixty-four percent of the respondents answered yes to the question, "Did study abroad reinforce your commitment to study language." This may be particularly relevant for American students who often do not speak a second language. One interviewee stated, "My ability to speak French has gotten me the ability to work on projects that I wouldn't have been able to do otherwise. And it has certainly influenced the way I look at the world and the way I look at what I want to do." It is also possible that awareness of communication gains across English-speaking cultures is not highlighted or facilitated as effectively for English-speaking sites. To date, there has been little research on this possible correlation.

Class standing

Alumni who went abroad as first-year students perceived more gains in communication skills, ability to learn new ideas quickly, broadening of worldview, and enhanced long-term career prospects than did the students who went abroad later in their undergraduate studies. This is intuitive, as these students have less life and academic experience than their older peers. Yet education abroad opportunities are most commonly created for upper class students. This finding may inform program design, as the first-year sample seemed to be capable and ready to benefit from an education abroad experience. An enhanced worldview early in an academic career could have a powerful impact on subsequent learning. In response, the University of Minnesota has developed a "Freshmen Seminar" series that incorporates more intentional group building and support. Internal data on students who studied abroad as freshmen between 2015 and 2018 documented that 93% are still at the university, pointing to retention as another possible outcome of education abroad early in academic careers, and the need to further study the possible impact or causation.

Duration

Similar to the findings in the Farrugia and Sanger (2017) research, longer program duration did positively impact skill gains. Yet, participants of shorter programs also benefited from going abroad. For example, all categories agreed or strongly agreed that they gained in ability to appreciate and interact with individuals different from themselves, and in self-confidence.

While the impact of duration is less evident in skill gains, it is more evident when linked directly to career trajectory, as is seen in responses for long-term career prospects and skill sets influencing career. This mirrors the Farrugia and

Sanger (2017) study finding that 68% of alumni who studied abroad for a year "reported study abroad contributing to a job offer at some point, compared to just 43 percent of alumni who went abroad for fewer than eight weeks" (p. 6).

Discussion

This research adds to evidence that an education abroad experience has a positive, long-term impact on professional competencies and career trajectory. There needs to be more research on how intercultural learning and challenge impacts career skill gains. There may be a relationship between growth in intercultural skills and successful navigation of the challenges inherent in education abroad, which leads to a confidence increase, in turn, facilitating skill gains. The impact of resilience on career skill gains could be investigated further. Study in a non-native language also has an enduring impact on skill development that should be further explored. In addition, the lack of association of communication gains with study in same-language sites should be a topic for further research.

Long program duration does not seem necessary for gains in certain skills, but students participating in shorter programs were less likely to recognise the impact of those skills on their career trajectory. Due to this finding, along with the disconnect between research on skill gains from education abroad and employers' perceptions of the value of this experience, we suggest that educators guide students to translate and articulate stories[1] of adaptability while abroad to career skill gains. One effective example is Smith's (2013) research on the impact that online mentoring during a students' time abroad had on their ability to articulate the experience. She found that students who took the course "Global Identity: Connecting Your International Experience To Your Future" while abroad, compared to those who did not take the course, had the ability to more clearly "identify and articulate their newfound skills and perspectives" (p. 137). Guiding students to translate their experience abroad in interviews and beyond may be the key to closing the gap between employer perceptions of skill development and actual education abroad student competency gains. This supports the findings of Farrugia and Sanger (2017) as well.

Conclusions

A review of the initial goals set for the career integration initiative makes it clear that University of Minnesota stakeholders now have a greater awareness of the career dimension to education abroad. Numerous intentional touch points, exercises, and resources have been developed and integrated into both the student cycle at the university and the student experience abroad.

The effort and methods of curriculum and career Integration at the University of Minnesota have led to a drastically increased participation by previously underrepresented students in disciplines across the university. Perhaps more importantly, these students have studied abroad with the support of a more intentional framework of pedagogical and program design choices created to maximise learning and leave far less to chance. By partnering with career colleagues, international educators have gained a better understanding of the role of experiences abroad in careers development in the long-term, and have developed strategies to help student better articulate what they have learned abroad.[1]

The associated research project has been an invaluable tool in gaining insights into the perceived value of studies abroad and skills gained by it that University of Minnesota students have developed or enhanced, both in terms of career impact and personal growth. However, there remain many lingering questions. Why did language study students perceive a significantly greater gain in overall communication skills than those who studied in English? Why is there a relatively low recognition by these English-only alums of the impact in terms of career path changes and choices?

The study can now be used as a baseline for further study, particularly as we change how we support career development for our students. The respondents for this survey all studied abroad before our initiative. Therefore, in future research, we will be able to compare the perceived impact felt by those who have benefitted from our enhanced career support and online instruction to the experiences of their predecessors.

Perhaps the best journey starts with a bit of flexibility in both the destination and the preferred route. Such is the case with this survey and interviews related to the LAC research project, which began with a focus on jobs, career advancement, and intercultural and global skills. While these gains were identified as clearly being enhanced by educational experiences abroad, they remain, to some degree, insufficient to telling the whole story. As the coded responses support, alumni consistently reported that their most important gains were a larger sense of independence and a pride in self-sufficiency, which they can clearly correlate to their time abroad.

One interviewee described the impact of time abroad on skill development as being gains in "Interpersonal skill, the ability to interact with people who are different from you and don't want to speak your language, the ability to be self-sufficient, because you do have to figure your stuff out on your own, be independent and learn those skills." The possibility exists that what we have accepted as a residual benefit and not the primary goal is, perhaps, the most important benefit to going abroad, from an employability perspective. As we move forward, it is this opportunity to continue to assist students in developing their overall resilience – academic, personal, and intercultural – that might guide our work and assessment efforts in the future.

Note

1. See also the chapter by Green et al. (this volume) on page 25.

Chapter 5

International education and employability

Perspectives of Ethiopians studying abroad

Wondwosen Tamrat and Damtew Teferra

Introduction

Discourses around employability are abuzz as institutional, national, regional and international organisations are frantically gearing up to respond to the ominous realities of youth bulge, "mass" enrolment, and graduate unemployment. Having enrolled some 20 million students in its rapidly massifying higher education system (Teferra, 2017a), Africa produces millions of graduates every year. This growth is, in turn, resulting in massive challenges at several levels, including in the preparation of graduates and their eventual employment.

It is reported that as many as 50% of Ghanaian graduates who leave universities and polytechnics will not find jobs for two years after their national service, and 20% of them will not find jobs for three years (Allotey, 2017). More than 71,000 graduates enter the job market each year, competing with an estimated 200,000 unemployed graduates in the domestic economy of Ghana (British Council, 2016).

In Kenya, about 50,000 graduates are produced in both public and private universities every year, increasing the number of unemployed youths in the country, which stands at 2.3 million. It takes a university graduate an average of five years to secure a job (British Council, 2015). Unemployment is especially high – in the area of 67% in 2015 – among those aged 15 to 34 (British Council, 2016). Of those with employment, a large proportion is reported to be engaged in jobs outside their field of study.

According to the British Council/Harvard School of Public Health report (2010), the situation is more serious in Nigeria owing to the country's large population. The report states that 3 out of 10 graduates of higher education are not working and that a highly educated Nigerian is not significantly more likely to find work than one with no education at all, while many are forced to accept jobs that do not fully utilise their qualifications. The job market for university graduates in Nigeria is very competitive and job openings suitable for university graduates attract a huge number of applicants (British Council, 2016).

Ethiopia's higher education institutions produce more than 160,000 graduates a year and many find it a challenge to get a job. According to a World Bank report (2016) 14% of the currently unemployed youth in Ethiopia are graduates of post-secondary institutions. Getnet (2018) indicated that among the 100,000 unemployed youth in Ethiopia's capital city, the majority are graduates from tertiary and technical and vocational institutions. A recent report published in *Ethiopian Reporter,* a major *Amharic* weekly, indicated that over 13,000 applications were received by the Water and Sewerage Authority for its 95 vacancies for audit officers and senior audit officers with a bachelor's degree and two years of experience, among others (Zenebe, 2018).

Though Higher Education Institutes (HEIs) are expected to respond to this systemic challenge (Tamrat, 2018a), little is known about the progress made, mainly because research on the subject is generally too meagre to provide a clear picture of the status quo. The same is true of the literature on international education and employability. While the subject of international mobility of students has received much attention within the realms of internationalisation – for instance, regarding the brain drain (Teferra, 2017b) – studies related to the perceptions and expectations of international students' employment remain limited (Johnstone, 2003; DiPietro, 2013). This is particularly so in the context of the developing world where there is a significant mismatch between the attention given to the subject and the available knowledge about it (Maharason & Hay, 2001; British Council, 2016). This study was conducted to bridge the existing gap in this area through a closer scrutiny of the Ethiopian context.

Objectives of the study

The study seeks to examine the profile and perspectives of Ethiopian students on the relevance and significance of their international education on subsequent employment opportunities. The key objectives of the study are to,

- Identify the profiles and trajectories of international students of Ethiopian origin; and
- Analyse the significance of an international study experience on the future employment of graduates.

Employability: concept and components

Over the last few decades, the concept of employability has become an important issue for graduates, governments, employers, and higher education institutions alike. Although the concept is used in various contexts and with different connotations, the most-oft invoked definition[1] identifies employability as "the propensity of students to obtain a job" (Harvey, 2001, p. 98). The domeneering "individual-centred," "supply-side" components of this definition presume the characteristic of graduates and the manners in which they make use of their job skills (McQuaid & Lindsay, 2005). But what are these skills?

Tymon (2013) notes that there may be no universal agreement on what constitutes an employability framework. In addition to the challenges of identification and definition, Moreau and Leathwood (2006) further argue the dangers of assuming skills as neutral elements, since their operationalisation could be affected by factors such as social class, gender, ethnicity, and disability. Furthermore, employability attributes and skills are assumed to vary depending on the type of worker, the circumstances of employment, and the perspectives of the particular employer being considered (Moreau & Leathwood, 2006; Tibby, 2012).

Despite the lack of agreement on what an employability framework should look like, the major emphasis in most cases seem to capitalise on areas broadly related to qualities, characters, skills, and knowledge of graduates (University of Glasgow, 2011; Tymon, 2013). Overall, employability comprises technical and discipline competence, and broader skills and attributes (University of Glasgow, 2011). Core skills, personal qualities, and subject knowledge combine to define the details of these requirements (Saunders & Zuzel, 2010; University of Glasgow, 2011; Tymon, 2013).

According to Yorke (2006) graduate employability refers to a set of achievements – skills, understandings, and personal attributes – that makes graduates, or individuals, more likely to gain employment and be successful in their chosen occupations, which benefits themselves, the workforce, the community, and the economy. In a similar vein, Harvey (2010) contends that the concept embodies the possession of basic "core skills" or a set of generic attributes specified by employers. Tymon (2013) echoes the same view on the importance of skills and personal attributes, with additional emphasis on the point that the demand for employability skills may differ depending on particular stakeholders in mind.

Having developed their list from the perspectives of students and employers, Saunders and Zuzel (2010) suggest that employability skills should include personal qualities, core skills, and subject knowledge. Helyer and Lee (2014), for their part, argue that the list should range from skills essential to obtaining a job (e.g., interview techniques) to generic abilities (e.g., teamwork), and include personal attributes (e.g., punctuality) and specific or subject abilities which are considered essential elements needed to carry out a job effectively.

McQuaid and Lindsay (2005), on the other hand, argue for a "holistic" perspective on employability and propose a much broader framework made up of three interrelated sets of factors: individual factors, personal circumstances, and external factors. While individual factors include what others earlier called attributes and skills, personal circumstances refer to a range of socio-economic factors related to individuals' social and household circumstances, and external factors that pertain to those factors that influence an individual's employability (e.g., labour demand conditions).

On the basis of the aforementioned different components that constitute employability skills, a variety of models have also been envisaged. Such models include one developed by Hillage and Pollard (1998) which includes employability assets, deployment, and presentation as its components; the DOTS model by Laws and Watts (Watts, 2006) which contains decision learning, opportunity awareness, and transition learning as its features; the USEM model by Knight and Yorke (2006) with understanding, skills, efficacy beliefs, and metacognition as its components; and CareerEDGE, developed by Pool and Sewell (2007), with different areas of emphasis, such as subject knowledge, understanding and skills, generic skills, emotional intelligence, career development learning, work and life experience, self-efficacy, self-confidence and self-esteem, and reflection and evaluation. The most important consideration in these types of models is the understanding that skills can change over time, indicating the need for "adaptability to the demands of a changing world" (Pool & Sewell, 2007).

The assumptions in the definitions[2] and models developed about employability underlie the fact that the value of university degree devoid of the skills demanded in the job market is at stake when issues of employability are raised. Academic qualifications without employment skills are not considered sufficient for securing a job, other than serving as a threshold requirement for applying. This has driven governments, graduates, and higher education institutions (HEIs) alike to contribute to the response to this new development.

On the part of governments, the issue of graduate employability has become a key objective in addressing unemployment and social exclusion (McQuaid & Lindsay, 2005; Tymon, 2013). The central place of employability in terms of informing labour market policies and as a mechanism of increasing national growth and prosperity are now recognised by many governments (Moreau & Leathwood, 2006). Since a knowledge-based economy and the concomitant competitiveness of the job market require graduates with the requisite skills, HEIs cannot be complacent about the employability of their graduates. As the concept of "job for life" is being substituted with the concept of graduate readiness for the market, HEIs need to be cognizant of what ought to be done in terms of employability skills. Among other aspects, HEIs must keep abreast of new developments and invest in employability development through such strategies as relevant training, curriculum design, and work experience (Saunders & Zuzel, 2010; University of Glasgow, 2011; Tymon, 2013).

Graduates are also becoming more proactive regarding the changing faces of the job world, developing concerns about the ways in which they are prepared for their future employment, and managing their own employability (Tomlinson, 2007; Saunders & Zuzel, 2010; University of Glasgow, 2011; Tymon, 2013). The concern for graduates is not only to earn employment after graduation but also to meet the ensuing demands of sustainable employability through the continuous acquisition and updating of skills (Mtebula, 2014).

International education and employability

According to OECD (2017), the number of foreign students attending higher education worldwide has exploded within a single generation, surging from 0.8 million in the late 1970s to 4.6 million in the 45 years since then. It is not clear, however, whether this trend is set to continue, as the pattern of internationalisation which has been driving student mobility is being seriously questioned and challenged (Cf. Altbach & de Wit, 2008; Tamrat, 2018b).

According to the French government's Campus France Agency (2013), which focuses on the international mobility of students from sub-Saharan Africa (SSA) and the Maghreb – with emphasis on France's contacts and activities – there were 380,376 African students on the move in 2010, representing about one-tenth of all international students worldwide.

The largest numbers of Africans studying abroad came from Morocco (39,865, 10.5%), Nigeria (34,274, 9%), Algeria (22,465, 5.9%), Zimbabwe (19,658, 5.2%), Cameroon (19,113, 5%), and Tunisia (18,438, 4.8%). This is followed by Kenya, Senegal, Egypt, and Botswana. According to UNESCO (2016), in 2013, students from sub-Saharan Africa were the second most mobile students in the world, with 264,774 students pursuing education outside their home counties. Top senders in 2015 include Nigeria, Cameroon, and Zimbabwe, representing three of the four sub-regions in Africa. In 2015–16, more than 35,000 students from sub-Saharan Africa studied in the United States – a 5% growth from 2014–15. With 10,674 students on U.S. campuses, Nigeria is the only sub-Saharan African country in the top 25 list. Ghana and Kenya are also large senders from the region, with more than 3,000 students each studying abroad. Over the past 10 years, student numbers from Angola and Ivory Coast have grown, more than doubling in the period from 2005–06 to 2015–16, each country sending over 1200 students to the United States in 2015–16 (IIE, 2017).

According to IIE (2015), Ethiopia reported to have sent 1472 students to the United States in 2014–15 alone, up from 888 in 2013–14. Ethiopian students also represent the largest African student population of the Erasmus Mundus program in Europe.

Studying abroad is generally assumed to provide a variety of advantages to students, including linguistic improvement, personal development, cultural experience, and global awareness, all of which have a direct impact on employability (Nilsson & Ripmeester, 2016). Foreign study is considered to have benefits in terms of employability in addition to its beneficial impact on students' academic work and life (Altbach, Kelly, & Lulat, 1985; Di Pietro, 2013; Nilsson & Ripmeester, 2016). International education creates opportunities for graduates to develop marketable skills (e.g., intercultural competence, global awareness, and foreign language skills) to which they may have been less exposed, given their background (DiPietro, 2013; OECD, 2017). International students are thought to offer employers additional skills such as diverse perspectives and diverse work culture, and be an additional pool of potential candidates to choose from.

Students themselves are aware of this importance and expect foreign studies to impact positively on their career and employability (Nilsson & Ripmeester, 2016). One of the major drivers of student mobility abroad is the prestige of the educational institutions in the country of destination (OECD, 2017), which offers students the opportunity to differentiate themselves among a growing pool of graduates in competitive labour markets.

The research context

Modern higher education in Ethiopia dates back to the establishment in 1950 of the University College of Addis Ababa (now Addis Ababa University)—the first public university in the country. Despite numerous efforts made over the next 40 years, little was achieved in terms of changing the elitist orientation of the system until the end of the 1990s. This was best exemplified by the limited number of institutions created for a large population and the low level of enrolment, both of which were major manifestations of the system. Until the beginning of 2000, the country had only two universities – Addis Ababa University and Haramaya University – and fewer than 20 colleges, which ran diploma and degree programs for a student population that did not exceed forty thousand. The gross enrolment rate (GER) at the national level was only 0.8 percent, far below the level in sub-Saharan African countries.

The Ethiopian higher education sector has exhibited phenomenal growth since the end of the 1990s. There are now 46 public universities and more than 130 accredited private higher education institutions, of which 4 hold full-fledged university status. The current gross enrolment rate (GER) stands at 10.2% at the national level (Ministry of Education, Federal Democratic Republic of Ethiopia, 2017). Higher Education in Ethiopia includes education programs offered as three- or four-year undergraduate degrees after completing secondary education, and special degrees such as master's and PhD programs.

Total undergraduate enrolment in public and private institutions has reached 788,766, of which 34% are female (Ministry of Education, 2017, p. 119). The rate of growth in the last five years stood at over 40%. The majority of students (85%) study in public institutions. The total number of students who attend programs in private institutions stood at 108,734. In 2016–17, engineering and technology programs had the highest number of undergraduate enrolments in regular programs. Agriculture and life sciences had the lowest enrolment, at 7%. The ratio of enrolment stood at 61% for natural sciences and 39% for social sciences (Ministry of Education, Federal Democratic Republic of Ethiopia, 2017, p. 124).

Study abroad: brief context

Although scarcely documented, Ethiopia's experience of sending students to study abroad is closely connected with the country's relations with the West, which goes as far back as the Medieval period (Zewde, 2002). Although missionaries of different backgrounds were mainly involved in sending Ethiopian students abroad – individually and in groups – prior to the establishment of modern education in the country, former Ethiopian kings, such as Emperors Tewodros, Menelik II, and Haile Selassie (especially the last two), had been instrumental in promoting foreign studies. For instance, between 1964 and 1973, 50% of the students studying abroad went to the United States while 11% went to the former Union of Soviet Socialist Republics (USSR). The United Kingdom and France each accounted for 5% of the 4143 students who studied abroad during this period (Commission for Higher Education, CHE, 1978).

Following the overthrow of Emperor Haile Selasie in 1974, the new military regime allied with the former Eastern European socialist bloc. During the years 1974–1977, the list of countries and the major destinations changed, with the USSR hosting 36% of the students, followed by the United States (18%), the United Kingdom (5%), the then Czechoslovakia (5%), Hungary (3%), and the then Yugoslavia (3%) (CHE, 1978).

International studies have further expanded without restrictions to foreign destinations since the incumbent government, which overthrew the Derg, assumed power in 1991. Despite the lack of reliable data, thousands of Ethiopian students are currently believed to be studying outside their country. In addition to government facilitation and support, family-sponsored and individually secured scholarships appear to be on the rise.

Graduate employability

Little is known about the effects of foreign training on employment in Ethiopia, but tertiary education continues to have positive impact on employment. Of late, however, graduates from these institutions are increasingly affected by a rising rate of graduate unemployment. According to Central Statistics Agency (2015), a significant reduction in unemployment was observed in Ethiopia between 2003 and 2014 for those with no primary education or secondary education while the unemployment rates significantly grew for post-secondary and university graduates.

Further to the rate of higher education expansion noted above, the growing mismatch between training and the labour market needs is contributing to the growing unemployment trend in Ethiopia. In fact, the World Bank's Enterprise Surveys (2015) data for Ethiopia identifies poorly educated workers as one of the 15 business environment obstacles as identified by business owners and top managers in 848 firms. This finding concurs with another assessment done on skills and competitiveness in Ethiopia, which revealed that vacancies for skilled production workers and managerial positions stay open for long periods of time, and that 57% of firms identify lack of appropriate applicants as the key reason for leaving vacancies open for a long time.

In a similar vein, the Ethiopia Skills Module Survey (World Bank, 2013), which involved 102 firms, revealed that one-quarter of them (27) reported vacant positions due to lack of skilled labour. For about 67% of those with vacant positions (18 firms), the positions remained vacant for more than four months. Among 21 firms, 12 (57%) mentioned lack of applicants for advertised vacancies while 8 (38%) cited a dearth of adequately qualified applicants.

According to the same survey (World Bank, 2013), employers reported diffi-culty in finding workers with requisite technical skills, ethical acumen, commit-ment, and computer proficiency—in that order. Skills concerns are especially on the rise for manufacturing firms, particularly in textile, garments, and food pro-duction, and exporters mention a shortage of skills as a key constraint for growth in productivity and expansion. The World Bank (2015) report noted above indi-cated that firms often report challenges in finding appropriate candidates with technical and soft skills.

Despite their increasing presence in Ethiopia, large firms and companies with foreign ownership view lack of skills as one of the major obstacles to their oper-ation and growth. A small sample survey of Chinese investors – who are sig-nificant employers in the country – conducted by the World Bank, showed that 93% of all professional positions and 67% of skilled production workers positions are held by Chinese employees (Salmi, Sursock, & Olefir, 2017). Only a limited number of the skilled and professional positions are held by Ethiopians. In addi-tion, more than 50% of Chinese firms indicated that an inadequately educated workforce remains a severe constraint to their operations (compared to 4% result for domestic firms), particularly in the manufacturing and construction sectors, forcing 75% of the Chinese firms to invest in the training of workers, compared to 27% for domestic firms (Salmi, Sursock, & Olefir, 2017).

Research methodology

This study sought to explore the perspectives of Ethiopian international students on the relevance and impact of international study on their subsequent employ-ment. It employed a mixed-methods approach. Data were collected using a sur-vey initially administered to members of Qine Association, a self-help association established by Ethiopian international students who pursue their higher studies in different parts of the world. Further, other subjects who were reached through a snowballing effect, through Qine networks, also participated. A preliminary list of the email addresses of 125 Ethiopian students studying abroad was developed and the survey was sent electronically to all the identified addresses. Sixty-five students (52%) responded to the questionnaire.

Following a sequential explanatory approach, Skype interviews were held with five volunteer respondents on the basis of their survey responses.

Study results

Participants' profile

The majority of the respondents (80%) were between 18 and 29 years of age. Only 11% were above 30 years. The majority of respondents were female (59%). In terms of their educational background, 88% had completed their secondary education in Ethiopia, while the remaining 8% attended high schools in the rest of Africa, and 4% studied overseas. Fifty-seven percent of the respondents attended high school in private schools; 21.5% studied in international community schools; and the remaining 16.9% studied at public and religious schools.

Foreign destinations

At the time of this study, the respondents were attending 39 different institutions in four major continents: North America (50.8%), Asia (21.5%), Europe (18.5%), and other parts of Africa (9.2%). They had employed a variety of strategies to identify their respective universities, as indicated in Figure 5.1.

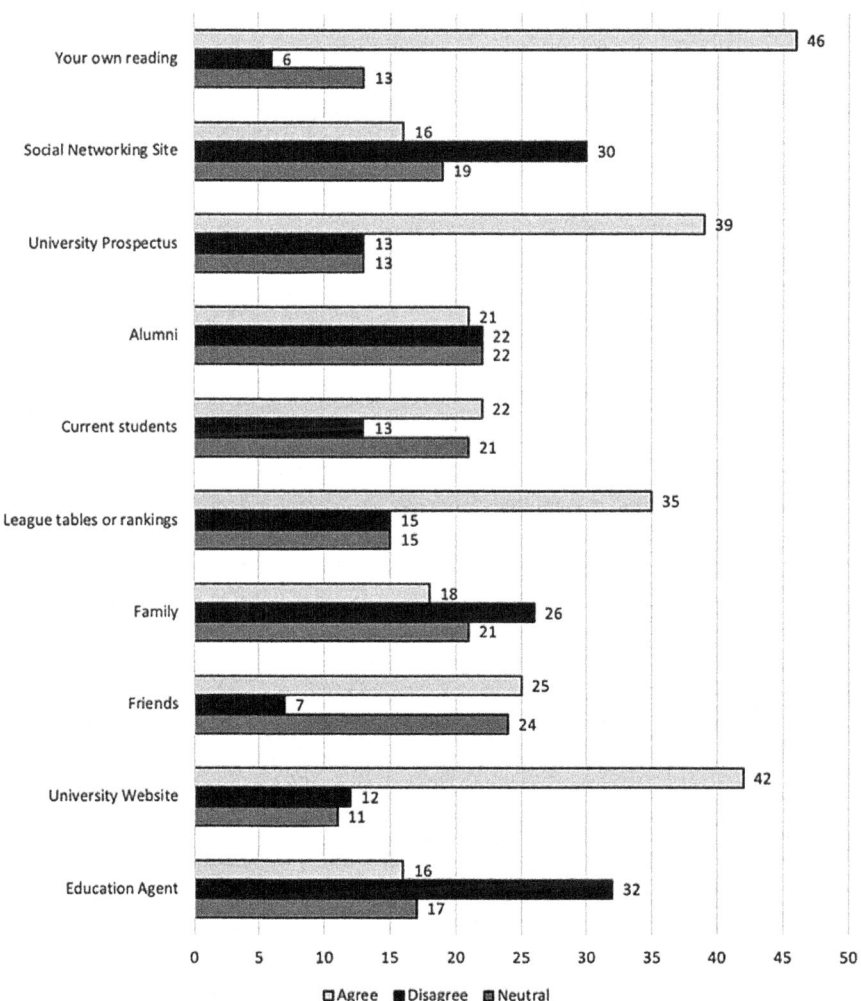

Figure 5.1 Strategies used by respondents for selecting universities.

Students' own readings and rankings were the major strategies employed to choose institutions, followed by university websites and prospectuses. This indicates active engagement of respondents in choosing their institution and host country. This was further substantiated by the respondents, who acknowledged the role of their schools in facilitating opportunities for foreign study. The influence of family, education agents, and friends appears to be limited, in this exercise.

Nearly one-quarter (16, 24.6%) of the respondents have stayed in their current location for less than 6 months, as many (17, 24.6%) stayed between 6 and 12 months, and 14 (21.5%) of them from 1 to less than 2 years. Overall, 60 (92.3%) respondents have stayed overseas up to 5 years and the rest (6.15%) from 4 up to 10 years.

Program of study

Among the respondents, 53.8% were studying for bachelor degrees while 24.5% and 20% were pursuing their master's and PhD degrees, respectively. The majority, 41 (63%), started their studies between 2016 and 2017 while 22 (33.8%) began between 2011 and 2015. The intended year of completion for 44 (67.7%) respondents ranges from 2016 to 2020; 17(26.6%) respondents plan to graduate between 2021 and 2025, and this mainly includes those pursuing a PhD.

At the time of the survey, 72.3% of the respondents were on full scholarships while 10.8% were on partial scholarships; 6.2% of the respondents were family sponsored. Only 1.5% of the respondents paid for their own education.

Motivations for foreign study

Respondents were asked to identify the factors that motivated them to study abroad. (see Figure 5.2).

The most important reasons that drive respondents to pursue international education are reported as being quality of training abroad, future career prospects, and broadening of one's experience. The same reasons were reiterated during the interviews with five of the respondents. These respondents felt that their foreign training would give them a competitive advantage by exposing them to a variety of skills and opportunities that they would not otherwise have obtained had they studied in Ethiopia. One of the responses to an open-ended question echoes similar views:

> I think foreign trained Ethiopians have a better chance [of employment] as they are likely to have gone through internship, co-op, or research programs to enhance their practical knowledge in their field of study, which enables them to have an edge in the competition. The credentials of the institution as well the international experience which broadens one's perspective also contribute positively towards the foreign trained Ethiopians.
>
> (A male respondent studying for his bachelor degree in mechanical engineering at the University of Toronto, Canada).

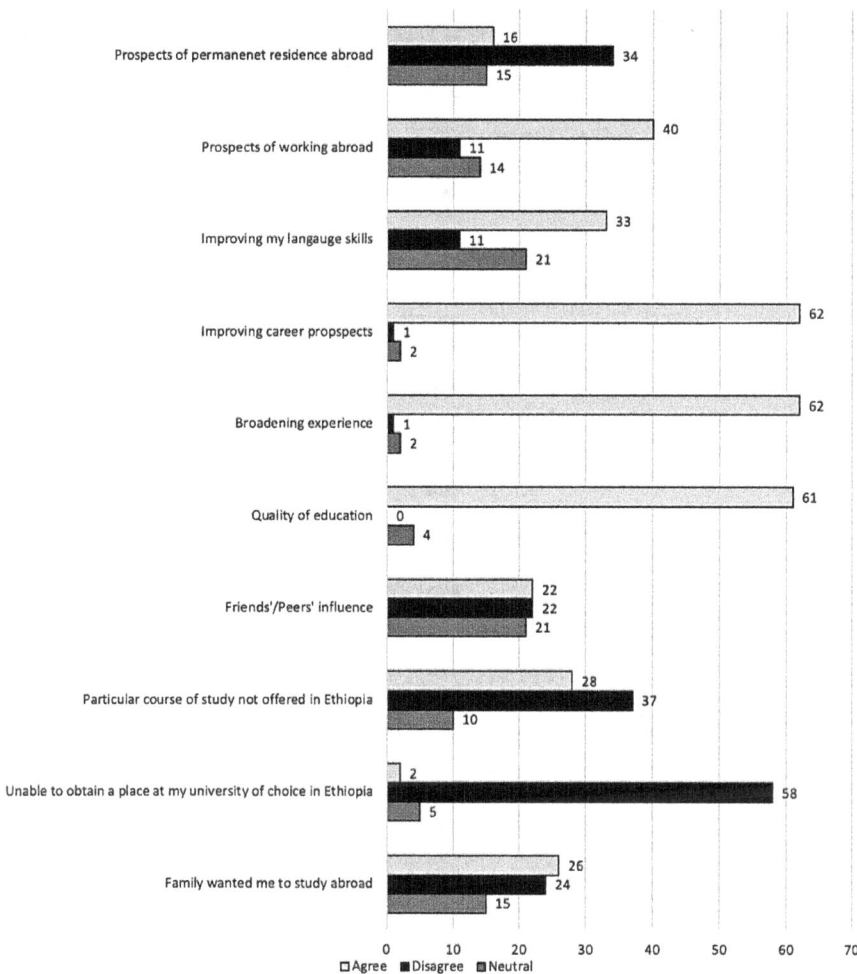

Figure 5.2 Respondents' motivations for studying abroad.

Other reasons for foreign study, such as friends/peers, absence of study programs, and failure to secure a place in local institutions in Ethiopia, were of limited significance in the decision of the respondents to pursue foreign studies.

Attributes and skills for employability

Respondents were asked to identify the types of attributes that they would consider critical for employability. (see Figure 5.3).

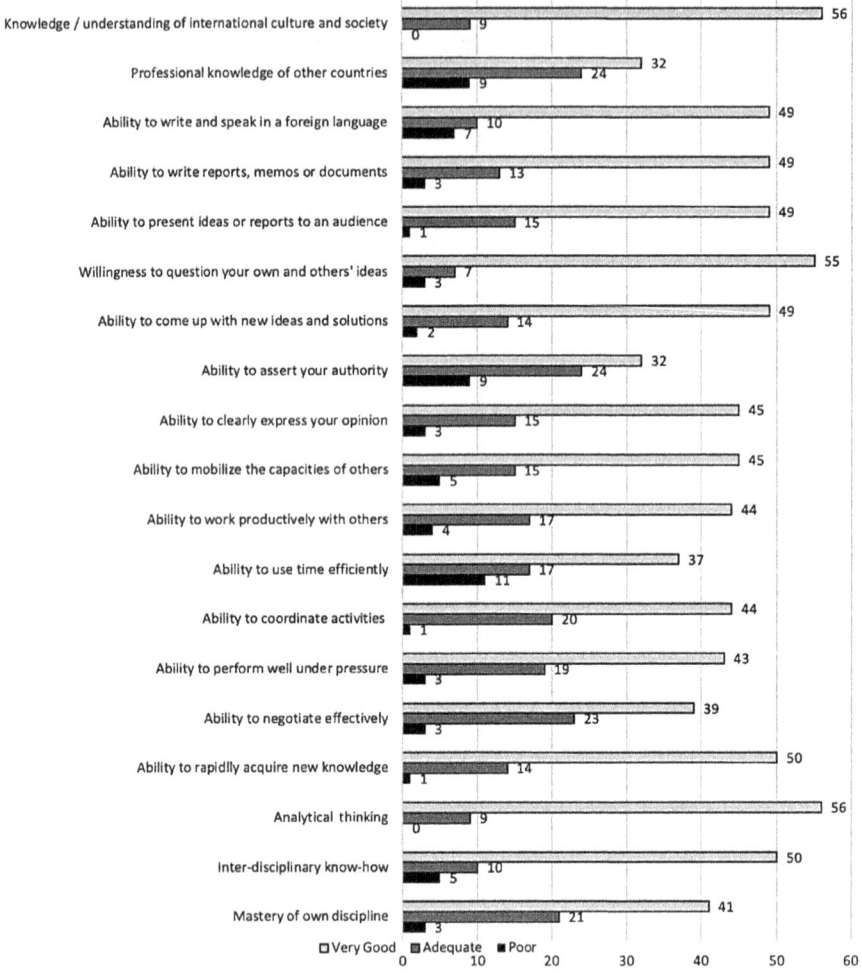

Figure 5.3 Respondents' views of the importance of skills and attributes for employability.

Attributes such as willingness to question ideas of self and others, ability to clearly express one's opinion, ability to write and speak in a foreign language, ability to rapidly acquire new knowledge, and ability to perform under pressure were perceived as key elements for securing employment. A response given to one of the open-ended questions further consolidates this by highlighting the competitive advantage of international training. According to one aspiring lawyer:

> Compared to what I know is the case for my friends going to Ethiopian law schools, the following attributes of my education at NYU Law prepare me better for employment in the future: the global reputation of an American

law degree from a top university, the skills of critical thinking and analytic research, summer internship and other clinical experiences that are part of my program, opportunity to network with practitioners in various legal practices while still in law school, and exposure to various mentors and role-models in my chosen field. All of these elements contribute to improving my substantive knowledge of my subject area but also my communication and negotiation skills that are key for landing at good employment (A female respondent studying for her Juris Doctor/JD New York University School of Law, New York, USA).

The major areas of difference in the training modalities in favour of foreign universities, which respondents reported as highly beneficial, include small student-faculty ratio, availability of committed faculty that help students, better system for accountability and compliance, predominance of skill-based training, and continuous assessment.

Mastery of employability traits

After having reflected on the attributes and skills they consider important for employability (using a five-point scale ranging from strongly agree to strongly disagree, which were later summed into three categories), respondents were asked to rate their own mastery of these attributes and skills. The ranking scale used for the perceived capacity of the respondents involved a five-point scale that incorporated poor, very poor, adequate, good, and very good, which were summed into three categories – poor, adequate, and good. The results obtained are quite instructive, as Figure 5.4 might reveal.

The respondents appear to be overwhelmingly confident of their preparation for the market place – particularly in terms of the ability to work with others, analytical thinking, ability to come up with new ideas and solutions, and ability to use time efficiently. The only exceptions in this regard were knowledge/understanding of cultural and societal differences and the ability to write and speak in a foreign language. These could be attributable to deficiencies associated with the recent movement of respondents to the country of study. It is important to note that these are included among the key areas which respondents identified as highly important in terms of employability.

The high level of confidence respondents seem to have expressed could be further understood in terms of their views on what they would do with the knowledge they have acquired. This was especially noted during the course of the interviews, as the following response indicates:

I think one of the biggest tools that I have gained from studying abroad is shaping the knowledge that I acquire in accordance to my experiences and upbringing. It had also exposed me to different people and, as a result, to different cultures, history, and policies. It has also pushed me out of my comfort

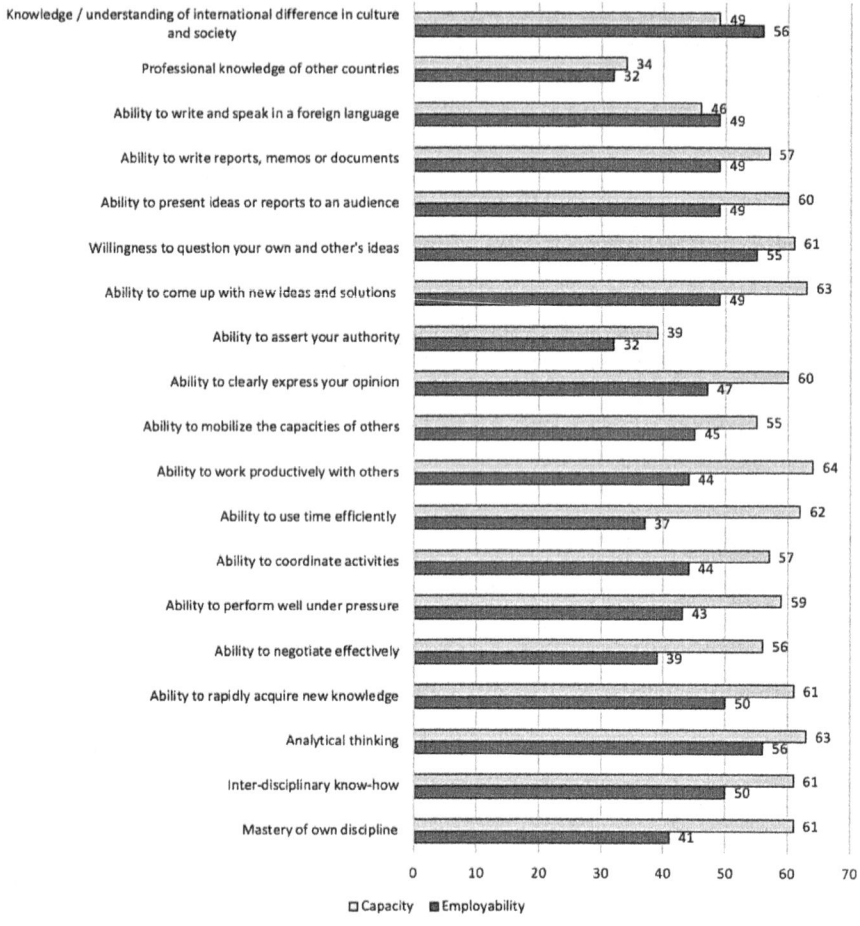

Figure 5.4 Perceived mastery of employability attributes and skills.

zone and has made me see the challenges that people face day-to-day in the world. Therefore, I think I can use the skills that I acquired here, first and foremost, to create awareness about several issues and to tackle them by professional activism. Additionally, I can relate the knowledge that I have gained to the world that I knew while growing up and can try to work in creating technological solutions for my country. Additionally, being here has exposed me to and taught me a lot about start-up culture, entrepreneurship, and the power of the youth, so I think I can use this knowledge for creating a platform for the Ethiopian youth in the form of a co-shared workspace, youth volunteer organisations, or creative urban spaces. (A female respondent studying for BA/BSc in Mechanical Engineering at Bogaziçi University, Istanbul, Turkey).

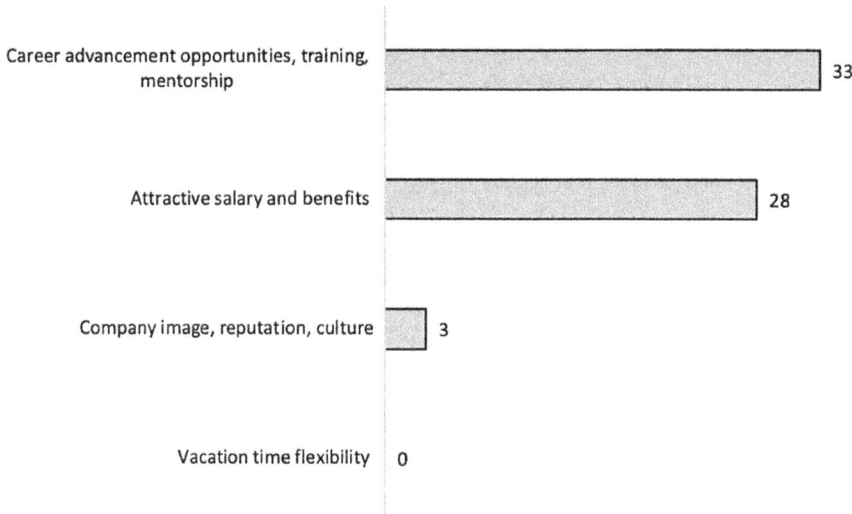

Figure 5.5 Preferred nature of job.

Job preference

When asked about a future job, which would interest respondents most, the majority identified the nature of the job, career advancement opportunities, and attractive salary and benefits (see Figure 5.5). It is interesting to note that attractive salary and benefits (28.1%) were rated third, after interesting and challenging work (35.9%) and career advancement opportunities (32%). Notably, vacation time and flexibility did not attract respondents' interest.

Plan after graduation

In terms of their plans after graduation (see Figure 5.6), quite a large proportion of the respondents (36.9%) were unsure of what they would do.

Both the survey and the interview response indicates that after graduation the number of those who intend to search for job opportunities in Ethiopia is nearly double the number of those who would choose to seek jobs in a foreign country. This is, despite the respondents' awareness of the prevalence of low-earning jobs, limited knowledge of skill deficiencies in the local market, and poor internet access in the country. Respondents are also aware of their significant contributions to their country after graduation and appear to be ready to give back to their community:

> Since I moved to the U.S., I have developed a better sense of my Ethiopian identity. Thus, I am currently pursuing an MPH in Epidemiology with hopes of addressing emerging community health issues in my native Ethiopia. Generally

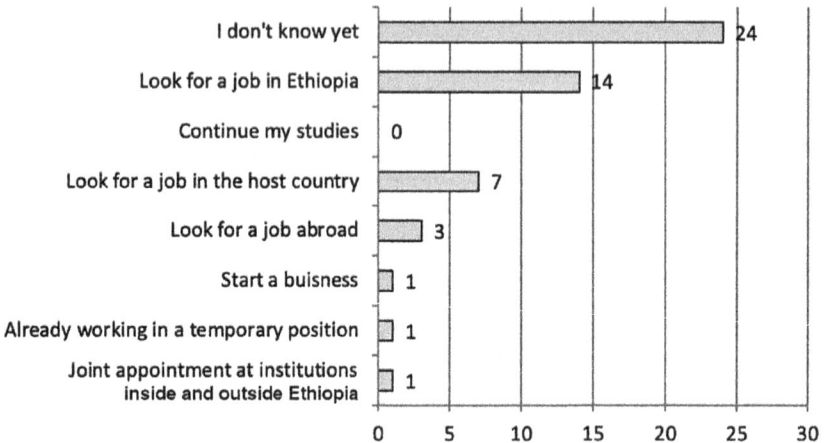

Figure 5.6 Plan after graduation.

speaking, I hope to elevate the ways in which I can be of service to my country through my academic and work experiences abroad. (A female respondent studying for her MPH in Public Health at Columbia University, USA).

I plan to come back to Ethiopia and open a policy advisory firm that works closely with the government to design policies that improve the energy sector. The firm will also hopefully have a strong mentorship program so that employees can improve their skills and advance in their careers. (A female respondent studying for her master's in International Affairs at Columbia University, USA).

Another 20% of the respondents still want to continue their studies abroad. This does not appear surprising given the greater share of respondents currently studying for their bachelor's and master's degrees.

Respondents also exhibited a strong interest in returning to Ethiopia if they had an attractive job opportunity. An overwhelming majority (72.3%) responded in the affirmative while the rest reacted to the contrary, except for a tiny number (1.5%) who said they "don't know." However, most of the respondents are unsure of the demand for their skills at the local level. This appears to be mainly due to disconnect between those studying abroad and the government and local employers who seem to have little knowledge about the profile and addresses of students studying abroad. Respondents were further asked what specific features of a job would attract them to go back to their country, and the responses are shown in Figure 5.7.

Interesting and challenging jobs and career-advancing job opportunities followed by attractive salary and benefits were the most common traits of job preferences. This suggests that it is primarily the nature of a job that matters most to respondents as compared to the financial remuneration that comes with it.

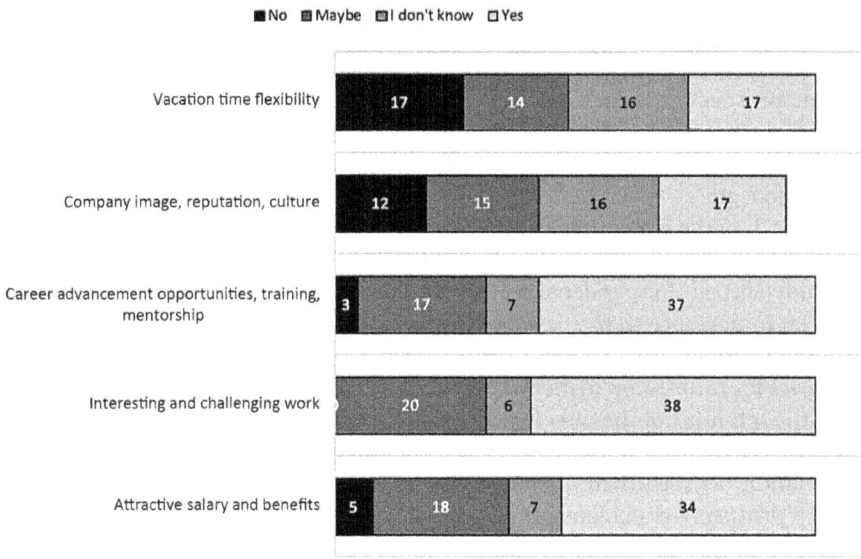

Figure 5.7 Respondents' views of attractive elements of a job.

However, in terms of a return home, 29.2% of the respondents noted that they had no immediate plans to return (see Figure 5.8), while the majority (49.2%) said that they intend to return in 5–10 years. The remaining 21.5% said they will return immediately after graduation. The overall interest in returning home among the respondents seems quite high, contrary to expectations and the wider literature that suggests that student mobility encourages "brain drain."

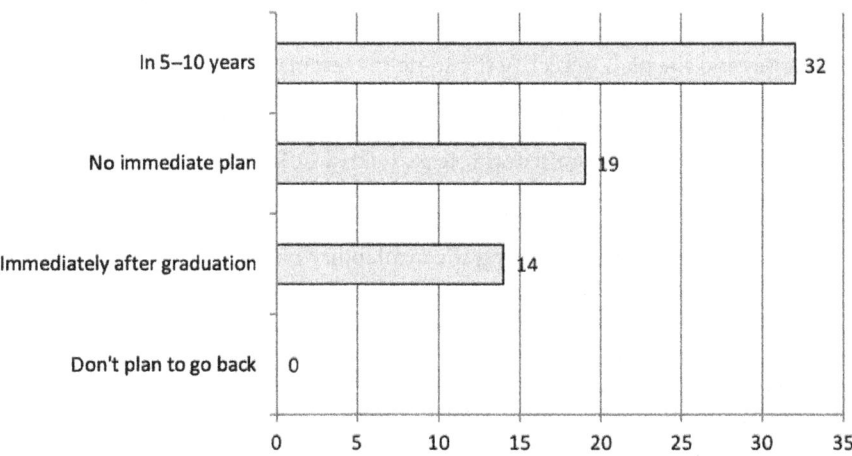

Figure 5.8 Planned periods of return.

Discussion and conclusions

This study explored the perspectives of Ethiopian students studying abroad on the prospect of their future employability by examining a range of factors, including motivations for studying abroad, employability attributes, respondents' mastery of these attributes, type of preferred employment, and respondents' plans after graduation. The findings reveal a variety of interesting observations about each of the issues under investigation.

The study has identified a number of factors that drive Ethiopian students to study abroad. Respondents realise the potential of foreign study in terms of its vital importance to the development of critical skills, such as analytical and communication skills, enhanced ability to acquire knowledge, and heightened prospect for future employment.

Although it is not the only factor, employment appears to be one of the overriding reasons for foreign study. From the perspective of respondents, a clear association between their current training and its potential to enhance future career prospects is evident. In this regard, the research concurs with earlier studies that have identified the career benefits associated with studying abroad (DiPietro, 2013; Tomlinson, 2007; Tymon, 2013).

The overall tendency of respondents to place the importance of the acquisition of skills and personal qualities over subject-specific knowledge is also in accord with other similar studies (e.g., Saunders & Zuzel, 2010; Tymon, 2013) and has been identified by respondents as the major point of difference between Ethiopian and foreign institutions in terms of graduate preparation. In this regard, the extensive reflections made by respondents on the manners in which their training at foreign universities are conducted might offer useful insights to local universities. In light of the increasing demands on graduate employability attributes, it is important that Ethiopian universities find mechanisms to cater to these additional needs often lacking in their subject-dominated curricula and methods of delivery. The recent recognition of these gaps by the Ministry of Education and the plan to rectify the same in the curricular and training provisions of public universities could be a change for the better (Tamrat, 2018b).

Although the literature on student mobility is replete with the impact of study abroad in the context of "brain drain" (e.g., Teferra, 2014), this research has shown an overwhelming interest by respondents to return home after graduation. This, however, seems to depend on the availability of conducive employment opportunities at the local level, including the availability of information on vacancies and skills needed. As noted in the profile, half of the students currently study in the United States – a country where many Ethiopians are pursuing their studies, and where most are known to stay at the completion of their studies. Given this underlying view, it may be appropriate to further undertake a comprehensive study to firmly establish the scale of this interest to return home.

It is now well established that international student mobility enhances graduate employability; and as such, Ethiopian students are not an exception. Wächter

(2017), however, cautions that studies on the professional impact of study abroad have recently noted "declining returns" of the anticipated benefits of mobility, which can be attributed to the growing number of students studying abroad. It may be relevant to reflect on the long-term implications of this observation given the overwhelming enthusiasm expressed by Ethiopian students in this study to return home after completing their overseas study.

It should be noted that the findings of this study are interpreted rather cautiously due to the limited size of the respondent group. Yet, the study will contribute to our scarce knowledge on interest, trajectory, and processes of academic mobility and foreign studies as regards Ethiopians. The study lays out a sound groundwork for a more systematic and comprehensive research to further enrich our understanding of Ethiopian students abroad in the process of pushing the frontiers of the discourse on the subject.

Furthermore, this knowledge is anticipated to contribute to national human capital planning and deployment, which has wider implications. There is significant opportunity for government, businesses, NGOs, and think tanks to both tap the huge potential of the highly skilled Ethiopian diaspora and explore how foreign study contributes to employability in different geographical and cultural contexts.

Notes

1. Other discussions about the definition or concept of employability can be found on pages 12, 25, 25, 92, 117, 164.
2. Other discussions about the definition or concept of employability can be found on pages 12, 25, 25, 92, 117, 164.

Chapter 6

Recent trends in learning abroad in the context of a changing Japanese economy and higher education situation

Hiroshi Ota and Yukiko Shimmi

Japanese government's policies on study abroad

During the post-war period, the central focus of the Japanese government's internationalisation policy was on attracting international students to come and study in Japan. However, with the decline, from the late 2000s, of the number of Japanese students studying abroad, the government (under the Abe administration) started prioritising the promotion of outbound mobility in order to foster a globally minded workforce for Japanese companies, leading to a revitalization of Japanese economy. Until that point, studying abroad had been mainly considered as a private choice, and governmental support for Japanese students to study abroad had been limited. In its effort to promote study abroad, first, the Japanese government set a numerical target of raising the number of Japanese studying abroad to 120,000 by 2020 under the Japan Revitalisation Strategy (Prime Minister of Japan and His Cabinet, 2013). Second, the government increased scholarships available for individual students, to expand the range of study abroad participants, and provided competitive funds for universities to develop outbound mobility programs and support systems in order to broaden the range of study abroad options.

With respect to scholarships, in 2014, the MEXT (Ministry of Education, Culture, Sports, Science and Technology) significantly increased (more than twofold) the budget for JASSO (Japan Student Services Organisation) study abroad scholarships,[1] which are targeted at students enrolled at Japanese higher education institutions who study abroad for less than one year (see Figure 6.1). Currently, this scholarship can be granted to students who participate in one of their university's study abroad programs with a duration of eight days to one year. The number of recipients dramatically increased from 627 in 2008 to 21,000 in 2018 (Minami, 2018). Moreover, a small number of scholarships for studying abroad for a degree were added within the JASSO scholarship programs; 252 scholarships to study abroad for postgraduate degrees and 78 for undergraduate degrees were provided in 2018 (Minami, 2018). In addition, in 2014,

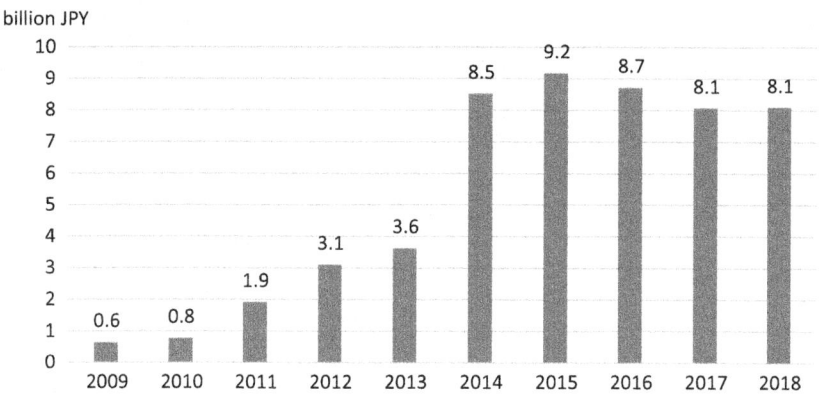

Figure 6.1 MEXT budget for study abroad scholarships.
Source: MEXT (2018).

the government established another scholarship program called Tobitate! (Leap for Tomorrow) Young Ambassador Program (A Public-Private Partnership Encouraging Students Studying Abroad),[2] with funding from both the government and private companies. Tobitate! scholarships are intended for students who study abroad for periods varying from 28 days to two years. By 2017, 3000 students of universities and colleges had studied abroad with Tobitate! scholarships (Minami, 2018).

Regarding competitive funds for universities, since 2011, the Inter-University Exchange Project has provided funds for two-way exchanges between Japan and regions that are specified each year. Through this scheme, by 2017 the number of Japanese students who had studied abroad reached 14,700, while the number of international students who had studied in Japan reached 15,200 (Minami, 2018; Ota, 2018). In addition, from 2012 to 2016, the Go Global Japan Project provided funds to 42 universities to develop study abroad programs for students to acquire competencies for the new global society. The aim of recipient universities was to send 58,500 students abroad through this project. Other programs—such as the Top Global University Project, started in 2014—also aim to stimulate Japanese students to study abroad (Horio, 2017; Ota, 2018; see Table 6.1).

Trends in Japanese students studying abroad

Due to these policy initiatives, short-term study abroad participants during university study are rapidly increasing. The number of short-term study abroad students, which was around 36,300 in 2009, rose to 96,600 by 2016 – more than

Table 6.1 Government's policy initiatives for outbound mobility with numerical targets

	2008	2009	2010	2011	2012	2013	2014	2015	2016	2017	2018	2019	2020	2021	2022	2023
1 Japan Revitalization Strategy (Doubling the number of study abroad students)								Outbound: 120,000 in total								
2 Inter-University Exchange Project (Two-way mobility)																
CAMPUS Asia and ASEAN					13 programs Outbound: 1,687; Inbound: 1,867											
North America and EU					12 programs Outbound: 2,484; Inbound: 1,873											
ASEAN						14 programs Outbound: 3,045; Inbound: 3,631										
AIMS with ASEAN						7 programs Outbound: 746; Inbound: 759										
ICI-ECP (EU)						5 programs Outbound: 69; Inbound: 61										
Russia and India						9 programs Outbound: 1,086; Inbound: 1,130										
Latin America & the Caribbean, and Turkey								11 programs Outbound: 1,159; Inbound: 1,295								
CAMPUS Asiaa and ASEAN									25 programs Outbound: 3,279; Inbound: 3,789							
Russia and India									9 programs Outbound: 1,157; Inbound: 1,084							
3 Go Global Japan (Outbound mobility)						Type A (University-wide): 11 univs.; Type B (Faculty-specific): 31 univs.; Outbound: 58,000										
4 Top Global University Project (Comprehensive internationalization)										Type A (Top Type): 13 universities Type B (Global Traction Type): 24 universities						

Source: As cited in Ota, 2018, p. 97 and modified by the authors.

Notes
1. CAMPUS Asia stands for Collective Action for Mobility Program of University Students in Asia and is a trilateral student exchange program run by China, Japan, and Korea, as the East Asian version of the Erasmus Programme in Europe.
2. AIMS stands for ASEAN International Mobility for Students Program and is a government supported multilateral educational program in the ASEAN region, launched in 2010 by coordinated efforts of Malaysia, Indonesia, Thailand, and the current members, including Vietnam, the Philippines, Brunei, and Japan.
3. ICI-ECP (Industrialised Countries Instrument - Education Cooperation Programme) refers to EU cooperation with Australia, New Zealand, Japan, and Korea in the field of higher education and vocational education and training.

double (see Figure 6.2). The number of those students participating in short-term study abroad programs, lasting from one week up to one month, in particular, grew significantly, reaching 60,100, or 62% of the total, in 2016, (more than tripled from 16,800 in 2009 to 60,100 in 2016). Also, those studying abroad for less than six months accounted for 82% of the total in 2016 (MEXT, 2017).

On the other hand, long-term, mainly degree-seeking, study abroad numbers peaked at 83,000 students in 2004 and had fallen by 35% to 54,600 in 2015 (see Figure 6.3; MEXT, 2017). Study abroad by Japanese students is shifting from study abroad for a degree to study abroad for credits (McCrostie, 2017). This reflects a growing global trend among college students, especially in developed countries (Institute of International Education, 2017; Universities UK International, 2018; Australian Government-Department of Education and Training, 2018).

Although those aforementioned study abroad scholarships for students and funds for higher education institutions were not meant for this in particular, universities specifically increased opportunities for short-term (up to one month) programs abroad, because, for a number of reasons, they appear to be preferred by Japanese students. First, the short duration of the program prevents time conflicts with other activities, such as looking for graduate positions

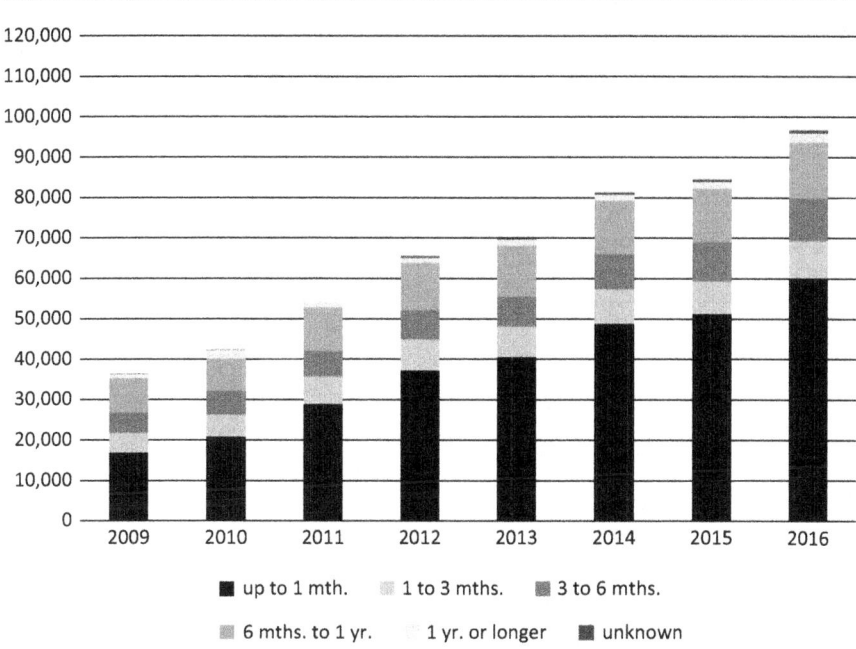

Figure 6.2 Short-term study abroad students.

Source: JASSO (2017).

Note: This graph shows the numbers of students enrolled at Japanese higher education institutions who study abroad. The JASSO collects data from the sending Japanese institutions.

at Japanese companies, typically conducted during a certain period in the year; preparing for national qualification examinations; and participating in extra-curricular activities, such as club activities. Second, short-term study abroad programs tend to require lower participation fees than longer programs. Third, short-term programs abroad that focus on foreign language learning at the basic level are popular among Japanese students because many students do not have sufficient foreign language skills to participate in longer exchange pro-grams where they are required to take courses at partner universities together with local students.

The recent government support has been effective in increasing the number of students studying abroad for at least short-term (up to one month) programs; in comparison, the number of participants in longer-term programs has not increased as much. Moreover, although participating in short-term study abroad programs can be a step for "inward-looking"[3] students towards becoming more open to other cultures (Bradford, 2015), short-term study abroad programs are considered too short to enhance the students' foreign language and cross-cultural competencies (Ministry of Internal Affairs and Communications, 2017), compared to longer-term programs in Japan where degree-seeking study abroad

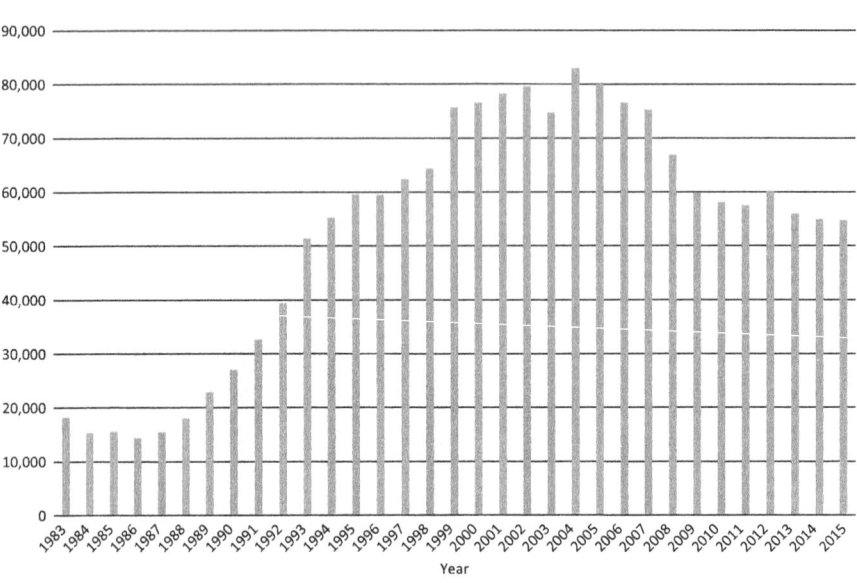

Figure 6.3 Long-term study abroad students.

Source: MEXT (2017).

Note: The MEXT compiles data from host countries, such as IIE Open Doors, and from international
organisations, such as OECD Education at a Glance and UNESCO Global Education Digest. Those
original data count mainly long-term international students based on their student visas.

was the norm before. Similar observations have been made in the United States
and other countries (Dwyer, 2004a; Kehl & Morris, 2008).

Study abroad and its impact on career development

Although studies on the relationship between study abroad experiences and
career/employability among Japanese students are limited, previous studies indicate that many Japanese students seem to perceive that study abroad experience
is beneficial for developing their career. The JASSO (2012) study, for example,
showed in a survey of 1506 individuals who studied abroad, 61.8% of respondents answered that their study abroad experiences were helpful in deciding their
career path and advancing through their job-hunting processes.

Later, as the key members of the three-year research project (2013–2015),
the authors of this chapter conducted a large-scale, retrospective online survey of the long-term impact of study abroad on career development and life
in 2015.[4] People who had studied abroad for three months or more were surveyed on a variety of topics, including their experiences and the improvement in their abilities while studying abroad, the effects on their subsequent
employment and careers, changes in their values and behaviours, and degree

of satisfaction with life. In addition, in order to act as a control group for comparison, people who had not studied abroad were also surveyed on their experiences and the improvement in their abilities while studying in undergraduate and/or graduate programs in Japan, and on their subsequent careers. For the purpose of comparison between those who studied abroad and those who did not, the research project recruited survey participants of these two types with the similar ratios of the four age groups, such as 50s or older, 40s, 30s, and 20s.

According to the survey results, those respondents who studied abroad for three months or more ($n = 4489$) perceived the higher impact of their study experiences on all the 10 items[5] related to the career development than those who did not go abroad ($n = 1298$) (Shimmi, Ota, Watabe, & Akiba, 2016).

By using the same dataset, Shimmi, Akiba, Ota, and Yokota (2017) examined the differences in current position and annual income as well as the abovementioned 10 items related to the impact on the career development among three groups (see Table 6.2). These groups are (1) those who studied abroad for an undergraduate degree (Undergraduate degree studied abroad, $n = 416$), (2) those who studied abroad for credits/other purpose at the undergraduate level (Undergraduate credits studied abroad, $n = 757$), and (3) those who obtained an undergraduate degree from a Japanese university without study abroad experience (Undergraduate degree studied in Japan, $n = 710$).[6] As Table 6.2 shows, the category "Undergraduate degree studied abroad" had both the highest annual income (5.47 million yen) and the highest percentage (32.5%) of in management roles,[7] followed by the "Undergraduate credits studied abroad" (27.7% and 4.79 million yen) and the "Undergraduate degree studied in Japan" (17.5% and 4.49 million yen). Similarly, as Figure 6.4 indicates, the "Undergraduate degree abroad" perceived the highest impact of their study experiences on all the 10 items concerned with the career development, followed by the "Undergraduate credits studied abroad" and "Undergraduate degree studied in Japan." The differences in the perceived impact on the career development among these three groups were statistically significant, analysing their weighted average efficiencies with the one-way analysis of variance ($p < .001$). In short, those results can be said to show that study abroad experiences have a positive impact on the career development and are meaningfully related to career success. Also, it can be inferred that studying abroad for a degree gives more positive influence on, and success in, the career path than studying abroad for credits at the undergraduate level.

Subsequently, using the same dataset, Shimmi, Yonezawa, and Akiba (2018) discussed that people who studied abroad for a graduate degree tend to report a higher impact on career-related aspects, both on the current annual income and position (management roles), than those who studied abroad for an undergraduate degree, as Table 6.3 and 6.4 show. Also, both foreign undergraduate and graduate degrees led to a higher impact on the annual income across all age groups and current position (employed by foreign companies[8] and the management roles) than their counterparts who had not studied abroad (domestic

Table 6.2 Current position and annual income

		Undergraduate degree studied abroad (n = 416)	Undergraduate credits studied abroad (n = 757)	Undergraduate degree studied in Japan (n = 710)
Current Annual Income (m = million)		5.47m yen	4.79m yen	4.49m yen
Current Position	Executive/board member class	14.2%	7.6%	0.3%
	Managerial class including heads of departments/sections, managers, professors, etc.	18.3%	20.1%	17.2%
	General staff class including assistant professors, etc.	43.4%	54.3%	67.8%
	Part-time/contract staff	15.0%	12.4%	14.5%
	Other	9.1%	5.6%	0.2%
Age	50s or older	56 (13.5%)	89 (11.8%)	144 (20.3%)
	40s	175 (42.1%)	208 (27.5%)	244 (34.4%)
	30s	145 (34.9%)	264 (34.9%)	227 (32.0%)
	20s	40 (9.6%)	196 (25.9%)	95 (13.4%)

Source: Shimmi, Akiba, Ota, and Yokota (2017).

Notes

1. Homemakers and unemployed were excluded for the current annual income.
2. PPP for GDP: US$1 = JPY 106 (OECD 2015), 1 million yen = US$9,433.

Table 6.3 Average current annual income by age and income gap coefficient

	Undergraduate degree studied abroad (n = 416) (1)	Undergraduate degree studied in Japan (n = 710) (2)	Graduate degree studied abroad (n = 353) (3)	Graduate degree studied in Japan (n = 528) (4)	Income gap in undergraduate level (1) / (2)	Income gap in graduate level (3) / (4)	Income gap in academic level (3) / (1)
Total	5.47m yen	4.49m yen	7.93m yen	5.53m yen	1.22	1.43	1.45
50s or older	6.54m yen	6.08m yen	9.94m yen	8.06m yen	1.07	1.23	1.52
40s	5.64m yen	4.71m yen	8.26m yen	6.55m yen	1.20	1.26	1.46
30s	5.40m yen	3.89m yen	6.43m yen	4.68m yen	1.39	1.38	1.19
20s or younger	3.50m yen	2.91m yen	3.73m yen	3.51m yen	1.20	1.06	1.07

Source: Shimmi, Yonezawa, and Akiba (2018).

Notes

1. Homemakers and unemployed were excluded for the current annual income.
2. PPP for GDP: US$1 = JPY 106 (OECD 2015), 1 million yen = US$9,433.

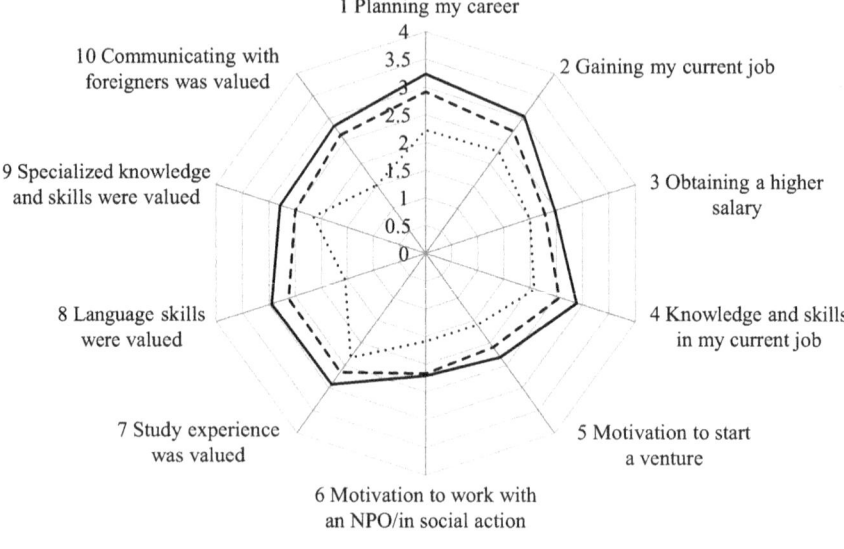

Figure 6.4 Self-evaluated career impact.

Source: Shimmi, Akiba, Ota, and Yokota (2017).

degrees holders). These results indicate that study abroad experiences are felt by graduates (foreign degree holders) to have an ongoing positive influence on their career.

Employers' perspectives on study abroad experience

Until recently, the main challenge for study abroad returnees was the unwillingness of Japanese companies to hire graduates of foreign universities, due to the fact that these companies often perceived such university graduates as unable to

Table 6.4 Ratios of employed by foreign companies and management roles

	Undergraduate degree studied abroad (n = 416)	Undergraduate degree studied in Japan (n = 710)	Graduate degree studied abroad (n = 353)	Graduate degree studied in Japan (n = 528)
Employed by foreign companies	24.6%	2.1%	22.4%	2.1%
Management roles	32.5%	17.2%	41.1%	18.6%

Source: Shimmi, Yonezawa, and Akiba (2018).

adapt to traditional Japanese business culture; for example, the lifetime employment system[9] and the seniority-based system.[10] This is felt to be because they had become too Westernised in their mind, meaning there was a greater emphasis on the individual abilities and performance and they were more self-centered rather than group oriented. Those students enrolled at Japanese universities who study abroad at partner institutions as exchange students for one to two semesters were also not always welcomed by corporate Japan because of the peculiar job-hunting and recruitment system. Japanese companies typically hire the bulk of college students as their future workers only once a year, while students are in the latter half of the third year through the first half of the fourth year.[11] Throughout that nine-month period from December to September, job-hunting students go through the whole screening process, including many job fairs, aptitude and knowledge tests, and several rounds of interviews.[12] If an exchange student studies at a partner university abroad from September (the third year) to June (the fourth year) as a typical junior-year abroad, that student misses the job-hunting season.

According to a survey of 1000 Japanese companies in 2011 on their recruitment plans for the following year (2012) conducted by a recruitment company, less than a quarter responded that they planned to hire Japanese students who had studied abroad. Even among leading companies with more than 1000 employees, fewer than 40% said they wanted to hire Japanese with an overseas education (as cited in Tabuchi, 2012).

However, the prolonged economic downturn and a rapidly globalising economy seem to be changing the situation gradually. Recently, Japanese companies have become more positive about recruiting graduates with study abroad experience in order to seek business opportunities and develop new overseas markets. For instance, a survey of 412 recruiters at Japanese companies on their perspectives of recruitment and study abroad experience conducted by the MEXT-Tobitate office in 2017 reported that 62.1% intended to hire graduates with study abroad experience. Also, 80.4% answered that study abroad experience would be useful in their jobs, and 75.3% said the delay of graduation or taking a leave of absence from school due to study abroad would not negatively affect the screening of job applicants (MEXT-Tobitate Office, 2017).

While, in general, employers are viewing study abroad experience more positively nowadays, another study reported that companies preferred long-term study abroad to short-term study abroad of a few weeks. As part of the policy evaluation of global human resources development, a survey of 980 companies was carried out by the Ministry of Internal Affairs and Communications in 2016. Of the respondents, 47.1% answered that a study abroad period of "more than one year" is necessary in order to develop various skills, including language ability, intercultural understanding, and the ability to accept a diversity of values, followed by a period of "more than six months to one year" (35.4%). Moreover, respondents mentioned that, from their experiences of human resources management at companies, a longer study abroad period would confer more foreign language skills and intercultural competencies that could be utilised at work. The evaluation report, therefore, pointed out a mismatch between the increase in short-term study abroad by university students and corporate needs.

In addition, the report recommended that the learning outcome of short-term study abroad programs for less than six months should be fully assessed to determine how much short-term programs have contributed to the development of those above three points; for example, language ability, intercultural understanding, and the ability to accept a diversity of values needed to foster globally minded workforce (Ministry of Internal Affairs and Communications, 2017).

Lack of opportunities to use foreign language skills at work

Beyond gaining a job or the hiring process, some studies describe that returnees from studying abroad often face difficulties in finding opportunities to use foreign language skills at work at Japanese companies partly because of the job (employee) rotation system[13] based on the membership-based employment.[14]

The JASSO's (2012) survey of Japanese students who studied abroad reported that 22.8% of those returnees faced difficulty in finding the opportunity to utilise their acquired foreign language skills at work, although 46.3% answered that such skills were useful in their jobs. According to Yonezawa's (2010) survey, office workers who studied abroad tended to use English at work, compared with those who did not study abroad. However, only about 15% of the surveyed workers said they frequently used English in their jobs. It seems that even though foreign language skills can be helpful in gaining a job in Japan after studying abroad, jobs which require foreign language skills are still limited at Japanese companies. However, since those two surveys were carried out more than five years ago, a follow-up study is needed to examine the current situation of this issue.

Nurturing "outward-looking" students (institutional efforts)

MEXT's support for universities' study abroad programs and scholarships for students has expanded the range of study abroad participants. Then a question is posted in institutions. How can universities encourage students to aim for the heights of academic and career success after their first short-term (typically up to one month) study abroad experiences as a springboard? This issue becomes even more critical when we consider the return on investment for study abroad.

In order to leverage the current increase in the numbers of short-term study abroad participants, it is crucial to provide opportunities for students to continue developing their global competencies after returning home. As an example, encouraging students to participate in longer programs could be a possibility, but efforts to reduce existing obstacles are necessary by providing adequate scholarships, solving issues related to companies' hiring systems, and developing mechanisms to allow students to transfer credits earned abroad easily. Opportunities for international exchange on home campuses should be increased both in curricular activities, including English-taught courses and extracurricular activities, such as language exchanges, tutoring, peer-support, and buddy programs.[15]

In addition, in order to respond to the current scepticism about the effect of short-term study abroad programs, it is important to conduct assessments to measure the impact of these programs as well as student learning outcomes, leading to quality improvement of these short-term programs. Collecting and assessing evidence on the value of the short-term study abroad experience to develop global competencies is necessary to build support. These recently developed short-term programs are meant mainly for students with a basic level in a foreign language; more advanced programs, requiring high competency in foreign language and cross-cultural skills (necessary for project-based learning with local students in a host country) can be an additional option for students to continue developing their competencies. Developing an environment for students to utilise and build on their experiences during short-term study abroad programs will be key to making this new trend an opportunity to nurture future "outward-looking" graduates.

Discussion and concluding remarks

From the review of the previous studies on the impact of study abroad on career, it can be argued that study abroad experience is helpful in enhancing employability and promoting career advancement. However, there are some issues to be considered. First, although the career-related impact of short-term study abroad for credits was smaller than that of long-term study abroad for a degree, and such short-term studies abroad lacked the impact at the time of recruitment by employers, short-term overseas programs are still important for the improvement of students' employability and career-related education. Considering the continuously increasing participation in short-term study abroad programs, it becomes imperative to examine the relationship between the outcomes of short-term study abroad and career-related benefits. At the same time, it will be necessary to enhance the quality of short-term programs.

Second, in order to leverage the acquired skills of study abroad returnees at Japanese companies, employers need to reform their hiring and employment systems to utilise those skills effectively in their jobs; for instance, by introducing a job-based employment system.[16] In other words, companies should give employees with study abroad experience more opportunities to use the skills acquired overseas, to increase their job satisfaction and motivation.

Nowadays, although employers have become more interested in hiring Japanese students with study abroad experience, they consider the learning outcomes of short-term study abroad experience to be limited, believing the experience to be too brief to allow students to acquire essential skills that can contribute to the expansion of their operations overseas. Accordingly, the Japanese government now emphasises the learning outcomes of short-term study abroad programs as an aspect of accountability for their funding schemes. This is because the Japanese government has invested significantly into funding and promoting outbound mobility, recognising the role that such mobility can play in revitalising Japan's economy.

Japan faces challenges in the transition from study abroad for a degree to study abroad for credits. In the Anglophone world, study abroad for credits is already the norm. Much importance has been attached to short-term study abroad as part of the university curriculum in the form of "education abroad." This has been further expanded to "learning abroad," which, apart from educational experiences at other higher education institutes, now also includes volunteer work, service learning, and internships. Assessments of the learning outcomes of study abroad and of the impacts on students' lives and careers are also carried out as part of the process. It is essential that Japanese universities collaborate with these initiatives. As the opportunities for students to gain study abroad experiences increase, universities should consider the whole period which students spend with them, from matriculation to graduation, setting out a roadmap which keeps in mind the stratification of study abroad programs and progression routes, relating study abroad to future careers or further study.

Notes

1. In 2014, the budget was increased to 8.5 billion yen from 3.6 billion yen in the previous year.
2. The Tobitate! (Leap for Tomorrow) Young Ambassador Program is made possible by contributions (donations) from supporting companies. For more information about the scholarship, refer to the website of the program, https://www.tobitate.mext.go.jp/about/english.html.
3. Bradford (2015) explained the inward-looking issues in Japan: "Around 2010, media reports, which proclaimed that Japanese students have a "fear of studying abroad" and "hinder [the] nation's economic growth," became regular. These reports were bolstered by a widely reported survey conducted by the Sanno Institute of Management in 2010, which found that nearly half of the new employees at companies in Japan did not want to work overseas" (p. 22).
4. The summary report of the survey can be found at http://recsie.or.jp/project/gj5000/.
5. Those 10 items are (1) Helpful in planning my career, (2) Helpful in gaining my current job, (3) Helpful in obtaining a higher salary, (4) I use knowledge and skills gained while studying abroad (or "at a Japanese university" for those who did not study abroad) in my current job, (5) I gained motivation to start a venture, (6) I gained motivation to work with an NPO/in social action, (7) My study abroad experience ("my degree was valued per se" for those who did not study abroad) was valued, (8) The language skills I gained through study abroad (or "my foreign language competencies" for those who did not study abroad) were valued, (9) The specialised knowledge and skills I gained through study abroad (or "at a Japanese university" for those who did not study abroad) were valued, and (10) My experience of communicating with foreigners was valued.

6. Regarding the ratios of the age groups in the three types of surveyed people, it is noted that the "Undergraduate credits studied abroad" had a larger proportion of individuals who were in their 20's than the "Undergraduate degree studied abroad" and "Undergraduate degree studied in Japan" (see Table 6.2).
7. The percentage in management roles is the total proportion of those in the "executive/board member class" and in the "managerial class."
8. In general, salaries are higher, promotion is faster, and more promotional opportunities are given at foreign companies than those at domestic companies in Japan.
9. Lifetime employment refers to a system in which a person is employed by the same company from getting a job after university graduation until retirement. Although this is not clearly stated within employment contracts, it is customarily expected in Japan that new recruits and companies tacitly agree to such practice (JASSO, 2018).
10. This refers to a system in which employees are assigned positions and pay increases in accordance with the number of years they have worked for the company and their age. The system is based on the prerequisite that employees will accumulate work skills and know-how the longer they work for the company and the older they get. Then these skills and know-how will be reflected back on the company performance in the long run (JASSO, 2018).
11. The Japanese academic year commences in April and ends in March.
12. For more information about the job-hunting and recruitment system in Japan, refer to JASSO (2018), Job Hunting Guide for International Students, https://www.jasso.go.jp/en/study_j/job/guide.html.
13. An employer rotates their employees' assigned jobs throughout their employment. It is designed to promote flexibility of employees and to keep employees interested into staying with the company/organisation which employs them. In Japan, the philosophy of this system is to build a cadre of generalists by rotating them through different locations and positions (Kopp, 2012).
14. It is a system of employment that does not limit duties, place of work, or working hours. The main feature of this style of employment is that employees are evaluated in accordance with their ability to perform all duties as generalists. Under this system, companies offer unlimited work in exchange for stable employment and treatment. The main feature of this system is that the jobs and workplaces they are assigned are not predetermined, so they can be relocated to any position at the discretion of the company (JASSO, 2018).
15. The language exchanges program is that two students with a different mother tongue teach their native language with each other by taking a turn. The tutoring program is that a domestic, graduate student provides an international, undergraduate student with academic support. The peer-support program is that a domestic student offers support to an international student enrolled in the same program and the same year. The buddy program is that a domestic student gives social support for a paired international student.
16. It is a system of employment that limits duties and place of work. Under this system, the job description is clearly defined and capabilities are evaluated in accordance with skill levels as specialists (JASSO, 2018).

Chapter 7

Understanding how international experiences engage employability

A game-based analytics approach

Dolly Predovic and John L. Dennis

Graduate employability is a key issue for higher education institutions. Industry recruiting strategies have evolved in recent years and the focus has shifted from graduates who have sound academic knowledge to graduates who can also demonstrate how they apply knowledge and other transferable skills in the workplace.

International experiences matter for employers but only if graduates can transform skills acquired into behaviours that are observable and translatable into value-adding workplace performance. We used game-based analytics to gain insight into hidden behaviours associated with skills that are valued most by employers. In doing so, this gave us an opportunity to think more creatively about employability development through international experiences.

In order to understand whether international experiences enhance graduate employability, it is necessary to reduce conceptual ambiguity and define employability. In fact, the operationalisation of employability from a theoretical concept to a measurable index is not a small undertaking. This chapter represents a tentative answer: game-based analytics. Most literature concentrates on the perception of different stakeholders on the development of employability skills, and our study tries to capture how well students can transform these skills into behaviours. We adopt a theoretical concept of employability under the processual perspective of ability to apply knowledge and skill, and we measured it by analysing behaviours with game-based analytics.

Employability definition[1]

The most widely investigated definition of employability is linked to a possession perspective, based on the assumption that employability is defined by skills and personal attributes that make graduates more likely to gain employment and successfully keep it (Yorke, 2006). Holmes, starting with his seminal work in 2001 (Holmes, 2001), challenged the possessive perspective on employability and based on skills, and built a "graduate identity" approach with a conceptual distinction between three explanations of graduate employability: skills "possession," social/cultural capital "position," and the "process" graduates use to present their claim on being a graduate worthy of employment (Holmes, 2013).

Several recent perspectives on employability are consistent with Holmes's idea of employability as a process. For example, Reid (2016) argues that employability must account for the social, political, and personal context of the recent graduates, while Jackson's (2016) concept of pre-professional identity is the result of a sense-making process where a "student makes sense of his/her intended profession through multiple memberships and differing levels of engagement with various communities." Similarly, Finch, Peacock, Levallet, & Foster's (2016) idea of an integrated dynamic capabilities view where a graduate's intellectual, personality, meta-skills, and job-specific resources are developed over time to give the graduate a competitive advantage and employability.

Measuring employability

Operationalising employability and finding an adequate assessment tool have been big challenges, and, generally speaking, employability assessments fall into three main categories: self-assessment, quizzes, and serious games (Employment Ontario, 2015).

Self-assessments have strong limitations, such as scoring accuracy and "content accuracy" (Panadero, Brown, & Strijbos, 2016), as well as social desirability bias, and, in fact, Kormos and Gifford (2014) find that 79% of the variance in the relationship between self-reported and objective behaviour remains unexplained.

Quizzes allow one to judge the quiz-taker's ability to demonstrate the skills being analysed (Darling-Hammond, 2014). Online, there are many such quizzes (mettl.com, centraltest.com, testofy.com) but very often they are simply poorly disguised self-assessment questionnaires (Employment Ontario, 2015).

Gaming is a new trend in psychometric testing and has been defined as "the use of game design elements in non-game contexts" (Deterding, Dixon, Khaled, & Nacke, 2011), and most employability related academic research in the field of gaming focuses on learning and developing employability skills through games – for example, the European Modes project (Haselberger et al., 2012).

Game-based learning and assessment

The largest body of research on game-based learning (GBL) investigates the learning potential of games (Boyle et al., 2016). Numerous studies analyse the impact of serious gaming on the development of employability skills: communication skills (Reinders, 2014; Romero, Usart, & Ott, 2015), critical thinking (Carolyn Yang & Chang, 2013), problem solving (Sung, Hwang, & Yen, 2015), conflict resolution (Ramón & Cristóbal, 2015), decision making (Savard, 2015), cultural skills (Romero et al., 2015), and leadership (De Freitas & Routledge, 2013; Lin & Lin, 2014).

Our focus is instead on game-based assessment, which can be achieved in three ways: game scoring, external assessment, or embedded assessment (Ifenthaler, Eseryel, & Ge, 2012). Game scoring focuses on the targets achieved during the game and is important for the player's motivation, which is a critical component of skill development and assessment (Keller, 1987). External assessments are not part of the game environment and are "real," through interviews, questionnaires, or essays (Chin, Dukes, & Gamson, 2009). Embedded assessments, or stealth assessments, are part of the game play and do not interrupt the game. Rich data about the player's behaviour while playing is the basis for the assessment of the skills. Implementing assessment features in a digital game-based environment is done only in a rather early stage of development because it is a very time consuming to step into the design process, and it needs to be tested in order for it to be reliable (Chin et al., 2009).

The KNACK

The KNACK suite of tests are stealth assessments that have been tested extensively and have been proven to have, both, very high reliability and validity indicators (Gray, Jerde, Prabhakaran, & Carroll, 2016). The United States Agency for Youth Development (USAID) has chosen the KNACK as being in the top 3% of the measurement tools they analysed (Galloway, Lippman, Burke, Diener, & Gates, 2017). Essentially, the KNACK, as a predictive analytic tool, helps employers find the right fit for employees by assessing the underlying processes that guide behaviour, thoughts, and emotions (basically one's psychology) and mapping that performance onto extremely well-known, well-tested, and scientifically sound measures (Galloway et al., 2017).

The KNACK as game-based talent analytics has been found to be a reliable and quantifiable predictor of workplace performance. Players' "micro-behaviours (e.g., the position and timing of screen gestures, user actions in relation to the state of the game, and so on) are logged at the millisecond level with such data density that we are able to recreate a given game session as the player made it happen." (Gray et al., 2016). From this data, within-game behavioural markers are generated that represent things such as how quickly a player processes information or how efficiently they attend to and see social cues, like facial emotional expressions, and then these markers are built upon to validate higher-level psychological constructs, such as intelligence or a growth mind-set. From these mappings, to numerous constructs, predictions to real-world outcomes are then generated for each individual player.

International experiences influence employability

The link between international mobility and graduate employability has been investigated from multiple perspectives: those of universities, employers, academics, and students (Crossman & Clarke, 2010; European Commission, 2014), students who have participated in learning abroad and alumni (Dwyer, 2004; Farrugia & Sanger, 2017; Mohajeri Norris & Gillespie, 2009; Potts, 2015) employers (Archer & Davison, 2012), employers and universities (Diamond, Walkley,

Forbes, Hughes, & Sheen, 2011), and signalling effect (i.e. students with international experiences are more likely to be called for an interview) (Petzold, 2017).

Jones argues that the benefits of internationalisation on employability, either through graduate mobility or through the internationalisation of the curriculum at home, are still not entirely understood by universities, employers, and even students (Jones, 2012, 2013, 2016). Discrepant perspectives on the value of international experiences among students, graduates, career development professionals, and employers are confirmed by Kinash, Crane, Judd, & Knight (2016).

Trooboff, Vande Berg, & Rayman's (2008) seminal paper finds that human resource professionals and non-senior management, contrary to common belief, place significant value on studying abroad. The main reason is that over 15% of the respondents have studied abroad themselves and by virtue of their own experience are positively disposed. Furthermore, among the different types of study abroad analysed in the research, findings show that employers have a strong preference for internships. More recently, the employers perspective on international study versus international internships in 31 European countries were analysed by Van Mol (2017) and this research confirms that employers seem to value internships abroad more than study abroad; however, this did vary across the countries in his study. For example, more than 40% of employers from Cyprus, Turkey, Luxembourg, Latvia, and Italy value international internships, while fewer than 10% of employers from Hungary, Croatia, Norway, Sweden, and the UK value international internships.

Present study

We conducted a study to determine how different international experiences affect employability. Considering our previous discussions, while we know that the KNACK measures employability, what we don't know is how the different international experiences translate into different KNACK scores and, therefore, into different measures of employability.

Data from 414 graduate students from 28 Italian universities was used and the study was conducted in conjunction with a project for a major multinational consulting company. The project's goal was to select 100 graduating students to be invited for a three-day talent program in the company's headquarters. The project was not a recruiting process for the consulting company, but a project aimed at identifying what tomorrow's top employable graduates should look like. Between November 2016 and February 2017, 28 Italian universities were visited. In order to participate in the selection process, students were asked to submit their resumes and motivation letters and to complete two KNACK games.

In all, 1973 resumes, motivations letters, and KNACK scores were received, and 414 candidates passed the first selection round and represent the sample used for the analysis. Of the sample group, 63% were male and the age distribution showed most participants (about 80%) were 23–25 years old. About two thirds of the participants studied economics, business, or management, while the remainder were enrolled in engineering (18%), managerial engineering (12%), and other fields (6%). Their previous experiences ranged from domestic internships (62%), domestic casual work (32%), international internships (23%), and international casual work (6%). Fifty-nine per cent had participated in study abroad prior to their participation.

Employability measures

Employability is measured by how students perform on 33 KNACKs, which result from playing the two KNACK assessment games, Meta Maze and Dash Dashi. The 33 KNACKs (see Table 7.1) are each measured on a scale, from 0 to 100, and they can be divided into five groups:

- Engagement: how you engage with the world and demonstrate professionalism
- Impact: how you make an impact on people and organisations
- Learning: how you learn new information and skills, and your motivation to learn
- Relationships: how you relate to other people and yourself
- Thinking: how you perform knowledge work and solve problems

Results

We conducted an analysis to assess whether KNACK scores differed as a function of demographic variables, (i.e., age and gender), internship experience (domestic or international), casual work experience (domestic or international), and study abroad experience.

Table 7.1 Factors in employability and the KNACKs associated with them

Engagement	Impact	Learning	Relationships	Thinking
Diligence	Leadership	Learning Agility	Social Intelligence	Logical Reasoning
Tenacity	Drive	Quick Thinking	Teamwork	Numbers
Self-Control	Self-Confidence	Growth Mindset	Customer Focus	Creative Problem Solving
Open Mindedness	Taking Ownership	Coachability		Creative Insight
Managing Ambiguity	Leadership Initiative	Intellectual Curiosity		Systems Thinking
Problem Solving	Inspirational Leadership	Data Fluency		Resourcefulness
Attention to Detail	Consensus Building			
Action Orientation	Executive Presence			

By using an exploratory factor analysis, it was possible to explore the structure of the 33 KNACKS and determine if they grouped together in a coherent fashion in relation to our independent variables – that is, international and domestic internships, study abroad, international and domestic casual work, gender and age.

Our analysis grouped the KNACKs into two main factors, revealing the underlying relationships between the 33 KNACKs. Factor 1 we describe as a social/effort factor that relates to employability behaviours defined by engagement (how one engages with the world) and relationships (how one relates to other people). Factor 2 we describe, instead, as a more cognitive factor that relates to employability behaviours defined by how one learns new information and motivation to learn.

What emerges from our analysis is that only international internships significantly impact the ability to successfully apply cognitive skills – like quick thinking, learning agility, data fluency, and creative insight – into workplace behaviours – that is, Factor 2. From our data, we argue that international internships are associated with higher-order capabilities; specifically, an enhanced power of learning (Rospigliosi, Greener, & Bourner, 2011), which is related to the highest cognitive domain in Bloom's taxonomy (Bloom, 1956) and is also exactly what employers seem to value the most (Finch, Hamilton, Baldwin, & Zehner, 2013). None of our independent variables significantly impacted the social/effort employability behaviours – that is, Factor 1.

The effect of international experiences on graduate employability has been extensively investigated with varied outcomes. Among intrapersonal competencies developed by study abroad, previous research has demonstrated that students self-rate as being more flexible, adaptable, and self-aware and as having developed better intercultural skills, while being more curious and having more confidence, while interpersonal competencies, such as communication, teamwork, and leadership are not rated as higher post study abroad (Farrugia & Sanger, 2017). Consistent with these results, Trooboff et al. (2008), found that while employers value team work more highly than any other skill, they believe that this skill is least likely to be enhanced through study abroad. Our research demonstrates that perhaps this previous research might not have taken into account those cognitive abilities, such as quick thinking, learning agility, data fluency, and creative insight.

All stakeholders (employers, academics, and students) seem to agree that international experiences do, in general, enhance learning, the acquisition of competencies, and the development of critical soft skills (Crossman & Clarke, 2010). Jones (2013) offers a very comprehensive review of literature on the influence of key transferable employability skills on international experience, divided between self-sufficiency/self-efficacy skills and people skills, and concludes that "it seems evident that transferable skills and capabilities are developed through international mobility, equally it may be the case that international mobility programs appeal to students who already possess, or have an advantage in developing, these skills."(Jones, 2013, p. 8) In fact, one limitation of our research findings is that since we don't have before and after snapshots of employability skills, we don't know whether those students who scored higher on employability skills post international internship had those very skills before they engaged in their abroad employment experience.

Conclusions

International experience matters for employers, but only if graduates can transform skills acquired into behaviours that are observable and translatable into value-adding workplace performance.[2] Unexpectedly, our research finds that an international experience translates into behaviours involving the highest order cognitive skills (e.g., quick thinking, learning agility, and creative insight).

Game-based analytics allow us to gain insight into the hidden behaviours associated with those skills that employers value most and offer us an opportunity to think more creatively about employability skills development through internationalisation. Our current research goes a step further by demonstrating behaviours that have not been typically found to be the expected outcome of international experiences – that is, higher-order cognitive skills.

According to Cavanagh, Burston, Southcombe, & Bartram (2015), students rate high-order skills as the most difficult to develop and to relate to work contexts. International internships might help with just that. Perhaps, those skills develop "under the radar" – such that students don't really know that they have developed them, and gaming analytics like the KNACK can help identify these hidden skill acquisitions.

There are also interesting prospects for internationalisation at home. Although collaborative online international learning is involved in an increasing number of programs, more could be done to actively simulate international workplace environments in virtual classrooms (Schech, Kelton, Carati, & Kingsmill, 2017). This would enable educators to offer such experiences to the entirety of the student body, not just to the mobile minority. Designing "international" internship activities into the curricula at home could yield unexpected and exciting findings.

This study underlies the importance of looking at employability from a behavioural perspective and looking at international experiences not from a social perspective but rather from a cognitive perspective. Our study could lead, therefore, to a paradigm shift where self-report data must be evaluated in conjunction with behavioural data, and where, for international experiences, the role of cognitive skills is evaluated in conjunction with social skills.

Notes

1. Other discussions about the definition or concept of employability can be found on pages 12, 25, 25, 60, 62, 117, 164.
2. This appears to be so; see impact on career development of Japanese graduates with international study experiences on page 82.

Part 2

International student migration and employment

Chapter 8

Open borders, closed minds

The experiences of international students in the Ontario labour market

Roopa Desai Trilokekar, Kelly Thomson, and Amira El Masri

Introduction

The idea of open borders, of welcoming international students (IS) and immigrants, is commonly associated with promoting national and global interests; mutual understanding; and, ultimately, global peace through the opening up of minds (NAFSA, 2003). However, in response to security threats post 9/11, the United States, with other countries following suit, have moved to a far more regulated and restricted immigration regime. Within such a global context – that is, "at a time of closing borders and closing minds" – Canada welcomes "students from around the world" (Universities Canada, 2017).

Canada's first international education strategy states, "International education, both incoming students and Canadians studying abroad, materially contributes to Canada's innovation strengths, such as by enhancing the development of qualified candidates for employment in both the private and public sectors" (Foreign Affairs, Trade and Development Canada [DFATD], 2014, p. 9). On one hand, IS recruitment and retention "help address the shortages of skilled labour that diminish Canada's long-term capacity for research and innovation and contribute to [closing] the 'innovation gap'" (DFATD, 2014, p. 9). Canadian students studying abroad, on the other hand, "bring back new ideas and discoveries" that contribute to Canada's success (DFATD, 2014, p. 17).

Barbaric (2017) notes that recent Canadian federal and provincial government commissioned reports recognise the importance of student mobility as a means of increasing experiential learning, employability, and the labour mobility of students. A new report titled *Global Education for Canadians: Equipping young Canadians to succeed at home and abroad* (2017) states,

> Young Canadians need knowledge, skills and experience to succeed in a more complex and competitive world. Relationships with emerging countries are becoming increasingly important to Canada's prosperity. The current generation of young Canadians will need to be comfortable working with people from different backgrounds. They will need self-awareness and

self-confidence, a willingness to take smart risks, and knowledge of the world and other societies. These are not luxuries in the 21st century; they are vital skills. (p. 5)

Similarly, Universities Canada[1] recognises the crucial role of universities in making Canada "globally competitive, [with] its newest graduates [needing] to arrive in the workforce equipped with international skills and experiences" (Chapuis & Fortier, 2016). Canadian employers are reported as "see[ing] the value of having staff members with a cross-cultural understanding and knowledge of the global marketplace. After all, about 60% of Canada's GDP is a result of international trade. To maintain and grow those trade relationships, a better understanding of the world is required" (Chapuis & Fortier, 2016). Canada may recognise and value open borders, but are Canadian employers "global ready," as the popular rhetoric around student mobility would have us believe? Are they valuing and, therefore, seeking graduates with international experience and intercultural and global competencies?

In an attempt to further understand the global readiness of Canadian employers, this paper examines the experiences of one subset of labour market hires; namely, international students (IS) who came to Canada to pursue their post-secondary education. IS represent Canadian university graduates with a wide diversity of international experiences and skill sets. They have studied and may have worked abroad. As a result, they may have developed global competencies, such as international language(s), intercultural communication skills, and comparative perspectives, to name just a few. This paper draws data from a pilot study conducted for the Ministry of Training, Colleges and Universities (MTCU) in 2016. The study examines the global readiness of Ontario employers by highlighting their hiring practices and their perceptions of the value proposition that IS represent.

Ontario is one of the 13 provinces and territories of Canada. Located in Ontario, Toronto is the nation's most populous city and hosts the largest IS population in Canada, over 60,000 students. The international student body has increased by 88.5% over six years, starting in 2010 (Crawley, 2017). With its 20 universities, 24 colleges, and more than 400 registered private career colleges, Ontario's post-secondary education sector is the largest in Canada. Ontario is the largest and fastest growing economy in Canada with strong manufacturing, financial, and service sector industries. Thus, Ontario provided an ideal context for our study.

Policy context – government

Canada is a country that is highly dependent on an immigrant labour force. According to Citizenship and Immigration Canada, "within the next decade, immigration is expected to account for 100 percent of net growth in the workforce, up from 75 percent today" (DFATD, 2014, p. 9). Canadian government policy positions international education as a tool to build human capital for a local-becoming-global marketplace.

> Our vision for Canada: become the 21st-century leader in international education in order to attract top talent and prepare our citizens for the global marketplace, thereby providing key building blocks for our future prosperity. (Advisory Panel, 2012 p. viii)

The first two goals of Canada's international education strategy are doubling the number of IS who choose Canada as their study destination and increasing the number of IS who choose to remain in Canada as permanent residents after graduation (DFATD, 2014); Ontario's goals are aligned with these national objectives. The recent discussion paper of the MTCU, *Developing Global Opportunities: Creating a Postsecondary International Education Strategy for Ontario* notes that, "Ontario recognizes that international students can help fill Ontario's need for skilled and talented workers" (Ministry of Training, Colleges and Universities [MTCU], 2016, p. 6). Similarly, Ontario's Immigration Strategy (2014) aims to "maximize the potential of international students" (Ontario Ministry of Citizenship and Immigration, 2014, p. 1). Within this context, the employability of IS who choose to stay in Ontario is considered pivotal to realising the policy objectives. Further, the recent introduction of the new Express Entry program[2] (January 2015) combined with the Ontario Immigrant Nominee Program (OINP) reflect a shift to a more employer-centred strategy in Canada's immigration policy (Papademetriou & Sumption, 2011). Under the revised OINP program, IS who have completed studies at a publicly funded college or university in Canada may apply for permanent residence status if they secure a permanent full-time job offer in a high-skilled occupation from an Ontario employer that offers a wage that matches Ontario's typical entry-level wage for that occupation[3] (Ontario Immigration, 2015).

Policy context – university

Paul Davidson, president of Universities Canada, states, "Students around the globe are increasingly choosing the internationally recognised quality of a Canadian university education, and the benefits for Canada are tremendous" (as quoted in Universities Canada, 2017, para 2). Universities Canada views this growth as "reflecting Canada's value proposition in today's global higher education market and institutions' concerted recruitment efforts…[as well as] Canada['s reputation] as a nation that values diversity and inclusion" (Universities Canada, 2017, para 1, 2).

Ontario universities align their institutional strategies and policies with federal and provincial government policies on IS (Trilokekar & El Masri, 2016). While there are a few exceptions, most Ontario universities are committed to recruiting and increasing IS enrolments. Most Ontario university campuses have invested in IS offices and provide support services. Several provide language programs;

on- and off- campus job, coop, or internship opportunities; career counselling; and networking services tailored to the needs of their ISs (El Masri, Choubak, & Litchmore, 2015; Morris-Lange & Brands, 2015). However, El Masri et al. (2015) report that there is a heavier concentration of programs offered to IS in the first year of study than in their later years and; therefore, there is limited support for the transition into employment.

Research study

Our pilot study engaged a qualitative research design with multiple data collection methods, including interviews and focus groups with 10 employers and 17 staff members (from career, cooperative education, and international education offices) at three Ontario universities, as well as observation of workshops and a job fair. We interviewed a "convenience sample" of 10 employers who were either recommended through university career centre contacts or whom we identified through their participation in university job fairs in Ontario. The three universities we chose for our study offered programs where enrolment of IS is higher than average and that were likely to attract employers. The three were situated in distinct geographic locations in Ontario. They included universities with student bodies ranging from 18,000 to 31,000 undergraduate students and from 2300 to more than 5000 graduate students. The percentage of IS ranged from 2.6% to 15% for undergraduate programs and from 7.7% to 36% for graduate programs. At the universities, we interviewed staff, observed on-campus workshops offered to students, and observed on-campus job fairs.

We conducted an inductive analysis of the observation, interview, and archival data using grounded theory and critical ethnographic approaches (Corbin & Strauss, 2008; Madison, 2011). Our research aim was to examine and develop a nuanced understanding of employer motives, perceptions, and practices, and of their interface and interactions with universities in facilitating or impeding the conversion of IS educational credentials into secure employment and access to Canadian citizenship. We report on select excerpts from our data to gauge the global readiness of Ontario employers by highlighting their hiring practices and their perceptions of the value proposition that IS represent.

Findings

Employer perspective

We present the results of our analysis of the interviews we conducted with employers in Ontario below. The employers vary in terms of size, location, and industry and, as we illustrate, in the relative ease with which they were able to attract students for temporary placements or post-graduation positions. With the exception of two, all the employers were "multinational" (i.e., operating in at least two countries, most often United States and Canada) but over half were "global" (i.e., operating in at least one region outside of North America), and one of the two that was not multinational at the time described their strategy as "trying to go global."

Despite the global nature of their businesses, as we show below, in describing what they looked for in potential employees, employers rarely mentioned anything that could be understood as "global skills." Instead, for the most part, employers focused on specific technical skills and more general attributes, such as being "professional," "a team player," and "able to think on their feet" as their priorities for screening and selecting students. Only one employer who had a high demand for employees with skills that were in short supply, and who described recruitment as "challenging" based on the company's location and size, spontaneously described having an interest in actively recruiting "international" applicants. One other elite employer, who was required to meet affirmative action targets to comply with federal regulations, actively sought out "diverse" candidates. Most employers did not mention IS among their potential hires until the interviewer introduced the topic. A few employers who were "unattractive" (see below for how we categorised employers) said that they hired IS in relatively large numbers. "Elite" employers, and even those who have a consistent demand for workers with skills in relatively short supply, did not actively recruit or consistently hire IS or workers with training and experience acquired outside of Canada. We begin by describing how we categorised employers and proceed to show how employers described "what they were looking for" in employees and how easy or difficult it was to successfully fill positions.

We have categorised employers in three ways: first, in terms of their "attractiveness," based on their own descriptions of how easy or difficult it was for them to attract employees; second, in terms of the overall ratio of supply versus demand – whether skills that they were looking for were in short or abundant supply; finally, based on their own quantitative descriptions of how many positions they attempt to fill versus the numbers of applicants they receive. As we show, using these criteria, three of the employers can be described as unattractive, with relatively high numbers of positions they would like to fill and few students who apply, often due to the nature of the job (low skill, customer service, sales) or the working conditions (e.g., low pay, seasonal). Three employers are medium in terms of attractiveness – they are able to attract applicants but positions are challenging to fill either due to locations (relatively far from urban centres) or working conditions (e.g., "dirty" work); finally, four of the employers we interviewed could be described as elite employers – they are well-known corporations and receive far more applications from students than they have positions available.

As Table 8.1 illustrates, even those employers that we categorise as unattractive are able to attract numbers of applications that far exceed the numbers of available positions. Those that are attractive cannot cope with the number of applications they receive and most have found ways to limit the number of applicants; for example, by only visiting a few specific universities. While the 2 larger employers that we categorise as unattractive invest more resources

Table 8.1 Characteristics of employers and recruitment behaviour with respect to global skills and international students

Employers	Attractiveness	Demand/supply ratio	Positions vs. applications	Global skills mentioned spontaneously	Actively recruit IS
N Tech	Elite	"We have a fair number of people that are interested in us, yes. So there are specialized skills sometimes that you do have to beat the bushes for but if I am looking for a new grad student I don't. I get lots of applications for it....I bring a lot more in for interviews than I hire."	"...looking at five or six interviews for a position I would think. I would think up to ten that you interview to get the right fit for you."	No	No
U Mfg	Elite	"...production team members, that is our biggest hiring and it is one that we do more on a steady basis so we just take them through a variety of selection stages...And skilled trades same way, there are not enough people out there to form pools, whereas in production we tend to have the ability to form pools, but we pull from them quickly so they are not sitting there very long." Q:...do you get a lot of applications for your co-op? A:...It is pretty healthy"	"our volume is anywhere from 40 to 50 a term [co-op placements]"; this employer does not hire graduates directly from university for full-time positions."	No	No

O Media	Elite	"So generally for that program we don't go out of those five schools; we've got enough applicants there to fill the roles. But for roles outside of that formal process we will consider applicants from other schools."	"So we actually have a university recruitment program where every year we bring in… generally it can range between five to eight new grads into our [job title]. I think for every school they are probably interviewing at least eight to ten individuals per school. And the nice thing about that too is so they pick their top five or eight."	No	No
S Fin	Elite	"About 300 students that apply to a job, the one job that I am recruiting for. How do I go from 300 down to 10? So … I look at the 300 names and I go through and I picked the 40 that are in my Rolodex… I will then look at their transcripts and their cover letter, and their resumes, and maybe I will get it down to 20. I will interview 20 to hire 10."	"So in our campus full-time programs we hired over 800 last year in Canada. So last year [S Fin's] website received over 740,000 applicants in North America, and we hire about 15,000. So how the heck am I going to go from 750,000 to 15,000?"	No	No
T Mftg	Medium	"And one of our challenges is the fact that … the location isn't overly appealing …because it is noisy down there and there is oil and some people don't want that environment, and so some people can select themselves out…, like is the wage the concern? And normally maybe I've gotten one response saying it is a little low but for most people that is not a concern."	"… for engineers because we do take four interns every year. We usually interview, I would like to say, ten to twelve and then we select four of those."	No	No

(Continued)

Table 8.1 Characteristics of employers and recruitment behaviour with respect to global skills and international students (*continued*)

Employers	Attractiveness	Demand/supply ratio	Positions vs. applications	Global skills mentioned spontaneously	Actively recruit IS
B Tech	Medium	"I wish I could say that I could find those resources to fill those needs; there is simply not enough of them... there is just so much demand. So for the government to say go and hire a Canadian and hire a new grad, well I would totally do that if I could get them."	"When you tell me there are 20 of them [students with the requisite skill set] that graduate in a year from my local school, and there are over 500 employers that are looking to secure them, what do you think is going to happen? [I] have 16 of them [Canadian applicants] and I have 89 that are not. So what do I do with that! You want me to ignore those 90 and only consider the 16; well I am but it is still not enough."	No	Yes
H Tech	Medium	"It's not hard to find but it's hard to compete against other companies; we are not Google, we are not Facebook, but we hire the same type of people so it is hard to compete against those huge corporations that offer these bells and whistles. So a lot of people get pulled in that direction rather than coming to the small and medium-sized companies. So that can be a challenge."	The employer did not specify the number of applicants or positions available.	No	No

U Tech	Low	"We are a large organization but we don't have the campus brand. ....we post on all of these job boards, but we don't have a lot of people apply to our opportunity so it all really comes through the school. Like, I really rely on the universities."	"I do over a thousand interviews a year; phone interviews.... I hired over 118 and next year we are forecasting over 150, and most of those are entry-level students; I would say 75 percent of those individuals come from universities right out of school because our role is an entry-level role."	No	No
G Tech	Low	"...it was a little bit of a struggle just because our business model is so unique [employees must sign a 2-year commitment], so I think the career centre representatives wanted to play it on the safe side."	"We received around 30,000 applications last year and that translated into a little over a 1000 consultants who were able to pass our recruitment process and then start working with us. In terms of just Canada alone, our target this year was 150 and we were a little bit below that; around 148. But we started off in Toronto with just 7, so we went from 7 to 150 in quite a short amount of time."	No	No
T Tourist	Low	Seasonal job	Hiring 12 "I think two or three weeks...we've gotten 12 to 15 resumes, all of them good."	No	No

in recruitment, only 1 of the 10 employers surveyed actively recruited international students (B.Tech). However, this employer actively recruits internationally, not to attract candidates with global skills but simply to meet their company's demand for technical expertise. Similarly, one of the two unattractive employers recruiting for full-time positions said that about half of their hires were IS, while the other also "...hire a ton of them [IS]"... we are a very, very diverse... So we will hire individuals from an international background. Do we have a lot of them apply? No, not really." It appears that many Canadian employers associate ISs not with a particular global skill set but with diversity. As one of the elite employers said, they have diversity targets to meet so they actively recruit IS:

> To me they're all part of the same pool when I am looking for all diverse candidates, now the majority [of international students], I don't want to stereotype them now the majority are part of a visible minority coming in, they have obviously demonstrated initiative to come to a school outside of their country, they have often had to get a scholarship or their parents have had to raise money or funds, it is usually the first born. You know, so all of that, so the people that I am meeting, these are the cream of the crop that are coming in. So, they have a lot to offer.

While this elite employer sees IS as "the cream of the crop" with "a lot to offer," only one of the unattractive employers described IS as having something positive that distinguished them from other students. She identified their resilience and, given the tourism business she operated, speculated that tourists might feel more comfortable with another person who was from out of the country. The larger, multinational employers, like the employer quoted above, treat IS as simply part of the "same pool" from which they select potential candidates, verifying the candidate's eligibility to work in Canada after they have been identified as a potential hire.

The majority of comments from employers related to IS framed IS within a deficit discourse. For example, they were often associated with having communication "problems," or as being risky to hire given the frequent rule changes by governments, which affected work permits both during their studies and post-graduation, or affected the student's mobility between countries (such as the United States) when international travel was part of the job. Since we conducted our interviews, the United States has brought in newer rules further restricting the mobility of citizens from predominantly Muslim countries, which may have further limited the number of employers who are willing to hire IS.

Overall, based on our interviews with a convenience sample of employers in Ontario who recruit at universities, global skills did not seem to be a priority that informed the recruitment process. Instead, IS were often seen as either part of the pool of potential hires, with no characteristics that were particularly attractive to employers, or seen as being somewhat less attractive than domestic students.

Table 8.2 Description of universities

University	Brief description
X	Consistently ranked high for providing comprehensive education combining traditional academia with experiential learning, co-operative education outside the classroom, and research opportunities that allow students to learn and work with faculty who are experts in their field.
Y	A distinctive career focused educational approach with emphasis on entrepreneurship and experiential learning. It is active within its community, serving societal needs.
Z	Home to the world's largest post-secondary co-operative education program, providing excellent links with industry, and it is considered a leader in university career education.

University perspective

Below, we briefly describe the three universities (see Table 8.2) in the context of their focus on experiential and cooperative education.

Each of these three universities had extensive contact and relationship with employers. The schools' employment rates for graduates ranged from 84.4% to 91.3% within six months of graduation and from 92% to 95% within two years of graduation. They represented a host of diverse disciplines, such as arts, agriculture, business management, communication and design, community services, economics, engineering, environmental studies, humanities, social and applied human sciences, mathematics, and veterinary science.

Commenting on employers' hiring practices, university staffers contend that employers look for the best candidates who have the skills they need regardless of their citizenship status. A staffer notes: "Employers who come to campus, not a lot of them are even thinking… about international students in particular, they want the best candidates and they could be domestic and they could be international." None of the interviewees reported that employers specifically searched for, or excluded, IS with specific set of (global) skills. One staffer notes, "I don't think I have ever heard an employer say 'I am not interested in an international student,' but I have also never heard an employer say 'hey, those [IS] were pretty special. I would like to get more.'" Employers, according to university staff, "just want the best talent," or want students who meet certain requirements, such as ability to speak another language.

When asked about the value they think IS have for Ontario employers, a few staff were quick to suggest attributes of IS that could be identified as global competencies. One staffer suggested that IS should be valued for their multiple international perspectives and their skills in working with diverse customers. They stated, "If you are hiring somebody who's already moved abroad, tried a new community and culture, you know they are resilient, and you know they are versatile, and you know they are agile, and those are some of the biggest things that employers are looking for." Another staffer spoke about a strong work ethic, stronger than those of domestic students', "that comes from their willingness to travel abroad in order to study...there is the willingness for experience, there is a willingness to put oneself out there little bit more and I think that can translate very well into the work force."

Staff could identify isolated instances when IS were valued by their employers for their international experience and competencies. One staffer recollected an IS hired in the Bay area of the United States being an asset to his employer as he was "able to leverage his family's connections in a particular business to the advantage of the employer." This employer valued IS for helping to expand their business's networks and opportunities for international deals. A few others spoke about IS as assets to their employers because of their home language proficiency. As confirmed by an employer in the financial services industry, "It's fantastic for us [financial services] to have students that can speak more languages [and] that understand the cultural context for new Canadians, who can then be representatives for us ...not a big challenge if their English skills aren't that great because we could put them in a neighbourhood where they would be liaising with their language colleagues or fellow citizens."

When asked, staff see the value of the following:

> intercultural competence, language skills, especially for major corporations and private companies that are looking to expand internationally, [because] how can you do that without international diverse staff members who understand the market in a very nuanced way?

While recognising the importance of international competence, most staff categorically stated that they rarely come across job postings that require or even consider international background or experience. Further, they recognise how they themselves are implicated, as they do not "suggest to international students that they use [their international background] as a selling point."

One staff member, himself a past IS, spoke about the need to educate employers about "the fact that these are graduates with different language skills; graduates who have pretty good solid sense of what intercultural competence means; graduates with contacts in different countries. I think we need to proactively educate employers on this rather than having them focus on the potential negative stuff." This staffer also discussed the role that government ought to play in incentivising employers to hire IS, and the need for government websites to say, "hey, we have a very diverse society here, whether you are talking about international students or newcomers to Canada, these are the different things that they come with."

However, in the majority of cases, staffers concur that employers see hiring IS as challenging, and IS are described using a deficit discourse. Whereas many IS come to Canada with rich work experience from their home countries or other countries, university staff report that Canadian employers are more interested in Canadian work experience. Lack of Canadian experience is perceived to be a deficit and poses a barrier to IS in accessing the Canadian labour market, because "when you look at small and mid-size businesses, they can be scared of something this different."

To address this perceived barrier, some career centre staff advised IS to pursue jobs in the retail industry in order to "start putting [a]... foot in the door." Others were directed to conceal their international experience or "lessening ... [its] impact on written documentation." Hence, different workshops are designed to help IS understand "the cultural norms, and the expectations of Canadian employers," "professional behaviours in the workplace," "how to do a handshake, how do you greet someone" in Canadian culture. After all, career centre staff "want them [IS] to be in the same competitive pool as any other student. So, ideally, an employer shouldn't notice... [whether] they are international or not because they should be educated the same, trained the same and still do just as good as a domestic student."

Within this context, the concept of "soft skills" becomes central. An IS "can have all of the right technical [knowledge and] experience," yet employers might perceive them lacking in terms of their English language and communication skills, accent, interpersonal skills, and how "integrated" they are. One staff member noted that IS need to "make sure they are doing it in the 'Canadian' way." Hence, the onus is on the IS "to speak to the frame of mind of Canadian employers in particular," and not vice versa. Thus, despite the discourse of the search for the brightest and most talented regardless of the status or nationality of the student, practices among career centres reveal another layer of complexity. In examining the types of services that career centres at the different universities offer, we noticed that the majority of these programs aim to familiarise IS with the Canadian job market and work culture, build Canadian work experience, and help IS translate their global experience into something more familiar to Canadian employers. In other words, "Canadianising" or minimising the international aspects of IS becomes the objective. Career centres note that career counselling for IS focuses on developing "cultural intelligence," where IS are expected to develop cultural skills to "get to the point where the employer is just focusing on the value of that candidate and not thinking 'oh it is an international student and I will have to think about x, y and z'. You want them to just see the person."

Conclusions

Universities Canada's 2014 survey of Canadian universities states, "among the most prominently discussed rationales for internationalisation is creating globally aware graduates with skills suited to the jobs of today and tomorrow," implying that Canadian employers are global ready – that they are looking for and in need of graduates with international and intercultural competencies. In fact, the survey reports that "82 percent of businesses that employ individuals with international and intercultural experience claimed that these workers enhanced their firm's competitiveness. Banks, manufacturers, law firms and resource industries told us their top performing employees were most often those with an international perspective. Some companies include international experience as a requirement for promotion, and others put their top performers on a fast track that includes an assignment abroad" (Momani & Stirk, 2017, para 4).

These findings seem contradictory to our pilot study's suggestion that most Ontario employers use Canadian, not international, experience as a key screening criterion in recruitment and selection practices. Contrary to the international education rhetoric of success in an era of globalisation, where international experience and the cross-cultural skills are required for success, it is the IS who are able to show higher levels of "Canadianness" that have better chances of being recruited than those who do not. IS need "to be able to really demonstrate that they get the culture of the company and when it is an international student of the local culture, of the country culture." Ironically, while the government speaks on the one hand of the many advantages of recruiting and retaining IS for their distinctive international experience, it speaks on the other hand the language of the employer by stating, "International students are well positioned to immigrate to Canada as they have typically obtained Canadian credentials, are proficient in at least one official language and often have relevant Canadian work experience" (DFATD 2014, p. 12). In other words, IS serve as an ideal pool of new immigrants because they have been Canadianised – they have Canadian education credentials, they speak one of the two official languages, and they have been trained by Canadian employers and acclimatised to the Canadian job market.

The reluctance of Canadian employers to hire international candidates has been identified by researchers. Momani and Stirk (2017) report that "while many of the business leaders we met wanted to see more cultural fluency in their workforce, they acknowledged they don't always follow through when it comes to hiring. Too many companies are still ambivalent about foreign experience, and they are unsure how to interpret or value foreign degrees, university credentials, and grading schemes. Although human resource departments may be familiar with the Ivy League or prestigious UK institutions, they may not know that China's Tsinghua University, for example, is the Harvard of East Asia and its graduates are an asset rather than an untested liability" (para 8).

So why then is there a push for the next generation to go "out into the world to develop new skills and build the intercultural fluency"? Chapuis and Fortier (2016) go so far as to state that, "as a truly global nation, Canada cannot afford to turn inward" (para 14). What our research suggests is that Canada does look outward but only in terms of recruiting IS, defining the best and the brightest for employment, and subsequently immigration, as those who successfully assimilate into mainstream Canadian society. This is quite the irony for a country that is "known worldwide as a nation that values diversity and inclusion" (Universities Canada, 2017, para 2). "At a time of closing borders and closing minds" (Universities Canada, 2017, para 1), while Canada does well in "opening borders," it clearly faces challenges in "opening its minds."

Notes

1. Universities Canada is a membership organisation providing its 96-member institutions with a unified voice for higher education, research, and innovation advances.
2. Express Entry Program, introduced in 2015, is an electronic application management system that applies to most of the immigration routes. In its first version, the program did not give extra points to applicants for their education in Canada. This was perceived to be counterproductive to Canada's efforts to attract and retain ISs as it withdrew an advantage they had in the previous system over other permanent residency applicants. Amendments were introduced in its second iteration (2016) where applicants with Canadian education received extra points.
3. ISs applying under the PhD graduate stream or master's graduates stream can apply without a job offer.

Chapter 9

Chinese student mobility, return migration, and the transition into the labour market

Saskia Jensen

Introduction

The internationalisation of higher education (HE) has increased dramatically over the last two decades and has largely become a market driven activity. There has been a major influx of Chinese students to British universities since the late 1990s, making Chinese students the primary engine for growth for international HE. This development raises the question about the main drivers for Chinese students to pursue tertiary education in the UK and the perceived benefits of an international education in the longer term.

International higher education (IHE) is an intangible and often expensive service that leads to complex and increasingly selective decision-making processes, which are largely influenced by information available, opinions of influencers, and reputational factors as well as structural factors, such as visa policies and costs. Choosing to be an internationally mobile student is a decision made on an individual level and, generally, the most important elements in the decision-making process relate to the course and the reputation of the education. Options for students to work, career prospects, and employability are, in general, other crucial factors that influence the decision making, and a 2017 study among internationally mobile students confirmed that 76% of respondents considered career-related aspects influential factors when choosing a suitable study destination.[1]

But does an international education really provide graduates with a competitive advantage in a highly competitive, increasingly global, and ever changing labour market? Literature on employability is usually focused on the national level, and the link between mobility and employability has been little researched. There are few studies available that look into international students' progress and their labour market transition (Huang, 2013).

This chapter elaborates on the link between international tertiary education, its perceived impact on future employability, and the role higher education institutions (HEIs) play in providing students with an extended set of skills. Focusing on Chinese students' motivations to study abroad, their expectations, and their study-to-work transition, this chapter investigates the role of higher education, the importance of future employability, student mobility, and graduate outcomes.

Drawing on the literature, the author argues that, despite a general understanding of the positive impact an international education has on the individual, a Western degree does not necessarily result in a successful study-to-work transition and does not guarantee a desirable job upon graduation. However, the increasing importance of an international perspective has become more apparent in China, and an internationally educated workforce is expected to make positive contributions in the changing context of China's position in a global market and it is increasingly in demand.

Employability and the role of higher education

The thought that the skill set of workers is a form of capital is one of the most important ideas in economic theory, and since the link between education and productivity was established in the human capital theory, this notion has become even more significant in the 21st century as human capital forms a key resource for competitiveness and development (Wang, 2012). Consequently, education at all levels is recognised as a contributor to a country's economic performance.

In information societies, knowledge is a key resource and both a formal and non-formal education are a necessity for economic and social development. The International Commission on Education for the 21st century stressed the fact that societies have to confront and overcome tensions between the global and the local, the universal and the individual, and modernity and tradition in order to foster the expansion of knowledge and facilitate progress (Delors, 1996).

The significance of the UK tertiary education sector to the wider economy is generally acknowledged and has been made more explicit in recent years. In his 1997 report, Dearing stressed the need for a globally competitive economy with highly skilled, trained, and motivated graduates who perform successfully on the world's stage. This, coupled with the further development of the human capital theory, has created a fertile forum for the discourse of employability. Consequently, the relationship between the economy and higher education has been a longstanding topic of debate, and graduate employability has become an aim that has been imposed on HE systems.

The Enhancing Student Employability Coordination Team (ESECT) delivered a widely accepted definition[2] based on their research with key stakeholders; it defines employability as "a set of achievements, understandings and personal attributes that make individuals more likely to gain employment and be successful in their chosen occupations" (Maher & Graves, 2008). Employability implies a relationship between education and employment in which education orients learners and workers towards employment. In order to understand this relationship, it is crucial to understand the broader changing context of societies that identify educational needs for the workforce. Dramatic changes caused by demographic trends and migration, new technologies, and shifts in the labour market have had profound implications for the workplace and, therefore, for the education that prepares people for it. Today, the education sector faces challenges that derive from ever changing demands of the (global) labour market, and this means undertaking multiple tasks to prepare learners for further and continuous education, employment, and career changes. This development creates the need for a more flexible and balanced education system, which combines both formal and non-formal education to enable lifelong learning and to promote employability (Wang, 2012). In 2006, the UK government published the Leitch Review – a paper that considers the UK's long-term skill needs and emphasises the potential of people as being the country's natural resource. The paper stresses the need to maximise skills in order to maximise the economic and social health of the UK. At a European level, the Bologna Process seeks to "create a European space for higher education in order to enhance the employability and mobility of citizens," and with the ideas of Bologna spreading well beyond European boundaries, the link between education and employability is now stronger and more "global" than ever.

Educational institutions are challenged with teaching discipline-specific curricula as well as supporting soft skills development, such as communication, creativity, leadership, teamwork, values, and ethics. Education itself is no longer the ultimate goal for learners. It imparts relevant skills that allow a smooth education-to-work transition. National and international competitiveness is another challenge faced by institutions in the 21st century: employability rankings, graduate outcome scores, and various international assessments present important benchmarks and performance measures (Wang, 2012). In academia, however, employability causes controversy as many academics feel the employability agenda is too driven by the government and economic motivations while faculty are driven to protect the "traditional liberal idea'" of education. Hence, many academics believe the curriculum should focus on making the students experts in the subject, with employability skills emerging as a by-product of the educational experience (Maher & Graves, 2008).

On the other hand, academic qualifications are often taken for granted and the "first tick" in the box before employers look at potential candidates in more detail and assess individual characteristics. Graduate employability has become a benchmark and a measure of success in the HE sector, and universities have acknowledged the "need for graduates to develop a range of personal and intellectual skills beyond specific expertise in an academic discipline", Shah, A; Pell, k. and Brooke, P. (2004). Institutions have increasingly shifted their focus towards graduate employability rather than knowledge acquisition, and degree-level studies now tend to focus on both subject-specific knowledge as well as transferable skills.

Employability and the role of education mobility

Internationalisation and student mobility present another layer of a dynamic that affects the labour market, the HE landscape, and how they interlink. Internationalisation and globalisation have increased the need for intercultural competencies in graduates. Employers have recognised that staff with an understanding of cultural issues and the ability to manage international relationships are a valuable resource, and universities talk more and more about curricula internationalisation (Crossman & Clark, 2010).

Research suggests that there is a link between an international experience, the potential for personal change, and the acquisition of a particular set of skills. Previous studies revealed significant improvement in areas such as open mindedness and the appreciation of diversity, as well as flexibility and cross-cultural adaptability, and highlighted the increasing understanding of foreign languages and culture (European Commission, 2014). These are all attributes that are highlighted as "important skills" in today's labour market. Social and intercultural competence, generally defined as "the ability to communicate effectively and appropriately in intercultural situations based on one's intercultural knowledge, skills and attitudes" (Deardorff, 2006) are important tools for graduates in the transition from education to the work place as intercultural competencies becoming deciding factors for employers in a globalised labour market. A study conducted by Hinchcliffe and Jolly in 2010 showed that over 75% of employers valued cultural and social awareness when hiring and promoting staff.

Education and employability in China

Since China moved from a state controlled to a devolved education system, investments in education have increased considerably, and despite the costs attached to it, the demand for university education is high and likely to increase with rising wealth. The government is moving towards a knowledge-driven economy and the majority of Chinese parents aspire to tertiary education for their children. The competition for places in top institutions is high, and tutoring to pass the gaokao[3] exam has become the norm.

As a result of increasing demand and substantial investments, China's higher education sector has expanded very rapidly. The number of HEIs has increased by around 8% since 2012, and with 42 million enrolled students in 2016, China now produces more university graduates per annum than U.S. and European institutions, combined. While China was largely an agrarian economy, the service sector has grown fast and has become the main economic driver. Today, China ranks as the second-largest economy in the world and represents an important consumer market. McKinsey reports that Chinese households are becoming more affluent: 78% of China's urban population is predicted to be "middle-class" by 2022 and the number of Chinese multimillionaires is forecast to increase by 75% (McKinsey, 2013).

The thriving economy paired with an improvement of employment opportunities and a more liberal lifestyle in China has resulted in an increase of returnees in recent years. The transition from a highly planned and restricted to a more mobile and flexible market has caused more young talent to enter China's labour market – many of them being *hai guis*, or "Sea Turtles" (foreign-educated, experienced, and highly skilled graduates) (Hao & Wen, 2016).

University graduates in China used to be guaranteed jobs in the public sector, but with the changing labour market situation and the increasing number of highly qualified graduates the public sector has become overstaffed and unemployment rates among graduates and youths is higher than the Chinese average. This situation is largely driven by an increasing tertiary education graduation rate which is flooding the Chinese labour market – unemployment and underemployment are both results of this development. While competition among graduates in government and the public sector is still high, graduates are also increasingly looking to the private sector and international firms for employment, and since the era of the planned economy and the "iron rice bowl" practice of guaranteed employment ended, indigenous Chinese university leavers are now also flooding the market. The economy, however, still doesn't generate enough jobs to absorb the high number of graduates each year (Hao & Welch 2012). Still, despite the surplus supply of graduates, employers report a lack of skills, poor attitudes, and unrealistic expectations and complain of difficulty in finding suitable talent. Young employees, on the other hand, report a lack of on-the-job training and of discrimination (Wang, 2012).

In an overcrowded labour market, Chinese graduates face fierce competition for graduate-level jobs and need to set themselves apart to successfully compete for desirable employment upon graduation. An international qualification is expected to be one way to facilitate early and mid-career gains – particularly for those who did not secure a place in one of China's top universities. Hao and Welch (2012) argue that international exposure is a unique treasure among the repertoire of personal skills and knowledge, and confers an advantage to the individual. In addition, formal endorsement through the government[4] and private enterprises has helped to create a positive external environment for returnees in recent years. Another policy that favours potential returnees is the conferment of a local *hukou*[5], a governmental system of household registration in mainland China and Taiwan, upon return which makes *hukou* transfers much more accessible for graduates with international qualifications as they may choose their preferred cities for employment in China and transfer their *hukou* appropriately. For domestic graduates, on the other hand, it remains difficult to transfer their *hukou* and gain formal status as a local outside their "area" (Hao & Welch, 2012).

However, physical absence from China for several years can also result in a certain loss of *guanxi* (Hao & Welch, 2012), and while there are clear connections between employability outcomes and an international education experience, recent studies have suggested that those who have a foreign (most often Western) degree often have overly high expectations with regard to their working environment and earning potential compared to their nationally educated peers (Hao & Wen, 2016).

Exploring factors influencing decision making

Caroline Knowles (2012) undertook a research project concerning young Chinese people in the early stages of their working lives in London. The study explores how mobility configures life and career planning among young professionals. Her findings show that most young migrants began their migration trajectories as students and identified multidimensional location choices. Reasons for choosing a destination are interconnected and shift over time.

A study undertaken by Anni Kajanus in 2015 confirmed that the main motivations for overseas study are language skills, the quality of education, and the improvement of career prospects both in China and abroad. Their survey respondents consider Western institutions to provide better education on critical and creative thinking, and highlight a lack in access to cutting-edge theories and methods in China (Kajanus, 2015). Even students who did not consider employment outside of China upon graduation did consider overseas study to be beneficial, as they expect to be better prepared to adapt in a dynamic and transforming work environment.

The characteristics of the family and parents' opinions play a significant role in the process of choosing a study destination. They are often the main source of funding and are, therefore, main influencers in the decision making. In 2014, HSBC commissioned a research series entitled The Value of Education. The study seeks to understand what parents want an education to provide for their children. The findings of the research were released in two stages. The first report, Springboard for Success, is based on the views of 4592 parents in 15 countries around the world. It focuses on education's value as a transformative force. Published in 2015, the second report, Learning for Life, is based on 5500 responses from 16 countries and focuses on parents' hopes and expectations for their children's education and beyond. Key findings of the research reveal that 43% of parents think that the ability to compete in the workplace is a key expectation of a good university education, and almost half of the sample agreed that enhanced confidence and social skills are the most valuable aspects of university education in preparing students for life after graduation (Learning for life, 2015).

Generally, university is seen as a springboard for success, and parents have high aspirations for their children with nearly 9 in 10 respondents wanting their child to pursue higher education. Education is considered an important enabler in a competitive and increasingly globalised employment market, and about 75% of parents would consider sending their children abroad for degree-level studies. Parents have clear ideas about the benefits to be gained from studying abroad in addition to academic skills: foreign language skills, international experience, and independence gains are considered key benefits by over half of the survey population. Parents in non-English speaking countries particularly value language skills (Springboard for success, 2014).

Largely, studying at a university abroad is seen as an important experience, with more than three-quarters of respondents thinking that this helps students to become more knowledgeable about the wider world, and parents valuing the opportunity for their children to experience different cultures. Parents in Asian countries are particularly receptive of the idea of sending their child abroad for tertiary education. Costs remain the main barrier for choosing a university, followed by the quality of education available in their home country. However, despite being conscious of the costs involved in study abroad, 80% of parents reported to being open to paying more for this than they would for educating their child in their own country. Chinese parents in particular are prepared to pay extra for their child to have an international university education: 39% of respondents would consider paying at least 50% more and 69% would consider paying at least an additional 25% for tuition (Learning for life, 2015).

The research also shows that 83% of parents have a specific occupation in mind for their child – this proportion is even higher for Chinese parents (94%). These career preferences are mainly based on income-earning potential, the job's benefit to society, and the child's individual strength. Particularly, Asian parents favour jobs for their children that are reputable and beneficial to society.

Generally, parents see the employment situation as increasingly competitive, and pure academic achievement is no longer seen to give students a competitive advantage. Therefore, parents expect HE institutions to equip their children with wider skills. The top five desirable outcomes are enhanced confidence, social skills, analytical thinking, independent study ability, and, lastly, independent living skills. Course-specific skills are considered less important.

Employers' expectations of the role of universities in educating "employable" graduates are also changing and they are quick to criticise when they feel that graduates are not well-equipped and lacking essential skills. Employers desire a consistent set of core skills – independent from subject-specific knowledge.

From an educator's viewpoint, students and parents are increasingly seen as customers who are aware of the financial relationship they enter into with an HEI. Therefore, the decision-making process and the buying decision become a complex process that considers a variety of expectations of a university degree which go beyond academic education (James-MacEachern & Dongkoo, 2016). The expectations of such a relationship include benefits in their future employment and wider opportunities. While there is evidence that university graduates are paid higher wages once in employment, increases in tuition fees and cost of living mean that salary expectations are now even higher.

The importance of future employability has constantly increased in importance over the last decade. Between 2007 and 2016 the proportion of students considering their future employment prospects as "very important" has grown by 12%. The author's own research with international scholarship recipients in London confirmed that these students' motivations to study abroad were to achieve academic excellence and reputation, but also to experience cultural diversity and creativity. A master's degree student from China stated, "I came to London because I wanted to see different culture policies in different European countries. China has a gap – it keeps improving but not as good as here. I want to see the best culture policy." Research with first-year students showed that students from Asia are more likely to want to study in the UK to broaden their horizon and improve their language skills than other groups of international students. Experiencing a better quality of education is also more important to them. Among first-year degree-level students, 57% also hope to improve their career prospects through international study in the UK – this share is expected to grow as students progress through their degree.

Study-to-work transition for international Chinese students

There is little research available about the post-study transition of Chinese students who undertook degree-level studies in the UK, and the relevance of Western-style career theories has been questioned when it comes to explaining the work experience of skilled migrants and the global labour market.

Whereas, in the West, job search networks are generally framed around "weak ties," in China, social networks are formulated around "strong ties," which involve social obligation and reciprocity. This makes Chinese graduates more likely to feel obliged to accept a job that has been offered within the *guanxi* network. *Guanxi* is a central idea in Chinese society which stresses the importance of "associating oneself with others in a hierarchical manner in order to maintain social and economic order." There is an emphasis on mutual obligations, trust, and reciprocity, which are the foundation of *guanxi* networks. While the concept of *guanxi* originated as a cultural phenomenon that refers to personal relationships, it was extended to the organisational level, and when it comes to businesses and the labour market these networks can help to open doors and find new opportunities (Luo et al., 2011). Consequently, career choices may be embedded in interdependent social relations rather than being the result of individual decision-making processes, and career development might, therefore, be more closely linked to the fulfilment of social roles rather than professional development (Dyer & Lu, 2010).

Chinese international students, however, have gained internationally recognised qualifications and have developed English language skills. In addition, they have been away from their *guanxi* networks for an extended period of time and are, therefore, entering the labour market as independent young adults. For middle- and low-income families in particular, having a child pursuing degree-level studies abroad is a source of pride and prestige, and students who have returned upon graduation are often proudly presented in social circles. Wei Shen confirms that the attraction of sending children abroad mainly lies in the prestige of foreign degrees and advancement in English (Shen, 2005).

In her article "Overthrowing the first mountain: Chinese student migrants and the geography of power," Anni Kajanus found that Chinese students pursuing tertiary education abroad feel obliged towards their parents to succeed. Prior to commencing their studies in the UK, they were convinced that an overseas education would result in superior career prospects and support their upward social mobility in China. The reality, however, is often characterised by marginalisation, feelings of alienation, and disorientation. Student life in the UK is often not what students had expected, and cosmopolitan competency isn't always acquired. A lack in skills and confidence paired with restrictive visa regulations result in difficulties in finding graduate-level work in the UK, and the transition into the Chinese labour market is often negatively affected by filial obligations, a different mentality, and competition for desirable jobs. On the other hand, students reported that living abroad had provided them with a feeling of independence and freedom and had equipped them with cosmopolitan competency; however, they feel under pressure to return to China in order to pay back the parental support (Kajanus, 2015). Particularly female student migrants often find themselves in a situation where they are expected to fulfil the traditional female role upon their return, which includes domestic duties, family support, and holding down a job (Bamber, 2013).

A study undertaken by Suzette Dyer and Fen Lu with Chinese student migrants in New Zealand revealed that most participants gathered a significant amount of information when deciding on a profession. Students spoke to parents, peers, academics, and career advisers and consulted the internet. Factors that influenced the decision making related to their course and personal interests and to values: "My values were possibly the most important thing to consider when I was choosing an occupation." (Dyer & Lu, 2010). The majority of respondents in Dyer and Lu's study confirmed that their jobs reflect their interests and beliefs as well as their career expectations. All interviewees highlighted the importance of their study experience abroad to gaining employment – particularly, networks that developed during their study years, extra-curricular activities, internships, and part-time employment were named, along with the acquirement of soft skills, such as decision making and teamwork skills.

While, for years, Chinese students would stay on to work abroad after graduation, the labour market for returning students is changing and foreign-educated Chinese nationals are now returning to China in greater numbers. A report by Forbes explains the increasing number of returnees with the strength of the Chinese economy and large venture capital investments. Another factor for returning to China is the so-called "bamboo ceiling" theory which posits that Chinese graduates have low career progression chances abroad. Third, many graduates feel obliged to return to China due to family ties. As a result of this development, over the last decades, hundreds of thousands of foreign-educated Chinese students and scholars, who constitute an enormous source of human capital for China, have returned home. Those returnees'(*haiguipai* or *hai gui*) are drawn by new opportunities in China, particularly in the technology sector, and put off by lengthy visa procedures and limited careers prospects in the UK (Kelly, 2018).

The number of graduates returning to China was over 480,000 in 2017 and as a proportion of the outbound students this constituted almost 80%. At the turn of the century the proportion returning was only 23% and this declined to a low of 14% in 2002. Since that time, there have been steady increases in the numbers and proportion of returning students. Outbound traffic increased sharply from about 2008 onwards.

Yet, a foreign degree is not always a guarantee for a successful study-to-work transition in China. Many Chinese institutions have climbed up the international rankings and league tables, and due to the high number of internationally mobile Chinese students and returnees, foreign degrees have become quite common among applicants.

However, despite high competition and comparatively low starting salaries, a Centre for China and Globalisation[6] poll showed that there are consistent perceived benefits of an international education among Chinese graduates. Returnees feel they have an advantage with regard to English language proficiency, intercultural communication skills, and global competence. Respondents also mentioned that the experience was life changing and improved their sense of empathy, and most graduates are optimistic that their salaries will see greater increase in the long run. Overall, returnees feel that their experience abroad is precious and outweighs the financial burden it has put on them.

At the same time, foreign-educated graduates are aware that study abroad puts a financial burden upon them and their families, and that opportunities which might have arisen at home during the period of their absence might be missed. They are also increasingly aware that career success is not a given and a degree from a university abroad is no longer a route into a great job. Other challenges returnees have to face are reverse culture shock and cross-cultural adjustment. Becoming comfortable with China's distinct form of networks and relationships (*guanxi*) again, becoming re-accustomed to the style and pace of working in China and getting used to local cultures in general have reportedly been major issues for many returnees (Hao and Wen 2016). Many foreign-educated graduates see themselves as special and show a degree of superiority, but upon returning to China quickly need to understand that they have to re-integrate into a rapidly changing contemporary society. While Jia Hao and Anthony Welch (2012) talk about "distinct advantages" the *hai gui* have, the increasing number of returnees, an improving quality of domestic graduates, and an incoming international workforce mean that not all *hai gui* have a smooth study-to-work transition upon return. In fact, many have to adjust their expectations when looking for jobs and re-embrace their home culture (Hao & Welch, 2012).

Over a decade ago, Cheng Li wrote about the status and characteristics of foreign-educated returnees in China and Chinese leadership. Their 2007 study showed that the percentage of foreign-educated returnees in high leadership positions in China was comparatively small. However, those who have returned to China after completing an international education played an important role in the country. Many established private enterprises or found work in research centres, educational institutions, consultancy companies, media networks, and the creative industries. With returnees growing in numbers, their influence has increased considerably. It is to be expected that this development will further shape both China's interaction with the outside world and the image the outside world has of China. While most returnees influence China's development outside the political establishment, Cheng Li highlights the increasing political influence of foreign-educated workers and their status in Chinese leadership. Li argues that Chinese leadership is in great need of foreign-educated individuals and of their expertise and knowledge. However, only a small percentage of returnees is appointed to high-level leadership positions. Most returnees influence China's development from outside the political establishment, but their growing influence is indicative of the increasing effect they have on officials and decision-making circles. It seems as though that Chinese leaders are still ambivalent about the foreign-educated elite, who still face a certain level of mistrust (Li, 2007). Nevertheless, Li observed a dynamic interaction between academia and political power. This relationship is characterised by a frequent solicitation of returnee-led think tanks that are affiliated with Chinese universities and leadership bodies. Leading think tanks and research centres often have strong ties with international academic communities. These relationships with the academic community outside of China and their ties with the Chinese leadership and the Chinese Communist Party within the country make foreign-educated returnees important contributors to China's coming of age. Due to China's rapid economic development and its integration with the world economy, more advisers with relevant expertise will become necessary and those positions are likely to be filled with foreign-educated nationals who understand China and its positioning in an international playing field as well as the ever changing global economic and financial landscape. The research also suggested that, with a Western degree, returnees are most likely to transition into a career in education and academic administration, science and technology, business (such as trade, banking and finance), and foreign trade and affairs.

More recent research has shown that returnees are believed to have greater confidence in their own abilities and are more open to diversity. Higher levels of maturity and independence are also associated with foreign-educated graduates – qualities that can translate into greater human capital and wider job choices (Hao, 2016). Recognising the need of a workforce with these refined set of skills, the Chinese government has emphasised the importance of international professionals and recruitment of returnees in their National Plan for Medium- and Long-Term Human Resources Development (2010–2020), signalling a genuine interest in successfully utilising the foreign educated. The Thousand Talent program mentioned earlier is only one of 10 national schemes that were designed to support the recruitment of highly skilled, experienced foreign talent – particularly foreign-educated returnees (Hao & Welch, 2012).

Concluding remarks

Since the 1970s, there has been a significant and more diverse migration flow from China that has been characterised by the emergence of student migration. With the opening of the Chinese economy, the need for highly qualified talent in the work force grew, and the prestige of foreign degrees and advancement in English language became key factors for securing a reputable job in China. Another push factor that has driven study abroad has been the fierce competition for national university entry examinations, along with family pressure for university education. In China, the UK has positioned itself as a desirable study destination through academic excellence, reputation, and the advantages of the English language from the very beginning. By the same token, China quickly became the main source country for international students in the UK and has been an important source of income generated by tuition fees. According to HESA,[7] in the academic year 2014–2015 about 90,000 mainland Chinese students were enrolled in UK HEIs, equating to 27% of the total overseas student population.

However, the British Council (2017) reports that the realities of UK visa policies and global economic conditions are likely to negatively impact international student recruitment. A shift towards inter-regional student mobility as well as alternative forms of provision (such as transnational education models), are likely to drive more UK institution to focus their efforts on delivering abroad, and prospective international students find themselves presented with a world of choice, making the decision-making process even more complex. Structural barriers, such as immigration policy, international tuition fees, and a lack of scholarships are factors that hinder student choice.

Consequently, universities have to operate in a market-orientated manner and understand their consumers and the competition. It is likely that educators will continue to face the challenge to align their courses and programs with (international) student expectations, and effectively communicate and deliver on these expectations. Understanding student demands is, therefore, critical and HEIs need to ensure they are matching student expectations. Career-related aspects are critical to both students and parents. A study undertaken by the Institute of International Education in 2014 confirmed that three out of four Chinese students identify career aspirations as a key motivating factor to study abroad (James-MacEachern & Dongkoo, 2016) and the ability to compete in the workplace has become a key expectation of a good international university education.

While a foreign degree is not always a guarantor for a successful transition into the labour market, the opening of the Chinese market, large investments and a growing economy have created a need for international expertise and present manifold opportunities for foreign-educated students. This development favours international study. Advantages around language proficiency, intercultural competence and personal development are likely to add to the employability profile of recent graduates and provide them with a competitive advantage in particular industries in China.

Employees with international experiences and exposure are in demand and highly valued, particularly in high GDP grow regions with vibrant development. However, those "Sea Turtles" are also presented with a list of challenges upon return to China. Based on survey results, Hao and Wen established a list of key challenges that included the ability to obtain or regain a necessary understanding of Chinese culture, inappropriate knowledge exchange, a degree of local resistance and resentment, as well as competitive counterparts from both China and overseas. These key challenges mean that returnees are required to adjust their attitude and positioning when returning to China. So, while international graduates might have a stronger entry point than their local peers, they also face a more challenging set of employment opportunities (Hao & Wen, 2016). Hao and Welch (2012) argue that knowledge and techniques that were gained overseas can be insufficient in China and need to be complemented by local practices. They advise that returnees utilise their advantages as bridges between China and the world by re-embracing their Chinese culture and appropriately employing advanced Western professionalism.

In order to continuously attract Chinese student to Western educational institutions and successfully recruiting students HEIs are increasingly challenged with teaching soft skills alongside discipline-specific content. Education itself is no longer the ultimate goal for learners, education is also expected to impart skills that allow a smooth education-to-work transition.

Notes

1. International Student Barometer, autumn wave 2017 (mean average: earning potential, work opportunities, opportunities to work while studying).
2. Other discussions about the definition or concept of employability can be found on pages 12, 25, 25, 60, 62, 92, 164.
3. The *gaokao* is an academic examination held annually and is a prerequisite for entrance into HE at undergraduate level.
4. The Thousand-Talent program for example emphasises the importance of international professionals and recruitment of returnees. (http://www.1000plan.org/en/)
5. *Hukou* (household registration) was introduced in 1951 and segregates the workforce according to regions, industries, and professions. Reforms have contributed to a gradual reduction in the traditional forms of labour segregation against a history of a planned economy that restricted people's movement within China significantly; however, obtaining an official rural-to-urban *hukou* change is still difficult. (https://www.thoughtco.com/chinas-hukou-system-1434424)
6. http://en.ccg.org.cn/
7. https://www.hesa.ac.uk/

Chapter 10

Internationalisation and employment

The case of the Kiwi overseas experience (OE)

Brett Berquist and Ainslie Moore

Introduction

As a nation of relatively small population and with sophisticated statistical reporting systems, New Zealand (NZ) has produced a remarkable set of data enabling a comprehensive look at the role of internationalisation and employability regarding both international students coming to NZ and domestic students heading offshore. In this chapter, we will review the NZ data and their impact on our understanding of internationalisation and employability. We will suggest areas for further research, call for more common metrics to facilitate comparison with other markets, and discuss how this information from the NZ case study can inform advocacy efforts in other markets.

Nation of immigrants

New Zealand is one of the latest land masses to be occupied by humans, beginning with the arrival of Polynesian peoples 700–900 years ago (King, 2003). Rapid colonisation in the 19th century resulted in a unique bi-cultural country. After a period of primarily European migration ended, nearly 30% of NZ's immigrants were from outside the British Commonwealth. A points system was introduced in 1991 with no weighting for ethnicity (History of Migration, n.d.).

The sustained post-colonial wave of immigration has transformed Auckland into one of the world's most culturally diverse cities with over 200 ethnic communities and 30% of the population speaking another language. At the 2013 census, nearly 40% of Aucklanders were born overseas (Statistics NZ, n.d.). Sitting on the southern edge of the planet, New Zealanders understand the importance of international trade and relations. John Key, former prime minister, used to say when promoting international trade alliances, "as a country, we won't get rich selling to ourselves" (Statements by the U.S. President, 2016).

Regional challenge

Immigration into Auckland has widened the gap between the country's only global city and the rest of the country, with Auckland now holding nearly one-third of the country's 4.5 million population and nearly two-thirds of the international education market. The immigration wave centred on Auckland contributes to the infrastructure challenges that come with rapid population expansion. Recent governments have developed policies to ensure the regions also benefit from the economic impacts of international education; for example, additional points are allocated for skilled migration settling outside of Auckland. In the new 2018–2030 international education strategy, the current government has explicitly emphasised the goal of making sure the regions benefit from international education (IE) enrolment growth (Education New Zealand, 2018).

Net migration

Net migration peaked in 2017 at just over 72,000 new residents (Statistics NZ, 2018). New Zealand has also been very successful in attracting international students, with one of the highest ratios of international students to tertiary education population among the main English-speaking destinations (MESD) (OECD, 2017). As the winds of nationalism have brought the role of international students in net migration to the forefront, the NZ version of this conversation was about finding the right balance, not shutting the door.

With a strong tradition of outward mobility, particularly through reciprocal work rights with Australia, the net flow of residents is responsive to economic shifts. Public opinion and government positions have varied considerably in interpreting the weight of returning kiwis in net migration spikes, as illustrated in Figure 10.1 below.

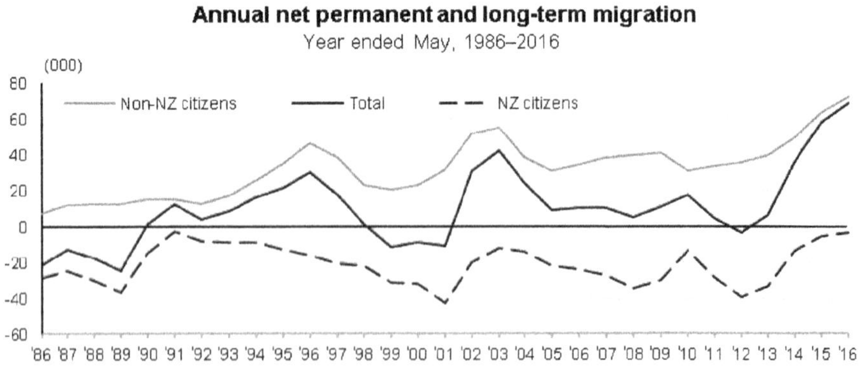

Annual net permanent and long-term migration
Year ended May, 1986–2016

Figure 10.1 NZ net migration patterns.

Source: Statistics NZ (2016).

The overall flow of people in both directions plays a very significant role in talent acquisition for the NZ economy. In 2015–2016, 45% of skilled principal migrants had been international students (Ministry of Business Innovation and Employment [MBIE], 2016). The international education field often reflects on the impact of mobility trends between the Global North and the Global South, and whether to interpret this as brain drain or brain gain, situating investment into mobility as a strategy to upgrade a country's knowledge base and technology, and to build capacity. The OECD posits that "students' mobility appears to more deeply shape future international scientific co-operation networks than a common language, or geographical or scientific proximity." (OECD, 2017, p. 287).

In the UK, 2011–2012 immigration restrictions have had a negative impact on the British economy, estimated at a loss of £8 billion in 2016 (Havergal, 2016). In NZ, the open flow of talent in both directions is seen to enrich a vibrant ecosystem, yet it also impacts the country's overall labour supply, housing availability, and, potentially, social cohesion. No surprise then that net migration featured prominently during the 2017 national election cycle with op-eds interpreting the data from opposing viewpoints (Hickey, 2017).

Robust NZ data sets on stay rates

New Zealand's strong statistical reporting systems have produced analyses of post-graduation behaviours that empower an evidence-based discussion on IE policy. Government is attuned to the comprehensive mobility question, particularly for young talent, as illustrated through a series of reports looking at post-graduation behaviour of young domestic (Park, 2014) and international (Park, 2017) students.

In a conference preview of the international report (Fabling, 2016), the Ministry of Education focused on how the export education strategy intersects with the national talent acquisition strategy, quoting the government's leadership statement (ENZ, 2011):

> As well as strengthening our education system, international education is expected to contribute to our goals for research, innovation, trade and tourism. International education also **encourages the immigration of highly skilled people** and helps to grow links with our major trading partners in Asia, Europe and the Pacific. These links are crucial to our ongoing success. (p. 2)
>
> Immigration policies can encourage the entry of students into high quality courses which equip graduates to take up **genuine skilled work opportunities after completion**. The need for such young and skilled migrants is expected to continue... (p. 5)[1]

The initial study of exit and stay rates of international graduates is unique for the size of the data set, examining 171,305 international students from annual cohorts 2003–2012 across 10 years post-study (Park, 2017; Ministry of Education, 2017). Surveying is the commonly used methodology for graduate outcomes, which presents

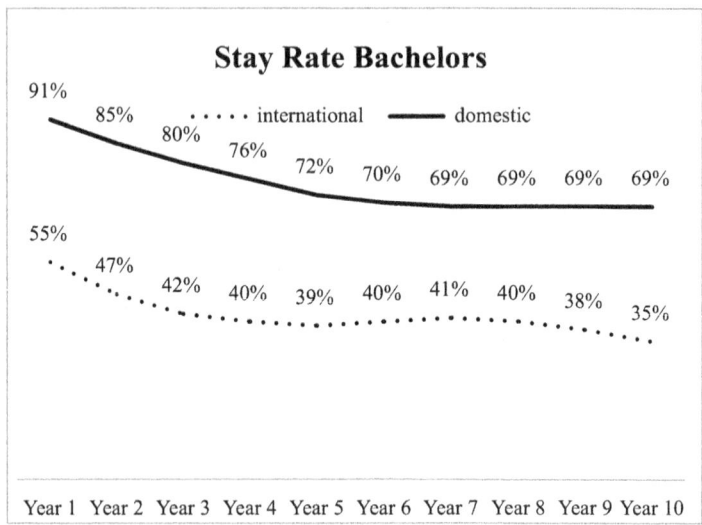

Figure 10.2 Domestic and international stay rates in NZ.

Source: Adapted from Park (2014) and Park (2017).

challenges of low response rates, respondent bias, etc. Not surveys, these studies are desktop analyses of existing government data sets capturing 56% of international students in NZ during that time period.[2] Analysts cross-referenced the Single Data Return (mandatory reporting for government funded educational organisations), student visa information, tax returns, benefits register, and, subsequently, census data. The study found a healthy overall stay rate of 33% for all international students five years after their first visa, exceeding the OECD average of 25% (OECD, 2011).

Government was interested in the outcomes of young graduates and set the "young" age filter at 24 years old for bachelor degrees, 27 years old for master degrees, and 29 years old for doctorates, first for domestic students (Park, 2014) and then international (Park, 2017), excluding up to nearly half of the international graduates for some cohorts. Nonetheless, applying the same methodology across the domestic and international analyses provides useful comparison. Long-term stay rates of international graduates are often examined without comparison to the domestic graduate pool. As shown in Figure 10.2, young domestic bachelor degree graduates stay in NZ at nearly double the rate of young international graduates. In this regard, the two reports together paint a picture of a vibrant and mobile labour market for both domestic and international graduates in NZ.

Data for Post Study Work Rights (PSWR) revision

New Zealand's sub-university sector is particularly active, with government-funded Institutes of Technology and Polytechnics (ITP) and the Private Training

Establishments (PTE) also offering bachelor and master degree qualifications. In 2013, international enrolments in the university sector and the PTE sector were nearly on par, at 24,000 students, respectively. A 2013 policy adjustment brought a 76% spike to the PTEs compared to 15% growth for the eight universities (Education New Zealand, 2017). Challenges and criticism from the opposition accompanied the rapid growth in the private sector.

In a surprise ending to the 2017 election cycle, the opposition Labour party negotiated a supply and confidence agreement with New Zealand First and the Greens to form a coalition government. The new government tasked the Ministry of Business Innovation and Employment (MBIE) with revising post-study work rights. MBIE undertook its own analysis of international tertiary student labour market outcomes using some of the same government data sets as the ministry of education studies but also Immigration New Zealand's "migration spells" data. Like the ministry of education study, it examined 10 annual cohorts but tracked their outcomes over 5 years post-study rather than 10. It did not filter for completion of the qualification, as the ministry of education study had, and it did not apply a young age filter. Finally, it also analysed visa pathways to residency. The scope was similarly large, starting with 187,233 international students in the migration spells data set for this time period (2006–2015). As with the ministry of education study, MBIE found that one-third of international tertiary students remained in NZ for five years post-study. Of these, half had transitioned to residency through skilled migration channels and one-third through a partnership visa (MBIE, 2018).

Previously, NZ's post-study work rights did not distinguish by level of study. Graduates had an open work visa for one year and could seek an employer-assisted visa for work relevant to their field of study for an additional two years. In 2018, the new government announced a three-year open post-study work visa for bachelor, master, and PhD degree graduates but left the duration at one year for lower-level qualifications. Confirming the previous partner work rights for master's and doctoral students, the new government took NZ to the forefront of international university student work rights policy (Immigration New Zealand, 2018).

The recent focus on international university graduate behaviours facilitates a broader understanding of graduate outcomes for both international and domestic students. In the next section, we will look more closely at outbound behaviours of domestic graduates.

The overseas experience (OE)

New Zealand counts 4.5 million people on-shore and an additional 15% of its citizens residing abroad (Statistics NZ, n.d.) many of whom are on their "Big OE," defined as minimum of nine months abroad in government data (Park, 2014). New Zealand university graduates have among the highest mobility rates in the world. One in three domestic university graduates are overseas within seven years of graduation, and 41% of doctoral graduates are on their overseas experience (OE) within 5 years of graduation. (Park, 2014) Traditionally, the OE has been a post-graduation undertaking, but the current generation is keen to start their OE during university and is particularly driven by employability outcomes, as evidenced by the phenomenal response to government scholarships for overseas internships. (Moore, Moore, Stephens, & Roberts, 2018).

Graduate longitudinal study New Zealand

In addition to the government-run large-scale analyses of graduate destinations, Universities New Zealand commissioned the Graduate Longitudinal Study New Zealand (GLSNZ), a 10-year tracker survey. The initial survey, in 2011, involved 8,719 final-year students, both domestic and international (of 35,000 in the graduating cohort). Seventy percent of these responded to the follow up survey in 2014 (Tustin et al., 2012). The GLSNZ provides a great deal of information about graduate destinations, employment, and social outcomes for both domestic and international graduates at all levels of study, but in the context of internationalisation and employability, it is specifically useful in corroborating the broadbrush data analyses from government data and enhancing this with information about student intentions.

The follow-up survey asked graduates about their work and living experiences over the previous two-and-one-half years and their intentions for the coming three. Half of all domestic respondents had spent at least one month living or working overseas and 47% indicated their intent to do so at some point in the next three years. Of these, 17% intended to work in Australia, reflecting the reciprocal free movement between the two countries. New Zealand also has working holiday reciprocal schemes with over 40 countries. Supportive government policies contribute to the high mobility rates of NZ talent and have implications for employability and internationalisation strategies for our higher education sector.

Learning abroad

The strength of the Big OE as a post-graduation undertaking traditionally hampered participation in modern outbound programming during university. In an initial benchmark of NZ IE, only two universities reported outbound activity outside of semester exchanges (Huckel & Ramirez, 2016). Similar to trends observed elsewhere (Potts, 2018), NZ university students are increasingly interested in starting their OE experience during their studies and are particularly motivated by potential employability gains. However, understanding of the value of learning abroad is clouded with misconceptions about its potential to derail study or delay graduation, as shown in surveys of year-13 students and their parents (Smart, 2017).

As with other markets, (Wright, Jones, & Welland, 2018; Potts, 2013), New Zealand students and their families sometimes see study abroad as a market distinguisher – a way to stand out from the crowd in the search for the first career job after university. They argue that a degree alone is not a sufficient career plan any longer, and an international learning experience could enhance future employability. NZ parental support for study abroad was more likely to be found where an overseas learning opportunity specifically served to enhance employability or academic success rather than the traditionally cited outcomes of personal growth and a wider worldview for Kiwis completing an OE after graduation (Smart, 2017).

Implications for universities' learning abroad agenda

Reflecting NZ's relatively recent entry into outbound learning abroad programming, there is a need to shift the promotional message from the destination itself to the potential learning outcomes, such as career development and academic progression. The national IE benchmark initiated in 2016 has contributed to an emerging focus on learning abroad among the universities rising from 5.7% undergraduate participation in 2015 to 7.7% in 2017 (Huckel & Ramirez, 2018) and 20% for the University of Auckland. The report also identifies growth in non-credit activity, reflecting internships as well as clinical and engineering placements.

Māori participation

With this increasing engagement with learning abroad during university studies comes a focus on access and underrepresentation, resonating with the universities' commitments to the Treaty of Waitangi. Underrepresentation among minority groups is prevalent across study abroad, globally. In the United States, the Diversity Abroad Network has developed guidelines for good practice for racial and ethnic minorities that are applicable in the New Zealand context.

Given the known correlation between learning abroad and positive outcomes in completion, academic success, and employability (Potts, 2016), the University of Auckland recently launched a Māori Strategy for Study Abroad: *he waka eke noa*. This includes dedicated staffing and outreach as well as internal and government funding. In a short timeframe, applications to the Māori and Pacific Study Abroad Award have tripled and learning abroad participation among Māori students is now at parity to representation in undergraduate enrolment.

New Zealand international education strategy 2030

The new government's IE strategy (ENZ, 2018), launched in August 2018, calls for "a thriving and globally connected NZ through world-class education." The strategy acknowledges the role international graduates play in bringing skills and professional and vocational qualifications NZ needs. It also acknowledges the value of learning abroad, calling for increased participation as a progress indicator and development of an outbound mobility strategy as a priority for the Ministry of Education.

One means of increasing access to learning abroad is removing barriers to participation. The most prominent perceived barriers to participation are, generally, the financial and opportunity costs (Gribble & Tran, 2016). The NZ government has implemented two scholarship schemes, The Prime Minister's Scholarships for Asia and the Prime Minister's Scholarships for Latin America, that seek to enable more New Zealanders to gain a learning experience abroad. The government funding usually covers most expenses, which has a substantial empowering impact on underrepresented populations. Further to this, the government has established three Centres for Asia Pacific Excellence (CAPEs) supported by four NZ universities to support business and community engagement in North Asia, Latin America, and South East Asia. The CAPEs have supported undergraduate student mobility programming as a means to further knowledge and relationships across these regions.

Flight risk[3] or labour market enrichment

Both learning abroad and the OE have the potential to contribute positively to personal development, intercultural competence, and other traits valued by employers. Recent immigration rates indicate significant numbers of Kiwis returning to NZ, many of whom may have increased skills and attributes of value to NZ society and the labour market. With an overall exit rate of one in three domestic graduates and stay rate of one in three international graduates, the internationalisation of both education and employment paint a picture of labour market enrichment welcomed by NZ government policy makers. At the research and doctoral level, this comprehensive mobility picture for domestic and international students enhances our understanding of NZ's vibrant research eco-system, with a revolving door at our border, welcoming international PhD students and bidding farewell to domestic students who leave to study and research at international institutions (Berquist, 2017). Recent streamlining of post-study work rights provides an impetus to engage NZ employers and public opinion on the complexity of NZ's highly mobile labour market and to deepen our understanding of how international education enriches our higher education system.

Evidence-based advocacy

New Zealand's strong data sets and comprehensive analysis enable clearer understanding of the factors influencing domestic and international student choices for study and employment, whether in NZ or offshore. This research assists us in understanding the impact of cultural phenomena, such as the OE, while also providing a solid evidence base for the formulation of policy for education and immigration settings. When considering this comparatively, or trying to compare observed phenomena in one country to another, we run into problems comparing like with like due to different metrics and measures used by various governments, analysts, and researchers. Commonalities in metrics and measures across countries will increase the utility of data analysis conducted in one country for the benefit of policy makers and international education providers elsewhere.

Universities New Zealand has been advocating for increases in funding to support international education and research through a commissioned paper examining the return on investment (ROI) to NZ of four aspects of universities' internationalisation – research, academic mobility, student flows (exchange), and work placement programs (defined as an addition to exchange). With respect to student flows, the paper extrapolates data on cost of living and tuition for Australian domestic and international students and applies this to a NZ model to determine value to the economy in movement of students over short- and long-term exchange programs. For every dollar of university or government funding, they posit an ROI of $1.06 for student flows and $5.87 for work placements over 15 years (Deloitte Access Economics, 2017). The paper considers work placements as an addition to student exchange rather than a stand-alone learning abroad opportunity. Along with the narrow definition of what is included in student flows (only semester exchange and longer), this limits the utility of the analysis given the larger interpretation of learning abroad used by interested governments. In the NZ context, growth in global internships and clinical and other professional placements has predominantly been as an alternative to semester exchange rather than an addition to the exchange.

Looking beyond the economic benefits towards a broader valuation of international education, Education New Zealand recently reviewed the literature and identified a higher propensity for international graduates to be drivers in the economy via increased participation in start-ups and higher-tech industries in the United States and other markets but did not locate NZ–specific data (Kalafatelis, de Bonnaire, & Alliston, 2018). Following 2018 NZ post-study work policy changes, employer sponsorship is no longer a visa requirement for international graduates. This change increases the possibility for international graduates to stay in New Zealand and establish start-ups or small businesses without needing an employer to maintain their visa status.

The revision of post-study work rights is a timely moment to evaluate if the immigration changes contribute to a similar economic impact in NZ. As these work rights are structured to remove the role of employers as sponsors, the changes may encourage greater involvement of new migrants in start-ups and STEM fields as evidenced in the other countries. The new post-study work rights were formulated with the benefit of the data and analysis of the major papers discussed here, and illustrate the potential for positive policy changes following evidence-based advocacy.

While governments and advocacy bodies rightly commission and utilize evidence-based analysis of education and employment to inform policy, it is also appropriate that universities do likewise if seeking to influence either public policy or public opinion.

Notes

1. Bolding by Fabling.
2. Only government-funded organisations are required to file the Single Data Return. The private training sector in New Zealand is particularly active compared to other IE markets and represented 44% of the international student enrolments during the time period of the initial Ministry of Education study (Park, 2017).
3. See also discussion on page 31.

Part 3

Transnational education and employability

Chapter 11

Employability in transnational education[1]

Elspeth Jones

Introduction

Transnational education has become a major element in international education in recent years both for those countries providing the programmes and the host countries in which they are delivered. In the United Kingdom, universities now provide qualifications to more students overseas than to international students within the UK itself (Boe, 2018, p. 59). Many different forms of transnational, cross-border, offshore delivery, distance education, international branch campuses, franchise, or partnership programmes exist, and the terminology can be confusing, with a variety of terms used for effectively the same kind of provision, while others are used interchangeably in spite of having different meanings. Knight (2016) seeks to provide a framework for those terms; however, for the sake of simplicity, transnational education (TNE) is used here, using O'Mahony's definition of TNE:

> Award- or credit-bearing learning undertaken by students who are based in a different country from that of the awarding institution. (O'Mahony, 2014, p. 8).

Yet, in spite of "exponential" increases in scope and scale, "there is a significant lack of reliable information regarding the nature and extent of TNE provision in terms of enrolments and ...modes" (McNamara & Knight, 2014, p. 1). As evidence of growth, Knight & McNamara (2017) note substantial proportions of higher education being delivered through TNE, such as in Mauritius, with 40%, and Dubai at 50% of student enrolments. Even in countries involved in TNE for longer and with increasing strength in local providers (e.g., Malaysia, Singapore, and Hong Kong), the figure still represents 10 to 20% of higher education (Knight & McNamara, 2017). Evidently TNE in its various forms is playing a significant role in the delivery of international education and thus it is crucial that we should understand its post-study outcomes in general and the link to future employability in particular.

And yet the dominant themes in TNE literature relate to globalisation, trade, quality, and regulation, with teaching and learning issues appearing to have a lower priority (O'Mahony, 2014), particularly in regard to student outcomes. Where outcomes are discussed, the emphasis is primarily quantitative, large-scale, and market-driven, such as in reports from Australia (Australian Education International, 2010; Banks & Olsen, 2008), or the UK (Boe, 2018; British Council, 2013b; HE Global, 2016). This chapter explores some aspects of TNE programmes, with particular reference to employability.

Some characteristics of TNE programmes

Quality assurance for UK institutions providing TNE requires that they offer learning and development, academically and through other experiences, comparable to those within programmes at the home campus. This means, amongst other things, that any employability development within a UK programme should also be provided in the equivalent TNE provision. Such programmes clearly have the potential to enhance employment-specific skills relevant to the local context, and gaining these credentials is an important driver for students to undertake TNE programmes (British Council, 2013b). Just as one example, (Chan, 2011) discusses the role of transnational education in developing professional skills for pharmacists.

Yet, circumstances in some settings for TNE delivery may be very different from the context of the home institution. Links with local business and industry may be more limited, while students may have personal circumstances which impact strongly on their motivations and perceived need for employability development; for example, if they are already employed. TNE alumni reported in a recent study that a programme delivered through TNE was their only option for an international qualification, as they needed to continue working in order to fund their studies (Mellors-Bourne, Jones, & Woodfield, 2015).

In respect of employability, the extent of equivalence with the same programme at the home institution is difficult to establish, since that same study revealed, "a paucity of literature relating to:

a)   graduate outcomes from international education and TNE in particular;
b)   support for enhanced employability, and specifically the incorporation of employability development in the curriculum, in TNE programmes" (Mellors-Bourne, Jones, & Woodfield, 2015, p. 4).

Motivations and profile of TNE students

The motivations of TNE students largely fit within "positional/transformative dimensions" (Pyvis & Chapman, 2007), where positional motivation is more directly work or job-related and transformative is more geared towards personal development. Beyond the "hard skills" requirements of specific jobs, several studies have noted those personal and professional motivations (Hoare, 2012; Robertson, Hoare, & Harwood, 2011). For one student in Sin's (2013) study, building their work skills was tied with an intrinsic motivation for personal development. Pursuing a UK TNE programme was a strategy to create distance from "a rigid culture of 'spoon feeding' and being 'spoon fed'; that is, of rote learning and teaching that were especially prevalent in public institutions" (Sin, 2013, p. 853). Work-related and competitive (i.e., positional) outcomes might be expected in TNE, especially at post-graduate level, but it is important to highlight that personal and professional identity can also be transformative dimensions motivating TNE study.

TNE reaches a different profile of students according to McNamara and Knight (2014). They find that TNE students are generally older; represent a relatively mature demographic, often with previous employment experience; and include a high proportion of students working full-time during their studies. They found, however, that career development is the main motivation for choosing TNE study, either in starting a career or in developing an already established one. In terms of employability skills, the opportunity to gain a more international outlook was seen to be the most positive attribute of TNE programmes (McNamara & Knight, 2014).

Employability skills in education abroad and transnational education

Employment and employability

The distinction between *employment* skills and *employability* skills is an important one; the former relating to specific professions for which qualifications and credentials are a key factor, while the latter indicates transferable skills which are not job specific. Employability skills have been defined[2] as,

> a set of achievements – skills, understandings and personal attributes – that makes graduates more likely to gain employment and be successful in their chosen occupations. (Yorke, 2006, p. 8)

Employability skills go by a range of names, including transferable, soft, generic, or transversal skills, and relate to generic personal and interpersonal qualities which are independent of the field of study. It has been found that employers tend to value these skills more highly than disciplinary-based understanding and skills (British Academy & University Council of Modern Languages, 2012; Davies et al., 2012; Yorke, 2006), and that 81% of employers in the UK rated employability skills as the most important factor when assessing potential candidates (Nunn et al., 2008). Across Europe 92% of employers were looking for such transversal skills, according to the Erasmus Impact Study (European Commission, 2014). Yet international students in Australia were unaware of the importance of these generic skills when seeking work, believing that credentials or qualifications alone would be key to future employment (Australian Education International, 2010).

As might be expected, there are many different lists of employability skills. While the descriptions may change and evolve, these lists are largely similar wherever in the world research has been undertaken into what employers are looking for. They include the following:

- Knowledge, intellect, willingness to learn, self-management skills, communication skills, team-working, and interpersonal skills (Harvey, Moon, Geall, & Bower, 1997).
- Effective learning skills, self-awareness, networking and negotiation skills, transferable skills, self-confidence, interpersonal skills, team-working ability, decision-making skills, and the capacity to cope with uncertainty (Knight & Yorke, 2006).
- Sense making, social intelligence, novel and adaptive thinking, cross cultural competency, computational thinking, new media literacy, transdisciplinarity, design mindset, cognitive load management, and virtual collaboration (Davies, Fidler, & Gorbis, 2011).

Although the lists may differ in wording, it is clear that they go beyond subject-specific knowledge or capabilities. Leggott and Stapleford (2007) report on a longitudinal study into student perceptions of their own transferable skills before and after a mobility period and then a year or more after graduation. As part of this they reviewed lists of generic employability skills (which they found could include up to eighty different skills) in a range of countries across Europe and China, and they claim that "employers' requirements seem to be broadly consistent internationally" (Leggott & Stapleford, 2007, p. 124). They suggest this means that,

> On the whole, employability interventions in the curriculum which are devised for home students planning to work in one country are largely appropriate for both home and international students who are planning to work in another. (Leggott & Stapleford, 2007, p. 124)

This is an important point in the TNE context as it suggests that if the employability skills which are incorporated into domestic programmes are then delivered in the offshore version of the programme, these will be equally valid for students who seek employment locally on graduation. It also means that those studying "abroad," in TNE locations but outside their home country, may develop a valuable skill set for employment on return (see section on *Employability skills in education abroad*).

Employability skills in TNE

Few TNE alumni respondents to a 2015 study by Mellors-Bourne et al. understood the difference between employability and employment, and merely gaining the qualification itself was felt to be developing employability. This contrasted with counterparts in the UK and suggested "a much less nuanced view of employability than comparable UK students" (Mellors-Bourne et al., 2015, p. 5).

There is further evidence of this in the second of an extensive three-phase study in Malaysia, where Fernandez-Chung, Cheong, Ching, & Hill (2015) found that, for TNE students and parents, "higher education institutions (HEIs) were perceived to have contributed little to enhance students' understanding of what constitutes employability" (Fernandez-Chung et al., 2015, p. v). Yet the examples given are not those which constitute employability in Yorke's (2006) definition, but rather skills for employment, including presentation of curriculum vitae, interview techniques, and engagement with alumni. "Soft" skills were seen as, for example, English language competence. Enhanced employability was expected to be provided by the international recognition and standing of the awarding university.

Employability skills in education abroad

Studies in countries around the world have identified profound transformational learning in students through international study, work, or volunteering experiences in a range of geographical contexts (Jones, 2013). Significant results in terms of personal growth, self-efficacy, maturity, and enhanced intercultural competence are widely reported (Black & Duhon, 2006; Bosley, 2010; European Commission, 2014; Hadis, 2005; Rowan-Kenyon & Niehaus, 2011; Sutton & Rubin, 2004). Such studies largely focus on the resulting personal transformation and academic benefits, although there is now acknowledgement of the link with more positional outcomes (Pyvis & Chapman, 2007) which impact on employability (Crossman & Clarke, 2010; Jones, 2010, 2012). There are similar results from varying visit durations, although for short-term experiences effective preparation and active engagement while overseas, along with reflection on return, have been shown to be important for success (Bosley, 2010).

In their three-way study of students, universities, and employers, Crossman and Clarke (2010) found that all stakeholders identified clear connections between international experience and employability. This finds echoes in a number of chapters in the current volume, the key point being that,

> many of the skills developed through international student mobility initiatives are precisely those generic transferable skills sought by graduate employers. (Jones, 2013, p. 8)

Equally, it may be that mobility programmes appeal to students who already possess these skills or "mobility capital" (Wiers-Jenssen, 2011). Noting this to be an issue, reaching 100% of students, not merely the mobile few, has even greater significance, particularly in a TNE context:

> "... a more important challenge is to consider how internationalisation of the curriculum 'at home' might offer similar opportunities for the static majority of students, who do not take part in an international experience as part of their programme of study. (Jones, 2013, p. 6)

However, Jones (2013) also argues that there is a need for employers, universities, and students to be better aware of this link, a point emphasised by a Finnish study, and precursor to a chapter in this volume, which asks:

> How can we make employers better understand the learning outcomes of international mobility? How can we make students and others more aware of the skills acquired during their international experience? (Leppänen, Saarinen, Nupponen & Airas, 2014, p. 6)

This is highly relevant to the TNE context since McNamara and Knight (2014) found that 49% of TNE students and graduates reported having studied abroad as part of their programme. As with other forms of mobility then, TNE students may need help in articulating the employability outcomes of their experiences in terms that future employers will understand and appreciate.

Mismatch between graduate skills and employer expectations

Studying on a TNE programme is often "a highly pragmatic choice, offering the prospect of a somewhat more valuable or prestigious qualification at a lower cost than studying abroad and, for many, in a much more practical way that could be fitted into their life" (Mellors-Bourne et al., 2015, p. 25). Yet the same study found that employers often misunderstood the nature and value of a TNE programme during the recruitment or promotion process (ibid.).

The mismatch of graduate attributes and Australian employer requirements, with the consequent implications for curriculum, has been the subject of research for some time (see, for example, Barrie, 2006; Barrie, Hughes, & Smith, 2009; Vu, Rigby, Wood, & Daly, 2011). Similar mismatches between graduate skills and employer expectations have been found elsewhere. Problem solving, team skills, communication, and management skills are seen to be in greatest deficit. Such research includes examples from New Zealand (Hodges & Burchell, 2003), Sri Lanka (Wickramasinghe & Perera, 2010), South Africa (Pop & Barkhuizen, 2010), Japan (Sugahara & Coman, 2010), China (Rose, 2013) and Malaysia (Daud, Abidin, Mazuin Sapuan, & Rajadurai, 2011) .

A number of reports for the International Education Association of Australia have emphasised the importance of engaging all stakeholders, universities, students, and employers in employability issues, particularly for international students (Doyle, 2016; Gribble, 2015; International Education Association of Australia, 2016). This is reinforced by a comprehensive three-phase study in Malaysia into TNE graduate employment which researched the perspectives of employers (Fernandez-Chung, Cheong, Ching, & Hill, 2014), students and parents (Fernandez-Chung et al., 2015), and senior management and academic staff (Fernandez-Chung & Leong, 2018).

A nine-country study by the British Council found that, "Employers understand the value of intercultural skills to their businesses. In fact, they value these skills above many technical abilities and formal qualifications" (British Council, 2013a, p. 19). However, employers do not often screen for them in the recruitment process (ibid., p. 14). This finding was echoed in Finland:

> international mobility produces the kind of competences that the employers are seeking, but they are not able to link these competences and people's international experiences at recruitment. (Leppänen et al., 2014, p. 5)

To address this, De Wit and Jones (2014) argue that we should "change the language of internationalisation" to emphasise the employability skills developed through mobility and an internationalised curriculum at home.

Embedding employability skills in the TNE curriculum

Curriculum interventions

As we have seen, there is clear evidence of employability skills being developed through international mobility and also being embedded in the domestic curriculum in countries such as Australia and the UK. Cole and Tibby offer a framework for reflecting on and addressing employability in the UK curriculum, and engaging colleagues and stakeholders with the process (Cole & Tibby, 2013). In Australia, employability skills as generic outcomes for graduating students may be reflected in the graduate attribute statements (Bowden, Hart, King, Trigwell, & Watts, 2000) of an Australian university.

As yet the evidence of systematic incorporation of employability skills into the TNE curriculum is more limited, even where it is evident at the home institution. This is in spite of the fact that, as we have seen, quality assurance requirements demand that any employability development within the domestic programme should also be provided in the TNE equivalent.

In this vein, work placements or internships have been highlighted as an opportunity to "bridge the gap between class teaching and the real world of work" (Fernandez-Chung et al., 2015, p. v). An article on TNE in Vietnam (Bilsland, Nagy, & Smith, 2014) offers useful advice on how processes around work-integrated learning (WIL) can be enhanced in TNE programmes, and see

Bilsland (this volume) for further discussion of how WIL can help span boundaries among TNE stakeholders.

Internationalisation of the curriculum "at home"

Discussion of internationalisation of the curriculum at home raises several issues as far as TNE is concerned, and indeed challenges the meaning and definition of internationalisation at home as:

> The purposeful integration of international and intercultural dimensions into the formal and informal curriculum for all students within domestic learning environments (Beelen & Jones, 2015, p. 76).

First, some TNE locations play host to international students as well as to local, domestic, students. This is particularly the case in countries such as Singapore which have set out to become an education hub. Second, and as a result of this, the answer to the question of who is "at home" and who is "studying abroad" is complex. Those deemed "international" by dint of coming from another country to study the TNE programme may thus be in a position to develop transferable employability skills simply through working in an international location, in an equivalent to the mobility studies noted above.

Third, there remains the issue of students who are domestic to the local delivery centre where the TNE programme is being delivered. What can be done through the curriculum to help develop employability skills for this group of students in particular? They are students studying at home, but for an international qualification.

Thus, there are policy, design, and delivery issues around internationalisation at home which need to be considered for TNE programmes and which do not appear to have been explored to date.

Embedding international and intercultural skills

It is perhaps more evident for some career paths than others that intercultural competence and/or global perspectives are crucial for future professional roles, but it is argued that in general "employers value graduates who have a global perspective" (Archer & Davison, 2008, p. 5), and Webb emphasises that all students need this dimension in their programmes:

> As part of their preparation to live and work in a globalising world, graduates need increasingly well-developed lifelong learning skills and attitudes, including an international perspective. They need to interpret local problems within a wider and global framework and to judge the importance of global phenomena for their own lives and work. (Webb, 2005, p. 110)

Clifford (2009) points to an increase in the prevalence and importance of interpreting the meaning of intercultural and international dimensions of the curriculum for individual disciplines, while Leask offers guidance for those wishing to embed it in practice (Leask, 2015). For specific professions, detailed advice on incorporating international and intercultural perspectives can be found for a range of STEM subjects, such as engineering (Bourn & Neal, 2008), medicine (Willott, Blum, Burch, Page, & Rowson, 2012), veterinary studies (Maud, Blum, Short, & Goode, 2012) and pharmacy (Murdan et al., 2014). Compared to what may be great diversity in the domestic and international student population on a home campus, cohorts in TNE programmes may be relatively "mono-cultural." Mellors-Bourne et al. found that, "in only a very few cases was the international composition of the students highlighted, which suggests that the opportunities for intercultural interactions will have been limited" (p. 49).

The TNE context is no exception to the need for international and intercultural aspects to be incorporated through an internationalised curriculum and associated learning outcomes. Simply because the programme itself is delivered in a different country does not mean that students will automatically develop intercultural competence any more than it can be assumed to be happening at the home university. There are limited examples which are specific to TNE but, for example, Fitch and Desai explore industry expectations of the intercultural competence of public relations graduates in Singapore and Perth, along with implications for the curriculum (Fitch & Desai, 2012). While Clifford (Clifford, 2010) considers student perspectives on interculturality within the same programme delivered in Australia, Malaysia, and South Africa and finds a mismatch between expectations and outcomes.

Employment and employability outcomes from TNE programmes

Hoare (2012) finds it remarkable that more research has not been undertaken to understand the opinions of stakeholders in transnational education, in particular since TNE is such "big business" for Australia. Where there is research, O'Mahony (2014) found,

> little evidence of any collaborative authorship or activity between host and provider, indicating the relative immaturity of transnational education as a research field. (2014, p. 4)

Hoare (2012) points out that TNE students' voices are only rarely heard as far as their overall experience is concerned, but offers a few examples (Chapman & Pyvis, 2005; Cuthbert, Smith, & Boey, 2008; Ziguras & McBurnie, 2011).

> Although many people are uncomfortable with the conceptualisation of higher education as a business, surely there is nothing sinister in attempting to understand whether or not this "service" is meeting its stated aims in the longer term

and at a human level… We know little about their preferences, even less about the outcomes that they attribute to their TNE experience and nothing in any depth about their longer term career and life trajectories. (Hoare, 2012, p. 272)

Hoare's longitudinal ethnographic study (2012) establishes that former TNE students have seen tangible transformative outcomes following their studies while also meeting or exceeding their original positional motivations. Participants talked of new-found confidence gained through "credibility," and that their confidence increased as they continued to apply the outcomes from their studies. This was in spite of the relatively low status of an Australian TNE degree in Singapore at the time.

It is important to note that employer perceptions of the value of TNE programmes can affect how valuable they are in obtaining employment. This was echoed by students in Sin's (2013) study, who observe that a "heavy display of UK cultural capital could be read as plain acts of social snobbery and pretension" (Sin, 2013, p. 861). Students in this study pointed to the need for "self-regulation and humility in cultural capital accumulation and activation" (pp. 861–2). Although studying abroad was seen as the gold standard, those who studied in the home country (Malaysia) identified that a TNE programme would provide them with continuity, helping them to be more in touch with Malaysian values, norms, and expectations that were essential for local employment, giving them a head start in the home labour market (pp. 859–60). In this respect, a UK education in Malaysia was seen as the best of both worlds.

> Aspects of local cultural capital that my interviewees believed were their strong points include spontaneity in using colloquial Malaysian English and willingness to adopt a softer, more submissive interaction style, indicative of Asian reverence for authority and seniority…… Their narratives reflect sensitivity and adaptability towards interactional and situational possibilities in their future employment. (Sin, 2013, p. 860)
>
> The participants believed that as much as western cultural capital was likely to give a positive impression of a candidate's technical and social competences, it had to be sensibly utilized because a display of excesses could backfire in the conversion to job entry and advancement. (Sin, p. 861)

This appears to be a valuable example of culturally situated employability skills, delivered through a Western approach to education but with an understanding of the local employment context.

In a study contrasting three groups of Singaporean students (Robertson, Hoare, & Harwood, 2011), one group studied in Australia to facilitate their migration, the second studied in Australia and returned to Singapore, and the third studied through an Australian TNE programme locally in Singapore. The researchers used Pyvis and Chapman's (2007) positional and transformative framework to consider both motivations for and outcomes of these three contexts, and their study offers useful insights into the outcomes of TNE study in comparison with studying overseas. In all three cases, they found that students' goals were not exclusively transformative or positional. Their long-term goals,

> encompassed work and career, financial security, home ownership, travel, personal development and overall life-satisfaction, all of which have a complexity of interdependence. (Robertson et al., 2011, p. 691)

The post-study career transition was framed differently for the TNE group, and although they described themselves as "late-bloomers," many had gone on to further study and had achieved transformational as well as positional outcomes from their studies. In contrast with the groups of student migrants and the students who had returned, most of the TNE graduates,

> attained the aspirations that had motivated them to enroll. Typical examples of intertwined positional and transformational outcomes included having escaped the boredom and frustration of subordinate or menial job roles for more interesting and highly paid careers. (Robertson et al., 2011, p. 694)

McNamara and Knight (2014) found that TNE graduates are highly skilled but not necessarily addressing local skills gaps. This depended on the type of programme being delivered, with niche topics having a positive impact, suggesting a focus on employment-specific skills rather than generic employability skills. In their study, TNE students felt that teaching methods on TNE programmes rely more on critical thinking and voicing of opinions compared with local programmes of study, so their analytical skills were better developed.

Overall, the TNE experience has the capacity "to develop an unexpected motivation for transformative learning, and postgraduate study," according to Hoare (2012, p. 276). TNE thus "provides a potentially rich experience for 'second chance' learners, which can change lives, often in situations where there are few other options" (ibid., p. 283).

So, these studies suggest that TNE can help develop employability, or result in positional outcomes, in domestic settings. This will partly depend on the local employers' views of these programmes but in some cases they may have advantages over domestic programmes delivered by a local university or indeed over students educated overseas. Being employable in the home country may require skills, knowledge, and attitudes which are relevant to the local context where there is an interplay between hard and soft skills requirements of employers. There is even the possibility that developing employability skills through study overseas could make some graduates less employable at home (Robertson et al., 2011) and that returning students may find it harder to reintegrate into the local labour market. If TNE is effective in developing employability skills it could help students to interpret their new-found knowledge and skills in the local labour market while also interpreting employability within the local paradigm.

Some key points

Employer involvement

- Relatively little employer engagement in TNE programmes has been reported. Employers may be failing to reap the benefits of such engagement, including input to TNE curricula which might address skills gaps, access to recruitment of work-ready graduates, potential gains from involvement in student projects, or employer-university collaborations.
- Few examples have been reported of formalised work-based/work-integrated learning in TNE programmes, although many TNE students are employed during their studies.
- Better employer understanding of TNE programmes might help them encourage innovation and development by their employees involved in transnational education.

Students

- TNE is often a pragmatic choice which is reaching a distinctive range of students. Limited opportunity to study abroad, affordability, and the possibility of working while studying are just some of the motivations and decision-making factors.
- Studying via TNE programmes can build personal confidence, develop flexibility, and enhance critical thinking, through different approaches to learning and curricula.
- TNE providers are not clearly identifying to their students the importance of generic employability skills in addition to skills for employment in their chosen field. Students therefore do not articulate to employers how their TNE programme has enhanced these skills.
- Students from "third countries" may gain greater benefits than those taking a TNE programme in their own country. They gain international experience by studying in another country, which may enhance their employability skills further.

Universities and academics

- Universities need to understand the nature of personal as well as professional, employment-related motivations to study on TNE programmes, providing opportunities for developing both dimensions for these distinctive groups of students.
- Universities and academics need to understand the importance of curriculum internationalisation, including intercultural competence development, and how this can be delivered in a TNE context which may be relatively monocultural.

- They need to understand in particular why and how internationalisation of the curriculum can help develop transferable employability skills, explaining this to their TNE students and providing appropriate staff development as required.
- Universities may need to reach a common understanding of employability skills development with their TNE partners and encourage partner involvement in adapting traditional employability approaches to the local TNE context.
- In discussion with their TNE partners, universities need to deepen levels of employer engagement in TNE curricula, including guest lectures, work placements, university/industry collaborations, and student projects.

Conclusions

This chapter has identified the limited nature of existing research on the development of employability skills in transnational programmes. It is clear that overseas study is often seen as the "gold standard," and TNE as second best. However, the complex array of factors noted here means that, in fact, TNE may offer a different kind of opportunity to students, beyond merely the qualification they will earn; namely, the ability to navigate these issues thorough a nuanced approach to employability which is sensitive to national and regional as well as the global labour market. Better support for students is also needed in helping them to understand the value not only of their qualifications but also of the transferable skills gained as they progress through their TNE programme, and how these enhance employability.

In order to engage with this agenda, more research is needed which looks both at the development of employability skills in TNE contexts and the outcomes for students on these programmes. Moreover, if the TNE programme also involves study abroad,

> the value that employers will put on it depends on how the graduates themselves articulate the added value that overseas study has given them. (Employer cited in Fielden, Middlehurst, & Woodfield, 2007, p. 15)

As TNE continues to expand across new provider and host countries as well as in traditional settings, this diversification should add to our current understanding, helping to ensure better outcomes for students in what can be transformational experiences of higher education, affecting both their employability and future employment.

Notes

1. Part of this chapter was written as the literature review for Mellors-Bourne et al. (2015). Relevant sections are reproduced with permission.
2. Other discussions about the concept or definitions of employability can be found on pages 12, 25, 25, 60, 62, 92, 117, 164.

Chapter 12

Boundary spanning in TNE

Building connections through work integrated learning

Christine Bilsland

Introduction

Universities worldwide face pressure to equip graduates with skills and attributes that match industry and wider social and community needs. Therefore, moves to integrate work integrated learning – course offerings that embed authentic work elements, such as internships and industry projects in order to enhance student employability – into higher education curricula are gaining strength. Running work integrated learning (WIL) is resource intensive (Universities Australia, 2015), making its implementation controversial in domestic university environments, let alone transnational education (TNE) contexts.

Concurrently, growth in TNE has sparked research into associated issues of quality and standards, general administration and management, equivalence and comparability, English language skills, teaching and learning, and student satisfaction. Surprisingly, given rising concerns about employability, research into employability through WIL and other curricular approaches in international education is only starting to be addressed (British Council, 2014; Mellors-Bourne, Jones, & Woodfield, 2015). Most TNE-related studies concern home institution perspectives; few studies consider host market stakeholder views, particularly regarding employability (British Council, 2014). Therefore, this chapter explores WIL from the perspectives of three key local external stakeholder groups of an Australian university operating in Vietnam (referred to as the AUV). It proposes that WIL generates learning benefits for students and wider organisational learning value through the boundary-spanning relationships established though WIL partnerships in TNE environments. Boundary spanning occurs when staff collaborate with external partner organisational staff in functional and cognitive activities (Prysor & Henley, 2017).

Quality, equity, and employability

A perceived neoliberal orientation, where market principles rule higher education provision, partially drives views of TNE as a threat to quality education (Altbach & Knight, 2007; Kosmützky & Putty, 2016). Altbach (2010) expressed concern about the limited curriculum offered on international branch campuses. Edelstein and Douglass (2012) echoed this sentiment, noting that in general TNE initiatives replicated selected program and curriculum elements, limiting meaningful curriculum development. Transnational students expect to receive the same quality in terms of curriculum, staff, and content (Shams & Huisman, 2012); if WIL is offered at the home campus, they will likely expect it also at the TNE campus.

Naylor, Bhati, and Kidd (2010) noted the subsector of TNE students who move to another country in order to undertake a TNE degree not offered at home, often in TNE "hubs" such as Singapore, Malaysia, and the United Arab Emirates (UAE). These students, and their future employers, value TNE degrees more if they are combined with overseas industry experience (British Council, 2014; Naylor et al., 2010). Authentic employability skills should be developed through authentic work situations (Cranmer, 2006); subsequently, researchers have underscored the essential nature of incorporating WIL into curricula (Billett, 2009; Gault, Leach, & Duey, 2010) and providing effective WIL support mechanisms (Smith & Worsfold, 2015).

However, offering equivalent experiential education opportunities such as WIL internships in offshore campuses can be difficult. The next section identifies challenges faced in the Vietnamese environment, and those that apply to wider TNE contexts.

Vietnam – challenges to employability in higher education

Vietnam, a rising player in the global economy, has a history of reverence for education. As stated by Kristy Kelly, former Director of the International Institute of Education (IIE) in Vietnam,

> Education is an important part of the society. It is a major preoccupation of government and is a highly valued and respected activity in Vietnamese society. The Vietnam education and training sector is large, present in almost every village and touches virtually every family. (Kelly, 2000, p. 5)

However, it has been left with a systemic legacy of separation between industry and education that has contributed to a chronic mismatch of skills desired by graduate employers and those demonstrated by graduates (Tran, 2014). Although internships feature in many Vietnamese university programs, internship processes are largely disconnected from the academic program (Bilsland, Nagy, & Smith, 2014; Cam, 2016).

Beyond Vietnam – challenges with WIL in TNE

Although generally considered valuable, WIL is resource intensive (Patrick et al., 2008). Therefore, its implementation in transnational education, where cost-effective operations can be critical to TNE strategy, is problematic (Naylor et al., 2010).

The viability of related processes established in the institution's home country to deal with WIL-related risks, such as partnership agreements and insurance coverage, cannot be assumed in offshore environments.

When adapting WIL activities to a TNE environment one often encounters visa-related legal challenges (Naylor et al., 2010). In international branch campus hubs such as Singapore, Malaysia, and the UAE, a restrictive, fluctuating legal environment around international students' legal working status makes embedding WIL internship placements into TNE programs uncertain and risky, limiting WIL implementation. TNE institutions often encourage offshore campus students to experience one or two semesters of a degree at the home campus where international student visas may enable students to work and undertake internship placements; however, international students without the means and inclination to study in the institution's home country may be excluded.

Alternatives to internships, such as industry projects, field studies, simulated workplace environments, and industry-partnered events, are offered in many offshore campuses. However, differences between home and host-campus environments, such as industry structure and resource constraints, can affect a university's ability to offer authentic, practice-based activities to students (for examples, see Wolf & Yong (2009) and Welch, Vo-Tran, Pittayachawan, & Reynolds (2012).

Boundary spanning – potential of WIL models in TNE environments

A scoping report on WIL (Patrick et al., 2008) concluded that a collaborative model that integrates voices of university staff, students, and employers within the higher-level context of government regulation and education policy is fundamental to effective WIL implementation. Underpinned by similar mechanisms that ground this collaborative model, boundary-spanning roles link organisations and create mutually beneficial relationships (Peach, Cates, Jones, Lechleiter, & Ilg, 2011) that facilitate knowledge exchange. According to Brink, Mearns, and Du Plessis (2014), a WIL process built on boundary spanning between academic (research), educational, (teaching, assessment), and professional (expertise, transformation of knowledge) agents requires clear linkages, mutual role understanding, mutual commitment, and sharing of relevant information. Aldrich and Herker (1977) emphasised the value of boundary-spanning functions but treated its implementation as problematic due to role boundaries existent in most organisational contexts. Prysor and Henley (2017) agreed that formal role structures typical of university bureaucracies create obstacles for boundary spanning leadership strategies. Nevertheless, Peach et al. (2011) posited that effectively implemented WIL boundary-spanning approaches help universities react to environmental uncertainty, an inherent element of offshore campuses. The following sections outline how research questions were formulated and analysed, resulting in a proposal of WIL's value as a potential boundary-spanning mechanism in TNE.

Background to the study context

The WIL internship unit was offered as a final-semester elective in the undergraduate business degree program at the AUV. Interns participated in 12-week, full-time placements in a range of local businesses. The unit incorporated several elements that differed from most local university internships: formal placement support and coordination by AUV career staff, academic visits to intern workplaces, and assessments linked to workplace activities and student reflections. Academic advisers facilitated several seminars throughout the semester where groups of 30–40 students shared their experiences.

Methodology

Grounded theory approaches are appropriate when there is a lack of theory about the research topic, and when the researcher is vitally involved in the research (O'Reilly, Paper, & Marx, 2012). This condition reflected the author's situation as a WIL academic in Vietnam. The research purpose was to gain insight into local stakeholder perceptions of the AUV and its WIL program in order to help students build locally relevant employability skills through WIL. Two broad research questions were constructed:

- What do local external stakeholders perceive about the value of internships and work integrated learning?
- How can transnational education institutions in Vietnam that offer foreign-developed curricula meet external stakeholder expectations of WIL?

Internal stakeholders, such as academics and students, were not included. The AUV employed few local Vietnamese academic staff; most lecturers came from a range of international backgrounds, and therefore their exposure to local employment conditions was limited. Students were initially considered; however, as their workplace experience was limited, AUV alumni were targeted due to their dual experience as students and as graduates who had transitioned into local employment. Work supervisors of AUV interns and local human resource professionals from external organisations comprised the other two external stakeholder group participants. See Table 12.1 for sample details.

Forty-six semi-structured interviews of 30–60 minutes were recorded, transcribed, and uploaded to a Nvivo 10 analytical software package, and iteratively coded and analysed in a manner typical of grounded theory (Patton, 2002). Rich memo writing and a structured research journal were incorporated into the analytic process and entered into the Nvivo program to form an audit trail characteristic of grounded theory process and quality mechanisms. The two stages of coding and analysis that shaped initial impressions around the stakeholder perceptions of WIL value and subsequent conceptualisation of WIL as a potential boundary-spanning activity in TNE environments are explained in the following section.

Table 12.1 Sample details

Sample	Sample criteria	Rationale for inclusion
Work supervisors (21) (W1-21) Recruited through AUV WIL academics	Had directly supervised at least two AUV interns on placement, and met with AUV academics on each placement occasion.	Front-line supervisor level. Have direct contact with both AUV interns and AUV academics.
Alumni (16) (A1-16) Recruited through AUV alumni	Had graduated from the AUV at least one year prior to interview.	Possess shared experience as past AUV students and current local industry employees in a range of organisations.
Human resource professionals (9) (H1-9) Recruited through LinkedIn and AUV careers	Human resource managers/ directors (7) and recruiters (2)	Influential human resource roles. Unlike work supervisors, they do not necessarily have direct contact with interns or academics, yet are instrumental in establishing industry partnerships and hiring graduates.

Findings and discussion

Findings generated from a content analysis of each stakeholder group's responses addressed the first general research question: "What do stakeholders perceive about the value of internships and work integrated learning?" A summary of key findings from each group of stakeholders is presented below.

Work supervisors

Eight work supervisors initially perceived AUV students as rich, privileged, and lacking the academic capability to gain admission to the top local universities and, therefore, were initially sceptical about AUV interns and the potential value in hosting them. However, these work supervisors revised their opinions after supervising AUV interns and meeting academic advisers, as quoted here:

> Before I have a chance to work with AUV students, I think they are over-confident … but after they come here and having a chance to work with them and know more about AUV students and know (academic) I know they have good knowledge and study at a good university (W5).

Twenty of the twenty-one participants mentioned the care extended by the AUV, demonstrated by academic adviser work visits and their ongoing communication with interns and supervisors. For example, one participant noted, "you come with clear information – it makes us feel you are very supportive both of students and us," (W9) and another mentioned how this approach benefits interns: "when we meet the AUV teacher we feel we can share more with the student" (W19). As young front-line managers, many work supervisors valued internships as opportunities to improve their own training and mentoring skills: "We learn how to coach, and also we have feedback from them" (W13). Eighteen participants wanted more information about interns' academic programs and further involvement with intern recruitment in order to provide interns with better training and supervision.

Alumni

All alumni recognised the value of WIL internships, whether or not they had participated in AUV WIL internship electives, and noted positive differences between local university internships and AUV internships: "It shows the responsibility of the university, helping the students orienting their career path, in comparison with my friends at Vietnamese universities they were left alone" (A2). Thirteen participants recalled feeling uncertain about how their Western education equipped them for a Vietnamese work environment; therefore, internships helped them adapt to local employment and to "network and get an idea of the Vietnamese system because at AUV we mostly focus on international things" (A5). A finding that went beyond the initial research questions was that many alumni sought greater connection with the AUV after graduation for their networking purposes and expressed willingness to support and mentor AUV students: "Alumni could mentor the new students, help them to see what is along the way, and after graduation. I would be very willing to do that" (A15).

Human resource professionals

Human resource professionals were the third stakeholder group interviewed in order to compare their perceptions with those of front-line supervisors who work directly with interns. Although foreign universities (including the AUV) were generally associated with a quality education, all nine participants identified that individual characteristics, such as attitude and motivation, shaped perceptions of a work-ready graduate to a greater degree than did educational qualifications or even skills. However, characterisations of some foreign university and AUV graduates as privileged and lacking motivation and commitment to their employers emerged. Typically, comments indicated that "most foreign university students are very good at English and computer skills" (H9) but demonstrate a lack of empathy – "they don't seem proactive in asking what the company needs…just 'what's in it for me'" (H5) – and a disinterest in developing along with the organisation – "they want quick wins" (H7) without "spending time to develop themselves" (H4). This ambivalence influenced reluctance on the part of some participants to partner with the AUV in WIL-related activities.

Value of WIL as TNE boundary spanner

As data collected across stakeholder groups were continually compared, the potential value of WIL as a boundary spanner in TNE was conceptualised. As the summarised findings across stakeholder groups show, positive feedback about AUV interns from work supervisors and about the value of the AUV degree experience and WIL internship reported by alumni contrasted with the more ambivalent perceptions about TNE graduates expressed by human resource professionals. An increased level of familiarity and contact with the AUV's WIL processes and people appeared to heighten work supervisors' knowledge of and commitment to WIL programs, and potentially to consider AUV graduates as work-ready recruits. Therefore, work supervisors and academics who have close contact with student interns and ongoing relationships with each other are proposed as potentially valuable "boundary spanners" that can not only build collaborative relationships with each other but also share insight about intern capabilities and their partners' processes throughout their respective organisations.

Figure 12.1 illustrates a potential boundary-spanning orientation for a WIL program in TNE. Five value elements are situated near the boundary-spanning relationships (identified by text boxes and relationship-directional arrows of varying shaded intensities) they are most closely associated with. WIL academics and work supervisors are identified as central boundary-spanning actors.

Interns form the linchpin of this orientation, connecting the two critical externally linked boundary spanners; the placement work supervisor and the WIL academic. They are not identified as central boundary spanners, due to the inherent role definition of an intern as one who is not an official employee and whose internship status is temporary. At this fundamental level, the first contribution a boundary-spanning orientation can make to WIL value is *improved employability* for its student interns. Work supervisors are critical to intern learning; hence,

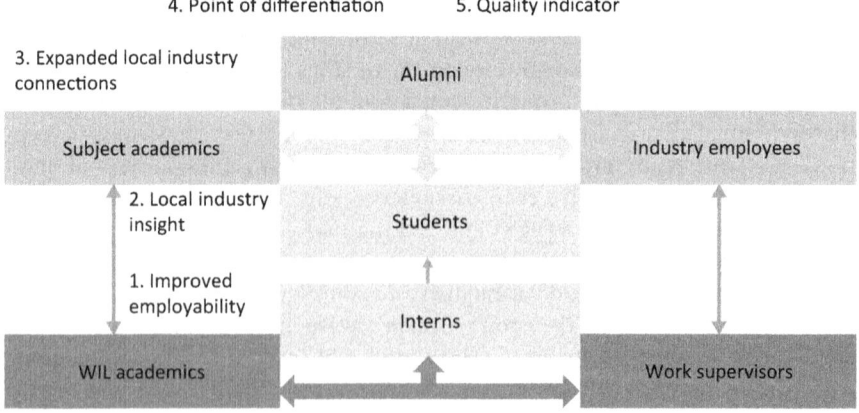

Figure 12.1 Value of WIL as boundary spanner in TNE.

it is important for TNE providers to support them as they guide intern learning. The study findings showed that work supervisors are positively inclined to provide increased support to interns through building strong relationships with the university and collaborating with the university to understand more about the interns' study program and goals.

The second benefit derived from a boundary-spanning orientation between WIL academics and work supervisors is the potential for WIL academics to develop enhanced *local industry insight* through relationships with interns and supervisors, and visits to intern workplaces and sharing these insights with other subject academics at the TNE campus who often come from international backgrounds. The benefits thus flow upwards to academics and students, as shared local practice knowledge can then be incorporated into other subject teaching to enhance local relevance, supporting the embedded employability value not only for interns but also for other TNE students.

A third potential benefit is that WIL academics can grow their local industry network through their boundary-spanning relationships with work supervisors, thereby *expanding local industry connections*. Enhanced connections can improve local industry insight and also generate contacts for potential WIL placement hosts, industry project participants, and guest speakers for the wider TNE campus, ultimately enhancing the student learning experience and generally supporting locally relevant employability initiatives. Local alumni are also incorporated into this level of a boundary-spanning orientation. As previous students who share an experiential connection with students, the AUV alumni interviewees expressed a desire for ongoing affiliation with the AUV and a willingness to mentor students. As their careers progress, they are well placed to provide ongoing links to industry, potentially as intern work supervisors, guest speakers, industry project sponsors and graduate recruiters and as overall TNE institutional ambassadors to local industry.

The marked contrast between the ambivalence about engaging TNE graduates in general expressed by human resource professionals and the willingness to collaborate with the AUV articulated by work supervisors indicates that front-line experience with WIL interns and collaboration with AUV academics can transform initially negative perceptions. Work supervisor insights into WIL practices and actual AUV intern performance can flow to other employees, similarly to the local industry insight exchanged by WIL academics and AUV subject academics, widening the relationships built with the AUV. An engaged alumni cohort would also, potentially, be part of this loop, as their collaboration in AUV WIL activities develops and involves their colleagues. Therefore, a fourth indirect but important outcome of a boundary-spanning orientation derived through WIL activities is the recognition of WIL internships in a local organisation as a *point of differentiation* that distinguishes the TNE graduate from other graduates. This point of differentiation marked by a collaborative WIL program where the TNE provider provides appropriate support to work supervisors and their interns may then represent a *quality indicator* of a TNE degree and a TNE graduate.

Conclusions

Despite resource constraints and other challenges encountered in TNE implementations of WIL, careful investment in offshore WIL resources appears justified. WIL not only supports equitable employability outcomes to a university's offshore students and community stakeholders, but it also can generate value derived from boundary-spanning relationships that transpire from WIL partnerships in TNE locations. The predominant factor that emerged around the transformed perceptions of work supervisors who initially expressed scepticism about AUV interns was the active participation in the WIL partnership. This contrasted with the more ambivalent stance of human resource professionals whose familiarity with the AUV and its WIL program were shaped from a greater role distance. Three general recommendations for further research are proposed. First, research into reciprocal benefits that industry partners stand to gain from WIL activities in general and from boundary-spanning collaborations in particular in TNE host locations is required. One example is for TNE providers to investigate how internship supervision might contribute to work supervisors' professional development goals related to coaching and leadership that both the supervisors themselves and their employers would value. Second, this paper focused on local stakeholders external to the AUV. Further research into internal stakeholder views is recommended to identify how WIL academics and other subject academics can collaborate to effectively incorporate local practice knowledge into subject units. This recommendation includes investigating curricula offered in TNE locations in order to discover workable adaptation. Finally, as a qualitative study conducted in one country, the findings justify future research that focuses on local stakeholders of other TNE host countries in order to incorporate locally relevant WIL activities.

Chapter 13

The contribution of imported programs in Vietnamese universities to graduate employability development

A case study

Tran Le Huu Nghia and Vo Phương Quyen

Introduction

Internationalisation in higher education is "the process of integrating an international, intercultural, or global dimension (e.g., a perspective, activity or program) into the purpose, functions or delivery of postsecondary education" (Knight, 2003, p. 2). Higher education institutions engage in internationalisation for different reasons, including commercial advantages, knowledge and language acquisition, curriculum content enhancement, etc. (Altbach & Knight, 2007). Internationalisation can occur in different dimensions (faculty, student, curricular content, international alliance) of the activities of a university (Black, 2004; Brookes & Becket, 2009).

Like many of their counterparts worldwide, Vietnamese universities are internationalising their curricula and pedagogical practices, seeing this as a way of increasing the employability of their students. Recently, a higher education (HE) curriculum and pedagogy internationalisation initiative has been implemented and endorsed by the central government (Government, 2008). Selected prestigious Vietnamese universities have been approved to partner with well-known foreign institutions to import and deliver target undergraduate programs (mostly in technology and engineering disciplines) in Vietnam.

These imported programs are known as "advanced" programs, which is literally translated from the Vietnamese *chương trình tiên tiến*. The initiative aims to produce high-quality graduates for national socio-economic objectives and to set an educational model for domestic university programs. Since their implementation in 2000, these programs have attracted tens of thousands of students; however, there is a lack of published research regarding how these programs help students increase their employability.

This chapter will report on a qualitative case study that investigated how the imported Advanced Aquaculture program offered by a Vietnamese university contributed to the development of graduate employability and career advancement prospects as well as identified challenges that these programs are facing. The study is important because it fundamentally addresses an "at-home" internationalisation initiative within the higher education context of a developing country. The study may raise implications for countries that adopt the similar initiatives regarding internationalisation of higher education curricula and pedagogical practices.

Graduate employability in higher education

In recent years, HE sectors around the world have witnessed the surge of the employability agenda. Several initiatives have been deployed to develop graduate employability, such as embedding employability skills into the curricula, using different forms of work-integrated learning (WIL) (e.g., simulations, internships, work placements, and field trips), organising extra-curricular activities, providing career education, international exchanges, career mentoring, etc. (Al-Mahmood & Gruba, 2007; Barrie, Hughes, & Smith, 2009; Jackson, 2015; Kinash, Crane, Judd, & Knight, 2016). These employability initiatives have been implemented as a response to government and regulatory body policies (Bacchus, 2008; McMahon, 2006; Staff, 2010), employers' complaints about a lack of skilled graduates (Briggeman & Norwood, 2011; Kavanagh & Drennan, 2008; Lowry, Molloy, & McGlennon, 2008; Rao et al., 2014), students-as-university-customers' expectations that university education can enhance their employment prospects (Labi, 2010; Stuart, Rios-Aguilar, & Deil-Amen, 2014), and universities' aspirations to improve their educational services, including preparing students as lifelong learners for an uncertain future (Hager & Holland, 2006, pp. 5–9).

Yet, the concept of graduate employability remains contentious. One of the most cited definitions[1] for employability skills belongs to Yorke (2006, p. 23), who defines employability as "a set of achievements – skills, understanding and personal attributes – that makes graduates more likely to gain employment and be successful in their chosen occupations, which benefits themselves, the workforce, the community and the economy." These skills are often referred to interchangeably as graduate attributes, generic skills, and transferable skills, to name but a few (Bowman, 2010).

Unfortunately, graduate employability is often interpreted as the readiness of students to obtain [first] employment. It is often understood in the simplest way as the knowledge and skills possessed by graduates that enable them to secure a job. This understanding equates employability with the narrow sense of human capital, which is often systematically developed through formal education (Šlaus & Jacobs, 2011). Therefore, the responsibility of developing employability is attributed to universities and other education providers.

Recent studies, however, have attempted to redefine employability to better capture its complexity. For example, Fugate, Kinicki, and Ashforth (2004) developed a heuristic model of employability that shifts the responsibility from the education providers to the learners and suggests that employability be treated as processual rather than as a possessed entity. The model shows that employability is at the intersection of three components: social and human capital, personal adaptability, and career identity.

According to Fugate et al. (2004, p. 24), human capital refers to a range of varying factors that "influence a person's career advancement variables such as age and education, work experience and training, job performance and length of time with an organisation, emotional intelligence, cognitive ability, and KSAOs [knowledge, skills, attitudes, and others]." All these factors have been found as determinants of the employment outcomes of graduates.

Social capital can be represented by the social networks that graduates have established, and contributes to employability via an "overtly social and interpersonal element" (Fugate et al., 2004, p. 23). Network size and network strength are the two most important characteristics of social capital with which graduates may be informed of occupational opportunities and be better positioned in the graduate labour market.

Career identity is a "more or less coherent representation of often diverse and diffuse career experiences and aspirations" (Fugate et al., 2004, p. 19). It defines "who I am" or "who I want to be" and may include goals, hopes, fears, personal traits, values, beliefs, etc. "Career identity provide a compass for the individual, thereby offering a motivational component to employability" (Fugate et al., 2004, p. 20).

Personal adaptability means being able to change personal factors – for example, knowledge, skills, attitudes, and others (KSAOs) – to meet the demand of the situation. Personal adaptability has been found to positively contribute to career satisfaction and career performance (Zacher, 2014). As a result, individuals with greater adaptability can become more employable and/or self-employed. By reviewing an extensive body of literature in the topic, Fugate et al. (2004) found that personal adaptability can be represented in five aspects: optimism to challenges, propensity to learn, openness to changes and new experiences, internal locus of control, and generalised self-efficacy (Fugate et al., 2004, p. 22).

In this chapter, this model of employability will be used as the theoretical framework for the analysis of how the advanced program could contribute to graduate employability. It is noted here that the authors deliberately separate human capital and social capital into two components to facilitate the analysis. Before analysing the contribution of advanced programs to Vietnamese students' and graduates' employability, it is important to understand the concept and implementation context of such programs.

Imported university programs in Vietnam

After Vietnam signed the World Trade Organisation's General Agreement on Trade in Services (GATS), the internationalisation of the HE sector has become more prevalent (Nguyen, Hamid, & Moni, 2016; Nguyen, Walkinshaw, & Pham, 2017). The launch of the Higher Education Reform Agenda (HERA) in 2005 and the granting of curriculum autonomy to Vietnamese universities, which was first mentioned in the 2012 Higher Education law, further politically primed the universities to begin internationalising their educational programs to improve the learning outcomes of students and to boost their graduates' employability.

One of the most notable internationalisation initiatives in the HE sector was the implementation of the so-called "advanced" programs in collaboration with a foreign institution (Government, 2008; Nguyen, 2009). These programs were developed to be flagship programs and have elevated the status of several Vietnamese universities regionally and internationally. This creates a spill-over effect that improves the quality of HE teaching and learning, which, in turn, improves graduate employability and attracts international students to Vietnam.

According to the Prime Minister's Decision 1505/QĐ-TTg (Government, 2008), advanced programs are defined as educational programs developed by Vietnamese universities that follow the curriculum structure and pedagogical practices of the top 200 universities in the world as ranked by prestigious university ranking leagues. These programs strictly follow the original content, pedagogical practices, organisation, and management of training activities and language instruction (preferably English), and include compulsory Marxist-Leninist subjects for Vietnamese students. Advanced programs are delivered following a credit accumulation system.

Staff from the foreign partnered institution can co-deliver the programs with qualified Vietnamese colleagues and participate in evaluating the effectiveness of these advanced programs. Either or both institutions issue the degrees for these advanced programs. To enrol in these programs, students must pass the national university entrance examination and demonstrate a high level of English proficiency. Finally, students are informed of the tuition fees, which are approximately 2.5 times higher than those for the "generic" programs in the same study areas.

Up until 2012, approximately 13,200 students had enrolled in 35 advanced programs offered by 22 universities (MOET, 2016). Their implementation was reported to have yielded positive results and to have produced exceptional graduates who were employed shortly after graduation and who successfully competed for prestigious international postgraduate scholarships in developed countries (MOET, 2016). Nevertheless, the programs also reported difficulties in terms of finding qualified teaching staff and appropriate facilities (MOET, 2016). There are no research publications available regarding the effectiveness of these programs from the students' perspectives, however.

The present study

The study reported in this chapter aimed to explore how imported programs at Vietnamese universities contribute to the development of graduate employability. The research questions were,

- How have advanced programs implemented in Vietnamese universities enhanced graduate employability?
- What challenges are the universities facing in implementing these programs?

The study was conducted as a qualitative case study of the Advanced Aquaculture program offered by a well-recognised university in the south of Vietnam. The multidisciplinary university hosts around 50,000 full-time students and is currently recognised as one of the best universities in Vietnam. The researchers had good connections within the university and with the school leaders and had witnessed the birth and development of the program. These elements enabled the researchers to approach participants and ensured the satisfactory completion of the study.

The four-and-one-half year Advanced Aquaculture program was launched in 2008 and follows the curriculum structure and training model of an American university. This 158-credit program was accredited by the Association of South East Asian Nations University Network in 2014 and is organised as follows: 108 credits for theory subjects, 27 credits for practice-based subjects, 3 credits for local and international field trips, 10 credits for the minor thesis/graduation project, and the remaining credits for English courses. The program offers students the opportunity to undertake a semester exchange abroad and has also hosted several international students attending a semester at the school. Successful graduates receive a degree conferred by the university and a certificate of completion by the collaborating university.

The data used for this study included a 10-year progress report of the program, which included information about how the program was established, the number of enrolments and graduations by years, a record of the teachers' and students' activities, and a summary of graduate employment and career advancement. In addition, the study also used data collected from interviews with 10 final-year students and four academics and leaders of the program regarding their experiences. All interviews were recorded and were transcribed verbatim to facilitate the analysis.

All the qualitative data was analysed using a content analysis approach (Hsieh & Shannon, 2005). The researchers read the report several times to understand how the program was operated, to identify the successes and challenges of the program implementation, and to recognise the aspects that need to be improved. The responses from each participant were coded separately according to the components of employability proposed by Fugate et al. (2004). The codes were then compared between participants and divided into themes based on their similarities and differences. It should be noted that in this chapter, participants' perspectives will only be considered to highlight issues found in the report.

Advanced aquaculture graduate employment outcomes and career advancement

The data from the interviews and the report revealed that the program added substantial value for final-year students and graduates. The academics observed that students and graduates were "recognisably dynamic, creative, and confident." Towards the end of the program, students were observed as being able to work in teams more effectively. The improvement in their English language proficiency was the most obvious learning outcome, with all participants reporting that they could communicate fluently by the end of the course. The students also felt confident with what they acquired from the program and appeared to be ready for career advancement as they had concrete plans for the future, such as applying for a job in a well-known organisation, competing for a scholarship program, continuing with their post-graduate studies abroad, etc.

In terms of tangible outcomes, the records of the Bureau of Academic Affairs showed that, until 2016, a total of 96 students graduated from the program. Among them, 16 students were ranked as "outstanding," 42 as "excellent," 35 as "good," and three as "average." Due to the quality of the program and the foreign university certificate of completion and the graduates' high-level English skills, reference letters from foreign teachers, international fieldwork, and internships, the career prospects of the graduates were very positive. The post-graduation survey conducted by the program coordinators showed positive employment outcomes and positive indications of career advancement for all graduates in the first three cohorts. All of them secured an employment position relevant to their expertise within one year after graduation. Regarding career advancement, 19 graduates from the first three cohorts were provided with further education by their employers or obtained a scholarship to study abroad.

The contribution of the advanced aquaculture program to graduate employability

The report and the interviews consistently indicated that the program substantially contributed to the development of graduate employability and enhanced their employment opportunities and career advancement prospects. The program's success in enhancing the overall employability of graduates was attributed to the following features.

Human capital

The high calibre students who enrolled in the program helped increase graduate employability. Up until January 2016, the university enrolled 217 students who satisfied the demanding entry criteria as specified in the admission requirements for advanced programs (Government, 2008). Prior to commencing the program, all students had to undergo an intensive English training course to ensure their English language proficiency met the demands of the program. This preparation and their high-level academic abilities and strong motivation for pursuing the program made them more likely to succeed and to maximise the opportunity for their future careers.

In addition, the highly qualified teaching staff involved in the delivery of the program contributed to graduate employability. The program leaders have to comply with the teaching standards set by the Ministry of Education and

Training (MOET) in terms of lecturer qualifications, teaching experience, and English language ability to ensure the quality of the delivery of the program.

In the first three years of its implementation, the program was delivered by lecturers from the collaborating American university, with local lecturers assisting. The report noted that up until the end of 2015 the program had invited 62 lecturers from the collaborating university and 20 lecturers from 10 other countries to co-deliver the imported program. All these lecturers had at least a PhD degree and were recognised experts in the field, an element that other local programs might not have been able to offer. Therefore, the students benefited from these lecturers' subject matter expertise and relevant specialised skills. As one student remarked,

> Enrolled in this programme, we have studied with many teachers, exposed to many enterprises, and got to know the latest technologies in the field. Then when we have acquired these technologies, we can apply them to the context of our country. (Participant 10)

Moreover, the program's pedagogical and assessment techniques contributed to the students' overall learning experience. The analysis of the interviews and the report revealed that instead of using traditional teaching methods, which are often seen in Vietnamese universities (Tran, Le, & Nguyen, 2014), the lecturers used a variety of student-centred teaching approaches, such as project-based and research-based teaching and field work. These techniques have been found to be conducive for the development of employability skills (Barrie et al., 2009).

The students were required to research and present their findings, which helped them explore and gain knowledge independently and increase their confidence and communication skills. The students were also taken for field trips, a form of WIL (Jackson, 2015), to understand how the theories could be applied in reality. In contrast to the conventional use of assessment for summative purposes in Vietnamese universities (Tran et al., 2014), formative assessments were frequently used throughout the course to provide the students with feedback so they could identify knowledge and skill gaps and areas for improvement. Two students reflected on the effectiveness of the pedagogical and assessment practices used in the program:

> Their teaching methods are interesting. They sent us out for field trips, then asked us to write a report of what we saw in the fieldwork. Then they pointed out what knowledge we missed and planned their lectures accordingly. (Participant 04)
>
> Assignments of most foreign lecturers are easy to understand. They gave us many things to do and we had to apply knowledge to solving situations. Vietnamese lecturers, in contrast, focus more on rote-learning, which I do not like because after their course, I have not acquired much knowledge and skills, just memorised things to pass the exams. (Participant 02)

A special feature of this programme was that students were involved in doing research with their lecturers. As a result, upon graduation, many students had experienced doing research, including seven students publishing articles in local academic journals, and 37 students presenting their work at or attending international conferences. Two of their projects received awards at the prestigious Vietnamese Young Talents for Science 2013 and Wilmar Agro Vietnam Award 2014. During the final semester, students were required to complete a research-based thesis to graduate. English was the language of instruction throughout the four years of the program, including the thesis and the thesis defence.

Furthermore, the effectiveness of pedagogical practices and students' development of human capital could be attributed to the learning conditions of the program. The classrooms and the laboratory were equipped with modern furniture, appropriate teaching-learning tools, and even air conditioners, which were only used for students of the advanced program. Learning materials, mostly in English, were given to students in advance so that they could have adequate time to read them prior to attending the lectures and discussing the subject matter in class. Student support services were also designed to support this group of students so that they had the best conditions for realising their academic potential. All the interviewed students were pleased with the facilities and the learning conditions.

In short, high calibre students, active pedagogical practices, the effective use of assessment for learning, an engaging learning environment, and favourable learning conditions all contributed to the development of the students' human capital, which, in turn, contributed to their employability and career advancement.

Social capital

The program offered students many opportunities to network with experts in their field of study. Both foreign and local lecturers who they had studied with could become valuable referees with relevant industry connections. The students were also sent to work with professionals in the field, who not only helped the students understand the industry, but who were also potential employers or contacts.

In addition, this international program provided students with many opportunities to network with international students. Up until December 2015, the program had attracted 45 international students on academic exchange (participating in courses) and 82 international students who participated in cultural exchanges, workshops, and seminars. The program also sent five Vietnamese students to foreign institutions for short studies and 101 students for field work or internships in Thailand, Malaysia, and Indonesia.

Within this international learning environment, students recognised that they could extend their social network with people in and outside of their field of study. They developed a sense of being global citizens, were able to tolerate cultural differences, and knew how to behave appropriately across cultures.

After the field trip in Thailand, I often compared what I have learned with the new one, as well as recognised the importance of self-studies. Generally, [in Thailand], there was a better positive learning environment in the class. They are not afraid of asking questions, of discussing with us as Vietnamese. We learned from them how to self-study effectively and then combine it with ours to have a better study method. (Participant 01)

In short, by participating in this programme, students were offered valuable opportunities to develop a large social network with professionals and influential experts in the fields, both in Vietnam and abroad. As indicated in Fugate et al. (2004), this social capital could connect them to occupational opportunities and strengthen their career prospects.

Personal adaptability

There was evidence that the program helped the students develop their adaptability to challenging situations, which is essential for the development of employability (Fugate et al., 2004). For many students, pursuing a program delivered completely in English was a significant challenge. Despite the intensive English preparation course and their prior English skills, most of the students struggled to keep pace with the lectures delivered by foreign teachers. This required significant effort and commitment by the students to improve their English, study in groups, and translate the lessons into Vietnamese to foster better understanding. This situation forced many students to improve their English, so they could survive in the learning environment.

Until the second year, when I studied some subjects with foreign lecturers, I could not understand them well due to my English proficiency. I intended to give up and transfer to another programme, but teachers and friends encouraged me to continue. [...]. I myself also invested to overcome the problem. (Participant 09)

In Vietnam, students are typically reluctant to ask questions in class due to their fear of revealing what they do not know, which is a feature of the face-saving culture (Leung & Cohen, 2011). Students are also reluctant to "challenge" teachers by asking them critical questions. Some students admitted that within the program's active learning environment, however, they were encouraged to speak their minds and engage with their learning in a meaningful way rather than just focus on academic results. This is an improvement that many Vietnamese university programs are not capable of. A student reported how their potential was harnessed within the program:

When we studied with foreign teachers, they paid much attention to ensure that we understood the lessons and assigned more assessment tasks throughout the course [...], so we had to spend a lot of time doing homework and studying in groups. Sometimes we had to stay up late until 3 or 4 am for these activities. [...] We were all stretched and forced to make great effort. (Participant 01)

This challenging learning environment may have helped students break away from their prior passive learning habits and become more autonomous in their learning, more willing to welcome challenges, and more resilient. Consequently, they become more adaptable, which benefits their employability and career development.

Career identity

All the students identified at least one career path they would like to pursue upon graduation. These included careers in research institutions, government organisations, and private enterprises. Notably, one student was inspired to pursue a career path outside the field of study after she participated in an international field trip. The report also indicated that all the graduates from the first three cohorts could secure jobs within the aquaculture industry and some of them enrolled in a PhD program within their discipline. All these outcomes provided evidence that the graduates developed a strong professional identity associated with the field of aquaculture.

As noted in the literature, career identity is a compass for students' and graduates' actions to achieve professional goals (Fugate et al., 2004). In this regard, the program seemed successful as it inspired and helped students identify career paths aligned with their aptitudes, interests, and qualifications. The program also helped students re-assess their career choices and develop a willingness to explore professional pathways that might differ from their original intentions.

Challenges of implementing the imported programs

Regardless of the positive contribution of imported programs to graduate employability, they face several problems that threaten their sustainability. The two interviewed program leaders reported that to sustain the "foreign elements" of this program, it is vital to keep a balance between international and local lecturers, which requires adequate resources to pay foreign lecturers. The central government only funded the program for the first few years, however, and then the university had to seek alternative resources to maintain it. In fact, the program leaders were outsourcing and attracting international lecturers, mostly from Southeast Asian universities, to reduce staff costs. They were also planning to increase the tuition fee, but this is not yet feasible as the program has not been well-recognised in terms of return on student investment. Increasing the tuition fee would, therefore, severely reduce the number of students enrolling. How to sustain the program in the context of constrained resources is a complex puzzle for the leadership:

> The MOET only funded the programme for the first few years, but later the operation of the programme had to rely on tuition fees. However, the majority of students are from [that region], so their families' income is not that high to bear a tuition fee that is almost double the normal university programme. So yes, the primary obstacle is funding and resources to maintain the programme. (Participants 11)

Another issue relates to English language proficiency. It has been difficult for program coordinators to recruit students that meet the English entry requirements and the quota allocated to the program, resulting in fluctuating student enrolment over the years. To address this, the program leaders had to advertise enrolment more than once to recruit enough students. This also caused challenges for the teaching-learning process as some students struggled to meet the demands of a program conducted in English. Two lecturers shared their views on these issues:

> One of the biggest challenges was that it was difficult to deliver the lectures in English to students whose English level was low. If they have an adequate level of English, it is easy, otherwise, they became so passive. (Participant 13)
>
> At first, I delivered my lecture entirely in English, but recently I had to switch to Vietnamese when I recognised that students were confused. (Participant 14)

Yet, apart from the intensive English training at the beginning of the program, there were no recognisable measures in place to help students improve their English skills. As revealed in the interviews, the students formed groups to study or attended private English classes to resolve their learning difficulties caused by the language barrier.

The teaching schedule was another difficulty associated with the implementation of this program. Lecturers from the collaborating university or other foreign universities could only stay for a short period to deliver their subjects in intense blocks. Therefore, the students had to complete these subjects in a short timeframe, which affected the quality of their learning and their learning outcomes.

In addition, the central government's funding cuts forced the program coordinators to replace international lecturers with local ones. This could be seen as a step backward for the program as it suggests that the university is unable to maintain academic delivery standards. A lecturer and program coordinator reflected upon the effect of reducing the number of foreign lecturers on students' learning outcomes:

> With the reduction of foreign lecturers, it is observed that students' activeness [in learning] was also reduced. Foreign teachers may not teach better

than local ones, but they know better how to guide students. Students of the first three cohorts were much more active than recent ones. It is easy for students of recent cohorts to study in English with Vietnamese lecturers, but when they have to work with foreigners, they fail to communicate in English. (Participant 11)

Looking at this issue from another angle, however, it could be seen as a step forward as the program has gradually become less dependent on external lecturers. Vietnamese lecturers participating in the program possess a relevant PhD in the field from a top university overseas and have completed their roles as teaching assistants for the American lecturers for at least three courses. Yet, the report stated that most of the Vietnamese lecturers did not possess an adequate level of English to be eligible to teach subjects in the programs, even for those who had previously completed their post-graduate studies overseas. They were not able to implement the teaching approach that their American colleagues used, possibly due to a lack of teaching experience or their own social beliefs regarding teacher-student relationships that are embedded in the Confucian educational heritage of the country (Tran et al., 2014).

Another lecturer also observed that while work integrated learning is a relatively prominent component in the original curriculum, it is less prominent in the imported curriculum. In her view, this is because not enough time is allocated to the four-and-a-half year program and there is a lack of connection with the industry (Participant 14). Changing the deep-seated attitudes to teaching and learning will only happen over time, however, as many of these issues are associated with organisational culture and beliefs.

Conclusions and the way forward for imported programs

This chapter has reported upon the implementation of an internationalisation of curriculum and pedagogy initiative in a Vietnamese university, with a special focus on its impact on graduate employability and career advancement. The study found that the initiative positively contributed to the students' development of human capital, social capital, personal adaptability, and career identity. Substantial growth in these components of employability can explain the success of the graduates from the first three cohorts of the program in securing employment within one year of graduation and winning prestigious scholarships to pursue post-graduate studies locally or abroad to advance their career.

The central issue now is that in the years to come, when expanding the program to meet growing student demand, the university will need to decide whether to keep its international dimensions or operate as a local program with an improved curriculum and pedagogical practices. This is a critical decision as it will have important implications for the sustainability of the program. If the former is chosen, there are several issues that need to be resolved urgently. These include the hiring of foreign lecturers, especially those from the collaborating university, reaching an agreement on how the degrees will be conferred in the future, increasing the number of inbound international students in the program, sending students outbound for international experience, and seeking alternative funding rather than relying on the government.

Alternatively, running it as a local program may result in a shortfall of enrolments, even when it is delivered in English by highly qualified Vietnamese lecturers. In addition, many international elements of the program are likely to vanish, including the English language instruction that Vietnamese lecturers and students find difficult. As a result, the students may be reluctant to pay high tuition fees if they feel they are not getting a return on their investment in the form of a superior learning experience and promising future employment prospects.

Regardless of the program's future status of operation, there are some issues that can be resolved to help improve graduate employability. First, the current program only enrolled high achieving students, but these students found it challenging to keep pace with the program. Although these challenges create opportunities for these students to develop several qualities and attributes, this could be a serious problem if the program accepts students with varying academic and English language abilities. As English is used as the language of instruction, the program, regardless of how innovative it is, will become meaningless if the students lack the required English language proficiency. Therefore, students' English skills should be continuously enhanced throughout the program. Likewise, students need to be prepared for different learning styles to ensure their successful transition into the program. This preparation would help reduce the students' timidity and dependence so that they can become more proactive, creative, and critical in the active learning environment.

In addition, although the current pedagogical and assessment practices are found to enhance graduate employability, the current curriculum has reduced WIL elements. The WIL experience has been found to significantly improve graduate employability and employment outcomes (Jackson, 2015), suggesting the value in the program, including greater WIL opportunities to expose students to more authentic work settings and workplace situations. To do this, university and program leaders need to forge a larger network with professionals and organisations in the field and connect with former graduates to seek WIL arrangement for current students. WIL activities will help the students reflect upon what they are studying, apply their knowledge and skills to authentic work situations, connect with more industry-based professionals, and develop their sense of belonging to the industry by fostering their professional identity. All these will, in turn, help develop the graduate employability of the students enrolled in the program.

Note

1. Other discussions about the definition of employability can be found on pages 12, 25, 25, 60, 62, 92, 117.

Chapter 14

Transnational education and employability

Lessons from a case study of an Australian degree in Malaysia

Fion Choon Boey Lim, Glenda Crosling, Greeja Hemalata De Silva, and Mien Wee Cheng

Introduction: the size and growth of transnational education (TNE) in Australia and Malaysia

Australian higher education institutions have been active in the transnational education (TNE) industry for several decades. While there are varied definitions of what constitutes TNE, most TNE activities involve teaching and/or learning activities in which the students involved are in a different country from the country where the institution providing the education is based (GATE, 1997). These students are commonly referred to as offshore students.

TNE operating out of Australian higher education institutions can be considered substantial in size. In 2012, Australian universities delivered 1027 transnational programs either in partnership with institutions in other countries, or at 22 overseas campuses (Universities Australia, 2012). In 2013, transnational higher education constituted 33.5% of the all international student enrolments in Australian higher education institutions (Department of Education and Training, 2014). While the size might be large in terms of number of programs and students, most Australian TNE activities are concentrated in a small number of countries: these are China, Malaysia, Singapore, Vietnam, and Hong Kong (Universities Australia, 2014; Department of Education and Training, 2015).

Of these major countries that import Australian higher education, Malaysia has long been a trading partner of Australia for education, with the relationship extending as far back as the 1950s with the Colombo Plan. The latest statistics reported by the Australian Department of Education and Training (2015) is that around 16,000 students are enrolled in an Australian degree in Malaysia. In 2014, the report by Universities Australia indicated that Malaysia delivered 24% of the 821 TNE programs offered by Australian institutions, or approximately 200 programs, in partnership with another local institution or through offshore campuses established by Australian universities. However, the scale of Australian TNE activities and the growth are not coincidental when one looks at the development aims of the Malaysian government, as explained below.

Background to the study

Malaysia is a developing country with aspirations of becoming a developed nation by 2020; that is, a nation with a high-income and knowledge-driven workforce. To achieve this target, the government aims by 2015 to increase the enrolment rate for tertiary education to 53%, and also to improve the graduate employment rate to more than 80% (Ministry of Education, Malaysia, 2015).

Given the degree of Australian TNE activity in Malaysia and the governmental aim to improve the graduate employment rate, the topic presented in this chapter, the preparedness for and employment outcomes for graduates of TNE higher education programs in Malaysia, is a valid and valuable topic for investigation. The topic reflects the interest and, indeed, the concern surrounding the employment of graduates globally, but its importance is magnified in the context of TNE. In the situation where educational programs are delivered by an institution based in one country to students located in another (McBurnie & Ziguras, 2006, p. 1), the geographic, national, and often cultural distances between the program designers and the students who undertake the program can manifest in a gap between the graduate outcomes and workplace needs of the country hosting the TNE program. This has implications for graduates' employment and career prospects. While successful completion of their studies provides students with the credentials and qualifications necessary for employment in their chosen field, it is well established in the literature that skills that promote employability are also required, and these may be areas where the gap can occur between graduates' skills and those required in the workplace (e.g., Lim, Lee, Yap, & Ling, 2016; Grapragasem, Krishnan, & Mansor, 2014).

Limited research and attention are available in the field about graduates who complete education offshore in Australian TNE programs. The research focus has previously been on labour market integration of graduates in Australia, but little attention has been provided to those who graduate in offshore countries. Of the limited number of studies available, one study of TNE in Singapore found that credentials primarily position graduates to enter the workforce, but transformative outcomes did arise for students from only having the credentials (Robertson, Hoare, & Harwood, 2011).

Employment and employability skills

The New Oxford Dictionary of English (2001) defines employment as the condition of having paid work. On the other hand, unemployment is viewed as an individual of a working age not having a job, and this is viewed as a serious social evil and at the same time as an important indicator of the economic health of a country. Graduates' lack of employment thus has serious implications in any country in which it occurs.

According to the Department of Statistics, Malaysia, (2016), the unemployment rate within the age group of 20- to 24-year-olds for graduates in Malaysia has risen from the 8.5 percentile in 2014 to the 9.3 percentile in 2015. The overall unemployment rate for 2015 is at the 3.1 percentile, while it was at the 2.9 percentile in 2014. Factors contributing to the above statistics include (i) an imbalance whereby supply exceeded demand; (ii) unrealistic expectations of graduates in terms of salary; and, according to the Graduate Employability Blueprint 2012–2017 released by the Ministry of Education in Malaysia, (iii) a lack of employability skills.

The literature makes a distinction between skills for employment and those for employability. Employment skills which are the credentials or academic qualifications required for particular jobs include technical skills. However, employability skills are broader, additional to and much more than qualifications and technical skills; they refer to the skills that will get graduates their jobs in the first place. Employability skills, also known as job readiness skills, include basic leadership skills, higher order thinking skills, and personal qualities (Robertson, Hoare, & Harwood, 2011). Key skills sought often by employers in graduates are critical thinking and problem-solving, as well as an appropriate attitude and proficiency in the English language. Authors such as Asma and Lim (2000) and Quek (2005) have noted that Malaysian graduates who lack tertiary training, communication skills, teamwork and interpersonal skills, and innovative and creative thinking are unlikely to find employment.

As a set of achievement skills, understandings, and personal attributes, Yorke (2006) explains that employability skills increase students' likelihood of gaining employment and being successful in their chosen occupations, with benefits arising for the students, the community, the workforce, and the national economy. Included in employability skills are what are termed transferable skills, such as personal and interpersonal skills, which are independent of the field of study. The value of these employability skills in current times is summed up by in Rafikul, Hamid and Manaf (n.d., p. 1) who write that "in the era of globalisation, employers are looking for versatile graduates who are able to drive their organisations to compete successfully in the market." Wilkinson (2017) elaborates further, pointing out that in preparedness for the workforce, graduates now require "the ability to self-promote and brand themselves, to work alone and as part of a globally distributed team, to take risks and remain resilient in the face of disappointments" (Wilkinson, 2017, p. 22).

A study by McQuaid and Lindsay (2005) that investigates the relationship between an unemployed person's employability and job search success pointed to a mismatch between the type of graduate produced by the institutions of higher learning and the requirements of industry. Hence, in a challenging economy, the role of higher education institutions is not only to produce graduates with specific disciplinary knowledge, but just as importantly, with employability skills which cut across all sectors of industry.

In Malaysia, employers have voiced concerns about graduate skills in relation to employment, and employers have stated that prospective graduate employees fail to meet employers' expectations in that they lack critical thinking skills and have poor communication and English language skills (Ministry of Education, Malaysia, 2015; *The Star*, 2012). Employers in Malaysia state that graduates require confidence in themselves and their abilities, and they note that in academic studies greater emphasis needs to be placed on team work and creativity in thinking rather than on information transfer and academic results (*The Star*, 2012). Cheong, Hill, Fernandez-Chung, and Leong (2016) explain from their study that graduates also require integrity and problem-solving skills.

The study and its design

The business degree program explored in this study is a twinning/franchise program between an Australian university that has operated since 1994 in Malaysia. Similar to most early forms of TNE, the syllabus and assessments were originally and continue to be fully managed by the university in Australia, with moderation being conducted for all assessments marked by the Malaysian college where the program is delivered. Teaching of the program is split between the university and the college, with the university lecturers flying in and out to teach in intensive mode. The underlying reason for such a form of collaboration is that the learning outcomes of the program remain equivalent, regardless of the site of delivery.

The study discussed in this chapter was undertaken by a quantitative research method. A structured questionnaire consisting of 17 questions was administered online to two cohorts of graduates (for the years 2014 and 2015) of the Australian degree offered in collaboration with the Malaysian University-College introduced earlier. Purposive sampling was used in this study as it allowed the research team to identify the participants who were most likely to provide detailed and relevant data (Oliver, 2011). Attempts were made to increase the response rate through active marketing of the survey on the alumni Facebook portal sites, through online newsletters, and through emails sent to alumni through email records managed by the college.

The aim of the questionnaire was to understand the employment outcomes of recent graduates, and their perspectives on how the Australian degree offered in Malaysia has prepared them for their work after graduation. The questionnaire consisted of three parts. The first part gathered information on the profile of the respondents and filtered suitable respondents by asking if they are currently in full-time work. Respondents who replied "No" to the question on full-time employment were directed to the end of the survey. The second part of the questionnaire consisted of questions that gathered information on the time taken for the graduates to find their current job, the profile of the job, the company, and the industry in which they worked. The last part of the survey consisted mainly of two key questions. The first question sought the participants' perspectives on the soft skills that they considered important in their current jobs. The soft skills that were listed on the survey were as follows: communication skills, people skills, ability to work independently, analytical skills, teamwork, problem-solving, organisational and management skills, English language skills, and cross-culture skills. Respondents were requested to rate the perspectives on a Likert scale from "very important" to "not required for my work." This question was followed by a question that sought the respondents' perception as to whether the Australian degree had prepared them sufficiently for their job. Respondents chose from the following selection as to whether the degree "gives a lot of training during my course of study," "insufficient coverage," or "nothing in my degree prepared me for the skill." The final question was open ended and asked respondents to indicate any soft skills they think are important for employment which were not listed on the questionnaire.

The graduates from the program from 2014 and 2015 were notified through email and invited to take part in the online survey. To improve the response rate, a lucky draw for five sets of gold-class movie tickets was provided to randomly selected participants who volunteered to give their email address. A total of 144 questionnaire responses was received when the survey was conducted in January 2016. This represents approximately 23% of the total number of 622 graduates in 2014 and 2015. Of these 144 responses, 141 were adequately answered and thus were analysed in this study.

Of the 144 responses, 84 respondents (58.3%) were female and 60 (41.7%) were male. The age group was highly skewed towards the representative age of full-time students in the Malaysian context; that is, those falling within the age range of 21 to 25 years old make up 93.3% (135) of the 144 responses. The group of students more than 30 years old was a minority, representing less than 3% of the respondents. Of the 141 completed responses, 43 (around 30%) indicated that they were not in full-time employment, leaving 98 of the participants to provide responses to the remaining questions. The percentage of unemployed respondents in this study is slightly lower than the industry average of 35.3% – this is the percentage of fresh graduates unemployed as reported by Leo (2016).

This chapter discusses the third part of the questionnaire. It examines from the perspectives of the graduates the nature of the soft skills that are, indeed, important and required for them to perform their work effectively. While many studies in the literature focus on employers' perceptions on the types of soft skills considered important or focus on graduates of public universities in Malaysia, few studies, if any, look at the relevance of transnational degree programs offered in Malaysia in terms of preparing graduates for their work in Malaysia.

Results of the study and discussion of the findings

Soft skills considered important

The graduates were asked to rate the importance of a number of soft skills in their current job as very important, somewhat important, important, not very important, and "is not required for my work." The findings from the respondents in terms of importance are summarised below:

Table 14.1 Soft skills considered important by Australian transnational graduates in Malaysia

	Number of responses for each skill set				
	Very important	Somewhat important	Important	Not very important	Is not required for my work
Communication skill	72	15	11	0	0
People skill	65	19	14	0	0
Ability to work independently	57	28	12	1	0
Analytical skill	59	23	15	1	0
Teamwork	57	18	21	2	0
Problem-solving skill	64	21	10	3	0
Organisational and project management skill	58	25	12	3	0
English skill	51	22	16	7	2
Cross-cultural skill	43	20	24	7	4

Table 14.1 presents the respondents' perceptions on what they considered as important soft skills needed for their current work. It is interesting to note the areas of convergence and divergence from the findings of other studies, particularly those that gathered data from the employers' perspectives, as we discuss in the section below.

In terms of importance, communication skill was given the highest level of importance by a large majority of the respondents: 72 out of the 98 respondents ranking it as very important. This is followed by people skill and problem-solving skill. These finding echo earlier studies that investigated the low employability rate of fresh graduates in Malaysia (Asma & Lim, 2000; Quek, 2005). This convergence in perceptions is particularly obvious in the top two soft skills rated as very important by the respondents – communication skill and people skill.

Communication skill has been widely recognised by employers in Malaysia as one of the critical skills they look for in fresh graduates, or the skill that is required at work. Recent studies that support the importance of communication skills for fresh graduates seeking employment include studies by Cheong et al. (2015) and Singh, Thambusamy, & Ramly (2013). Communication skills are a longstanding need, as seen in an earlier study of oral communication for graduates in the workforce in Australia (Crosling & Ward, 2002). Similarly, in this study, communication skills are the soft skill considered important by a large number of respondents (74%).

People skill received the second highest response rate perceived as important. People skills refer to the attributes and competencies that allow one to "play well" with others. It incorporates the elements of ability to communicate well with others and interpersonal skills. Specifically, the ability to communicate in "communication skills" is singled out as the most important soft skill in this study, as has been noted in a number of previous studies (e.g., Thiru & Ang, 2012; Ranjit, 2009). Studies by Thiru and Ang (2012) and Ranjit (2009) have reported similar perceptions of the importance of people skills by employers. According to Smith (2013), people skill is one of the most critical skills required for one to succeed at work.

Another prominent soft skill identified as important and commonly cited in other studies was problem-solving. In the National Graduate Employability Blueprint 2012–2017 by the Ministry of Higher Education (2012a) in Malaysia, the inability to solve problems was identified as one of the issues employers faced in hiring fresh graduates. The importance of problem-solving skill was echoed by the respondents in this study. More than 95% of the respondents have either rated this skill as very important, somewhat important, or important in the survey. The same skill, or the lack of it, was again raised in the Malaysia Education Blueprint 2013–2025 (Ministry of Higher Education, 2012b).

Difference in perspectives between graduates and employers

It is interesting to note that the study discussed in this chapter also revealed findings that point to some areas where the graduate respondents' opinions differ from those of employers as revealed in other studies. First, the data of this study pointed to an interesting difference in the importance of English language proficiency. While previous studies, such as that by Hanapi and Nordin (2013), indicated the lack of English proficiency as one of the key reasons for rejection for employment by the employers, the respondents in this study appeared not to place this soft skill as critically important (English skill is ranked the second-least important soft skill by the respondents). One possible explanation could be that most of the previous studies have been conducted with graduates from public universities in Malaysia, where English language is not necessarily the medium of instruction. Given that the graduates from the Australian degrees are required to meet a relatively high level of English proficiency before admission, and that the course was conducted in English, English language proficiency could be less of a concern to these cohorts of students in the study.

The study also revealed other soft skills considered important by the respondents in the work place. Some of these areas of importance and need have been uncovered in earlier studies on graduates' employability skills in Malaysia; they include the ability to work independently and organisation and project skills.

The study allowed the respondents to list other soft skills that they considered important when they started work but which were not mentioned in the survey, and it is interesting that some of these findings have received some coverage in the scholarly literature. One example is emotional intelligence, which was cited by at least two respondents who listed positive attitude and emotional intelligence in their responses. The other skills reported as important by the respondents include time management and being well-groomed. Indeed, the final two attributes above echo one of the reasons why graduates are rejected by employers in Malaysia; that is, the attribute of bad social etiquette (Salina, Nurazariah, Noraina, & Rajadurai, 2011).

Conversely and somewhat surprisingly, despite operating in an increasingly globalised workplace, cross-cultural skill is not seen as an important skill by the respondents. This is an important point to note because most Australian degrees emphasise the importance of preparing the graduates to be global citizens. It may be that the respondents in this study have assumed that cross-cultural skills are integral to life in multicultural Malaysia and thus not an issue of concern.

Soft skill where training is insufficient

If soft skills are considered important for and in employment, it is also logical to ask if the Australian degree provided sufficient training in these areas. Table 14.2 provides the findings gathered from the respondents regarding sufficiency of training in the soft skills that they perceive as required in their workplace.

The responses indicate two key points when they are considered in conjunction with the findings from Table 14.1. First, a soft skill could have been considered as important or very important by a majority of the study respondents, but the Australian degree could be lacking in providing the training, either through the content of the academic program, the assessment tasks, or the pedagogical approach utilised. This is most obvious for the topic of people skill. While people skill is ranked as the second soft skill perceived as important by most of the respondents, about 54% of the respondents perceived that there was not sufficient coverage of this skill or that no training was provided in their course to prepare them for this in the workplace. The implication is that the Australian university could improve the program design and delivery to better prepare their offshore graduates for the workplace with soft skills, such as people skills, cross-cultural skills, and even English language skills. As mentioned earlier, the perception of

Table 14.2 If there is enough soft skills training in the Australian degree

	Enough training during the course of study	Insufficient coverage	Missing in the course
Communication skill	62	32	4
People skill	45	45	8
Ability to work independently	55	38	5
Analytical skill	51	41	6
Teamwork	66	26	6
Problem-solving skill	56	37	5
Organisational and project management skill	57	37	4
English skill	48	43	7
Cross-cultural skill	44	41	13

the training concerning English is interesting; despite being taught in English, respondents have perceived that there was insufficient training in this area. Given the importance of English language competency in and for employment, further investigation would enable better understanding of this need from the perspectives of the graduates.

Second, there are some soft skills for which it seems that the Australian university has prepared the graduates well. The questionnaire results indicate that the Australian degree program has provided sufficient training in the skills of communication and teamwork. However, this outcome is not surprising, given that Australian business degrees more often than not emphasise the ability to communicate clearly (in writing and commonly through speaking in oral presentations) in the program learning outcomes and the related assessment tasks. Teamwork is a common form of assessment in a business degree, where students are required to work together with other students to complete an assignment. However, employers have held controversial perspectives on the importance of teamwork as a soft skill (Singh, Thambusamy, Ramly, Abdhullah, & Mahmud, 2013; Ngoo, Tiong, & Pok, 2015). Employers have, at times, demanded a leader rather than a follower or a team player.

Conclusions

The study discussed in this chapter was conducted from early to mid-2016 on graduates of an Australian TNE program delivered to students in Malaysia by a Malaysian institution. Although the number of participants in the study was not large, the survey respondents did constitute a representative sample of the graduates from two years of the degree. While there were slightly more female respondents compared to male, the difference was not significant, and the analysis did not indicate any particular gender biases. Hence, the findings reported here are specific to a particular group of graduates at a certain place and at a certain time, and while interesting and indicative, should be used with caution in generalising to other groups of graduates from other programs. Nevertheless, as stated above, the analyses of these participants' responses offer broad insights into what graduates in Malaysia perceive as important employability skills and indicate how well their undergraduate studies have prepared them in these skills.

The participants' responses also brought to the surface other important employability skills, such as emotional intelligence and time management, which were not addressed in this study. Studies on graduate employability in Malaysia also suggest the importance of other skills, such as proficiency in English, critical and creative thinking, and the ability to work with others (Asma & Lim, 2000; Quek, 2007; Cheong et al., 2016). What do all these soft skills mean in the context of a graduate being employed in their "first job" and in Malaysia? Again, more research into these areas will hone our understanding of graduate employability in Malaysia, but this study does provide us with the understanding that employers and graduates might differ in terms of their perceptions of important soft skills but agree on other areas.

Extending from the above points, what do these soft skills mean for Australian universities and their twinning programs with the objective of preparing their graduates as global employees and citizens? With TNE programs offered by Australian and other foreign institutions growing rapidly in number in Malaysia and elsewhere, globally, these questions and others warrant more studies on the types and extent of employability skills embedded in TNE curriculum and the level to which graduates are trained or prepared in such skills for employment. At a global level, the same question should be asked of TNE programs delivered in countries such as China, which has its TNE activities developing rapidly, at a rate unseen before.

Finally, the present study suggests further study is needed to ensure that institutions reconsider their curriculum design for the needs of transnational students as they prepare them with soft skills that are critical for their employment. To a larger extent, the issue of insufficient training in people skills and communication skills is common for transnational education students and international students who study on their home campuses. This suggests that, despite the opening up over several decades of the international market and internationalisation of the curriculum, the needs of non-English speaking learners might not be catered for in institutional degree offerings.

Part 4

Internationalisation at home and employability

Chapter 15

Collaborative Online International Learning (COIL)

Now preparing students for international virtual work

Jon Rubin

Introduction

This volume focusses on the relationship between university internationalisation and employability, and it is important to contextualise that topic within the shifting landscape of academia. Technology and the internet are changing the ways we teach, learn, research, and communicate, just as they have already dramatically affected the way that businesses operate. In some ways, the university is playing "catch-up," as higher education institutions (HEIs) are usually more adept at researching and discussing innovation than they are in implementing it.

Internationalisation is the term usually applied by the university to its outreach across national borders, traditionally through the physical mobility of its students and professors. More recently, the practice of internationalisation has expanded to include on-campus or near-campus activities that engender intercultural sensitivity and engagement. When organised as programs, they are often described as "internationalisation at home" or "internationalisation of the curriculum." In this chapter, I will mainly focus on the curricular aspects of internationalisation.

While many large universities collaborate internationally on research, few have significant experience with intensive collaborative networking in pedagogy. I will argue that there is an emerging need for networked international classrooms – virtual spaces where students and professors can share, teach, and learn together across national borders, thereby creating an authentic and interpersonally dynamic pathway to an international curriculum.

Standley (2015) states that, "International mobility placements enable students and staff in Higher Education to enhance transversal and employability-related skills." As argued by Jones (2016), "we need to prepare students effectively for future employment needs, which means operating in multicultural and multinational contexts, both locally and globally" (p. 108). Furthermore, many of the studies (see, for example, European Commission, 2014) and the broader discourse around this topic emphasise the role of learning abroad in the development of critical "soft skills." I will argue that the Collaborative Online International Learning (COIL) model described below not only supports students developing similar soft skills, but also provides actual training for students seeking employ-ment in the expanding virtual teams' marketplace.

I will base most of my comments on recent developments in networked education, as exemplified by the COIL model which I helped develop at the State University of New York, and which has been adopted by universities around the world. I will discuss the affordances of the COIL format and its practical application, and then will follow with a more detailed explication of how engaging COIL can aid students to prepare for international virtual work. However, first I will summarise some of the limitations of more traditional internationalisation formats.

The limits of physical mobility

Very few university students, and fewer instructors than one would like, will ever have the chance to blend study and research with travel. Overall, in the United States, only about 5% of all college students will participate in study abroad or student exchange during their college years (NAFSA, 2018). In Europe, the num-bers are slightly higher, around 10%, but in most of the rest of the world the figure is less than 1% (Association of American Colleges & Universities, 2018). So, what about the other 90–99% of the HEI student population who cannot participate in this form of mobility? We must help them to become more cross-culturally sensitive and better global citizens, especially in the current political climate.

Additionally, those who do travel are often the more privileged both in terms of their economic status and cultural capital, so one might argue that these sojourn-ers are the students who least need university internationalisation. Compounding the problem is a shifting demographic in many countries. For example, the aver-age age of a U.S. college undergraduate is now 24, with quite a few in their late 20s or 30s (National Center for Education Statistics, 2018). Many are married by this age and are holding down jobs, so cannot possibly undertake extensive travel abroad. For most students, physical mobility is either not an option or something that other students do.

In addition to the role that demographics or economics play in limiting who participates in physical mobility is the growing sense that it is dangerous to travel to all but a few "safe" destinations. This can be verified by the limited country choices that most students make when they choose to study abroad (NAFSA, 2018). This perception, therefore, severely limits the range of cultural experiences of those who do participate in physical mobility, and similarly tends to limit the geographic range of university partnerships developed for student study abroad and exchange (Rubin & Tippett, 2018).

Internationalisation of the curriculum

Curricular internationalisation is a response to the issue of relative low student mobility. Internationalisation of the curriculum is "the process of incorporat-ing international, intercultural and global dimensions into the content of the curriculum as well as the learning outcomes, assessment tasks, teaching methods and support services of a program of study" (Leask, 2015, p. 9). Its goal is to infuse the entire curriculum with affordances that will allow all students to have an opportunity to develop intercultural competence and transversal or soft skills. This will aid them to grow into global citizens and guide them as they seek employment in the global workforce. Because such interventions are often directly compared to physical mobility, this is a daunting task. How can a university transform what is typically a closed system, where most student needs are provided under one roof, and which must also be sustained by local or national funding, into a more diverse experience for its students? How can local classes and activities engender experiences comparable to visiting another country, travelling down unfamiliar and sometimes exotic pathways, and being able to socialise with peers far away?

Obviously, directly replicating most aspects of physical mobility is not the answer, so educators have developed an array of responses to this challenge. These include assigning multicultural texts and media in their teaching, engaging international students present on campus in meaningful classroom dialogue, working with the diverse communities that may exist near the university, and many other internationalising approaches that can be implemented locally.

But as such internationalisation-at-home strategies are being developed, the world is also changing, and technology is a big part of that change. While most higher education institutions superficially appear much as they did fifty years ago, many aspects of their daily activities have been transformed. Whether we look outside the classroom to recruitment activities and admissions processes which are now typically driven through the university's online presence, or inside the classroom to the expanded use of learning management systems, smart classrooms, and online learning programs, technology is changing the way HEIs function.

What is COIL (Collaborative Online International Learning)?

COIL courses (often called "COIL-enhanced modules") are embedded in the curriculum, so they are available to students as part of their regular university program. Every COIL-enhanced module links at least two classes in two different countries so that students work together on academic projects and get to know each other at the same time. As a form of experiential learning, it is attractive to many students; once they have taken a COIL course, students often ask to take more. At the same time, as discussed in Rubin (2017),

> COIL is not a technology or a platform, but rather a new teaching and learning paradigm that develops cross-cultural awareness across shared multi-cultural learning environments. Unlike more typical online distance courses provided by one higher education institution to students nearby or

around the world, COIL is based upon developing team-taught learning environments where teachers from two cultures work together to develop a shared syllabus, leading to experiential and collaborative student learning. The courses give new contextual meaning to the ideas and texts they explore, while providing students new venues in which to develop their cross-cultural awareness. Classes may be fully online or more often are offered in blended formats with traditional face-to-face sessions taking place at both institutions, while collaborative student work takes place online. (pp. 33–34)

The COIL model takes advantage of internet technology to authentically engage other cultures from within the local classroom, providing a unique approach to internationalising the curriculum. It offers an innovative pathway for students and instructors to interact with the world that was not possible in the past. By utilising rapidly expanding internet connectivity and increasingly widely available and less expensive technology, it has become possible for classrooms to be networked with those in faraway countries, even where physical mobility is limited.

But without proper guidance and structure, many people utilise the internet only to interact with those like themselves. There is some research that confirms the bubble which encloses most of us when we are online. (Filter Bubble, 2018). COIL is an attempt to use the university classroom setting as a vehicle for connecting and interrogating these cultural and social bubbles for the benefit of students.

This model has been developing organically over the past twenty years, often driven by inspired teachers working with colleagues abroad, until recently often without significant university support. However, in the past five years we have seen a dramatic shift, as senior international officers and other campus leaders at many higher education institutions are taking the lead to launch COIL initiatives.

Collaborative online international learning is an inherently networked model of education as COIL courses cannot exist on a single campus – they require an international partner. This differentiates them structurally from many other curricular internationalisation approaches. Developing a COIL course means engaging another institution, working with international professors and lecturers, and sharing the local classroom with another group of students far away. It also means understanding other approaches to teaching and learning and being responsive to them. It is at heart a bi-lateral engagement, a two-way street, enabled by technology, but ultimately focused on enhancing human interaction across cultures.

This means that COIL is not a single template, one-size fits all model. As discussed in Rubin and Guth (2015), it is a framework which must be adapted to specific courses, disciplines, and cross-national partnerships:

For example, some classes make intensive use of video conferencing, while others have little real-time interaction or use simpler synchronous technologies like text chat. Most focus primarily on asynchronous tools developed for conventional distance learning courses, such as discussion forums, and use synchronous tools, like Skype, more occasionally to build community. But the selection of appropriate tools depends on the partners, the language skills of the students, the time zones where the schools are based, the technology that each school has available and many other factors. Occasionally, course work takes place on smart phones, in situations where students lack access to computers. The collaborations can last an entire semester – but more often they last 5–7 weeks. Shorter engagements are problematic because it takes time for students to develop trust, and thereby become comfortable engaging one another.

Cooperating teachers work closely with all students, but in most cases these students are enrolled, charged tuition (if there is any), and are awarded grades only at their home institution. This revenue-neutral model reduces the administrative complexity of bi-lateral institutional agreements, while linking and enhancing international classrooms through collaborative coursework. These courses do not require expensive technology, and they also work effectively as portals to increase student interest in mobility for students who have the time and resources to travel (p. 18).

COIL also directly engages innovative instructors and instructional designers in the exchange process as they participate in developing joint COIL-enhanced courses. For that reason, COIL is also a powerful method for internationalising teachers and staff. COIL courses have been mounted in most academic disciplines and have become increasingly interdisciplinary in nature. They are also well suited to institutions that primarily serve less well-resourced students, such as community colleges in the United States, as there is usually no additional cost for student participation.

COIL methodology and virtual teams

Many students will likely have careers in which they must work with other nationalities or with clients or partners in other countries, often at a distance or as part of virtual teams. Esbin (2017) projects that "by 2020, more than 1.3 billion people will work remotely. Many will find themselves on virtual project teams, which will generally be cross-functional, cross-cultural and cross-generational in makeup." Jones (2008) offers a further definition of a virtual team: "An inter-dependent group of individuals who predominantly use technology to communicate, collaborate, share information and coordinate their efforts in order to accomplish a common work-related objective." The problem is that very few institutions teach the skills needed to be successful as a member or leader of a virtual team. This is in part because few institutions practice COIL or any form of networked education.

While the COIL model was not designed specifically to meet this demand, there are many parallels between the activities, processes, and potential pitfalls of COIL course implementation, and the typical dynamics and activities of virtual teams, such that almost any COIL course could be utilised as appropriate training for participating in or leading a successful virtual team. However, an academic COIL course does not have the same drivers as do most virtual teams, which are usually set in corporate contexts, so we must also acknowledge where the two models sometimes diverge.

More broadly, in most traditional university classes, students respond to the content and issues put forward to them, but their local knowledge is often not sought out, nor can they easily discuss their cultural perspective regarding the topics at hand, because few courses see intercultural exchange or team building as a goal or learning objective. Therefore, most courses, even those that are online and reach beyond national borders, do not serve to deeply connect the world, any more than does television, even when students from many countries are enrolled. The COIL model is all about understanding the perspective of those with whom one studies and works collaboratively, so it can also set the stage for working in international virtual teams.

Convergences

Designing and implementing a COIL course and constructing and managing a virtual team present many of the same opportunities and challenges. The following section examines a few salient and shared issues in order to understand how participating in a COIL course can provide preparation for working in virtual teams.

Collaboration and group work

Ferrazzi (2012), writing in the Harvard Business Review observes, "There's a world of difference between merely working together and truly collaborating with one another. Collaborative activity is the 'secret sauce' that enables teams to come up with innovative new products or creative, buzz-worthy marketing campaigns."

The "C" in COIL stands for collaboration. To develop meaningful intercultural experiences for groups of students physically far apart, it is critical that they engage each other at a deep level. Simply being in the same online classroom sharing common course material is not enough. One way to develop insight and community with others is to work collaboratively on projects. In COIL-enhanced modules this is most often done through group teamwork, where, for example, two students from each classroom join with their peers far away to undertake a research project, culminating in the submission of a co-written paper. Alternatively, two teams may co-produce a photo essay on a common topic, reflecting on each other's choices as the project develops, and later presenting their final project to students in both classrooms.

For many students and professionals, working in groups poses challenges. In order to be successful, there needs to be adequate structure and a commitment to shared responsibility so that all participants have a designated role, while providing room for innovation and creative process to take place. And while virtual teams typically construct their working groups somewhat differently from a COIL course where bi-lateral intercultural exchanges are foundational, both demand the production of an actual collaborative result which can be assessed. This makes participation in COIL an excellent rehearsal for virtual team collaboration.

Developing rapport and trust

One of the potentially painful deficits of working online can be the lack of informal, casual, and chance social interactions that are so typical of face-to-face environments. According to Esbin (2016), this creates a major challenge which "stems from lack of trust between employees who are essentially 'virtual strangers'. This is despite the fact they may work for the same organisation, share common goals, and be members of the same virtual team" (p. 314). Face-to-face environments and water-cooler, elevator/hallway, and lunchroom encounters, allow student and workplace colleagues to get to know each and to gradually develop rapport. Here the conversation may be more personal than would be appropriate in the office or classroom, or it may provide a chance to let off steam or complain on neutral ground about what is going down in those same environments. Through these social interchanges, one lays the groundwork for developing trust in others, or alternatively deciding from whom one may want to keep some distance.

In a project that included both local and remote participants, Armstrong and Cole (2002) give an example of how a lack of personal contact can yield a negative result:

> A post-mortem analysis of one cancelled international project zeroed in on the lack of casual connections: "There was no day-to-day coffee machine conversation, which was needed to make it succeed." Remote group members felt cut off from the key conversations, over lunch or in the hall, that often-followed videoconferences. (p. 170)

For teachers developing a COIL course and for virtual team leaders laying out a project, there is the same tendency to expect that their students or team members should get right down to work as soon as they have been onboarded. When first introduced, these individuals often know little or nothing about each other, and typical formal introductions, such as providing their names, positions, classes or home locations, is only a minimal starting point. It is critical that space be provided for the students or team members to get to know each other before they are expected to work together productively.

This can be accomplished through many techniques, each of which must be tweaked to fit the specific cultural and course or work environment. First, it is often a good idea for all students or virtual team members to create profiles visible to all, where they are asked to include some of their personal interests, something about their family and home, and possibly their thoughts about being part of the project/class. Not all of these are appropriate in every case. Often it makes sense to request a photo, but this need not be a head shot. It can simply be an image that each prefers, or which each feels represents them.

An "ice breaker" is the general term for the introductory techniques which may follow. These can be structured as large group activities but are more often undertaken by pairs or in small groups. For example, each student/team member can be asked to contact another by Skype (or with a similar online tool) to introduce themselves and interview their colleague. They then share with the group what they learned about the person they interviewed. In this way they all have a chance to interact outside of the larger group environment and to share some information with all. It is also important for the teacher or leader to suggest norms or limits so that the discussion not become too personal too quickly.

Getting to know someone from another culture, whom one has never met, and with whom one typically shares no prior friends, may be a new experience for many. While this struggle to connect personally may seem far away from the technology that links participants, it is of the essence of both a successful COIL class engagement and of becoming comfortable working in a virtual team environment.

Engaging technology

There is a tendency to assume that everyone under 30 or even 40 years old is a "digital native" and will almost instantaneously become comfortable with whatever online technology they are provided. This is rarely the case, and when launching a COIL course or initiating a virtual team project it is critical to provide time for all participants to become familiar with the tools they will use. Furthermore, because these tools will often be used in group work, without the concurrent presence of the teacher or leader, they need to be explored in the context of group work – not simply by asking everyone to open the software and look around.

One way to do this is to begin using a new technology for the ice breaker activity, perhaps followed by another small project, which takes advantage of a second tool in the course/project toolbox. As new tools are emerging all the time, it may be interesting to ask class/team members to suggest software they think would aid them in their project work, as this active participation will engage them further into the project. Of course, opening the toolbox has some risks, as it raises the question of who will support a new tool proposed from the group should that tool become troublesome if adopted?

No matter how one manages the technology, it is critical to give everyone time to become comfortable with the tools. The assumption that all are "good to go" from day one may sink a COIL course or a virtual team project. Going through such exploratory processes in the networked classroom prepares those students for similar challenges in virtual teams.

Time zones and communication modalities

There are many communication modalities that can be utilised in COIL-enhanced modules and virtual team projects. The content and learning objectives of the course/project may partially determine which of these modalities are most propitious, but the geographical location of the participants may also drive these decisions. For example, if a COIL course is offered between a university in Western Europe and one in South Africa, despite their great physical distance, both are in the same time zone, making synchronous communication (audio and video conferencing, texting, etc.) logistically comfortable. However, if a virtual team includes team members from New York, London, and Shanghai, synchronous communication will need to be scheduled for participants living in three disparate time zones. To have a group meeting may mean the New Yorker will need to be available at 7 a.m., the Londoner at 2 p.m. and the team member in Shanghai at 7 p.m. Such potentially complex scheduling similarly influences group dynamics in COIL courses and virtual teams, so navigating this in the networked classroom is direct training for the complexities of the online workplace.

The choice of communication modality extends beyond the scheduling of synchronous meetings to the comfort level of all participants conversing in the chosen lingua franca of the course/project. While most virtual team projects and many COIL courses are managed in English, the level of English spoken may vary widely among individual team members. In the case of some COIL class groups, English may be the second or third language of all students, so great care must be taken that their level of fluency is respected. For that reason, it may in some cases, be best to avoid face-to-face videoconferencing between classes, as this modality may be stressful to some members of the group. In this situation it may be preferable to shift much of the exchange and project work to an asynchronous mode, where the participants less fluent in English have more time to translate and interpret complex information.

While such a situation is somewhat less likely in a virtual team, where a level of lingua franca fluency is more likely a prerequisite, there will still almost certainly be different "Englishes" spoken by different team members. These variants can occasionally be misunderstood by some team members who are not familiar with a specific usage or accent. Such unfamiliar or less fluent speech can also sometimes lead to a fundamental attribution error, where fluent speakers falsely assume that others are less competent or capable, simply because their use of English is different than theirs. Garton and Wegryn (2006) make a similar observation:

> The extent to which your associates understand English might vary widely. Some might be able to read and write in English exceptionally well but might not have mastered the spoken word. Do not assume that because you understand each other well in email, you will also do so in person. Some people might be shy about speaking, as they are nervous about making a mistake. You might

find that the quietest person in a group understands and can speak English better than the others. That person is just embarrassed and afraid to speak. (p. 123)

Needing to get past this type of misjudgment is also an important aspect of COIL
courses, thereby readying such students for work in linguistically complex virtual teams.

Flexibility and adaptability

It has been remarked that Charles Darwin said, "It is not the strongest of the spe-
cies that survives, nor the most intelligent that survives. It is the one that is the
most adaptable to change." In traditional face-to-face team meetings and university classes, stable physical surroundings provide a consistent technological and
work environment. At the same time, the relatively easy scheduling of solely local
participants supports group concurrence in time; when requested, everyone can
generally be expected to be in the same place at the same time. Bad weather or
the illness of a team member may occasionally disrupt that continuity, but this
is the exception, not the rule. Additionally, local meetings may or may not bring
together a relatively homogeneous group of participants, but even when the class
or team is more diverse, they are likely to have acquired a strong sense of common cultural norms by residing in or near their university or business setting.

In contrast, COIL classrooms and virtual teams are composed of students and
team members from different cultures, who are physically dispersed, and who
are also based in different institutional settings. This means their expectations
when beginning their course or project are likely to be very different, so mis-
understandings are more likely. In addition, participants must communicate
with each other through technology that provides fewer interpersonal cues than
does a face-to-face setting, and all too often that technology does not function as
expected. In some COIL courses the internet connectivity at partner institutions
is intermittent, requiring the regular scheduling of back-up plans and meetings.

This means that as one gains greater cultural diversity through networked education and virtual teams, one must at the same time be clear to everyone involved
that they must be flexible and adaptable, so they can respond to the unexpected –
whether it be technological bumps or unexpected responses to requests and communications. It is through navigating these variables that participants gain
greater understanding of each other, of themselves, and of the online work environment, preparing COIL experienced students for virtual teams.

Education and the workplace: different drivers
for different outcomes

This chapter examines some of the areas where COIL courses tread similar
ground to virtual teams, thereby providing informal training for emerging
online career opportunities. In some cases, COIL courses have been formally

organised to perform as actual virtual teams, so the congruence and training model is then even more closely aligned.[1] However, COIL courses exist within a higher education context, and are usually designed and managed by two professors from different cultures who have worked together to create a joint curriculum that must be gradable, and which provides college credit to their enrolled students. Because the participants are students, the work they are assigned must be somewhat process oriented, allowing different students to learn what they can from the class projects and intercultural interactions. And because COIL modules usually run between five and seven weeks, their lifespans are shorter than those of many virtual teams.

On the other hand, virtual teams are usually managed by a single project leader, within a corporate context, where the desired outcome is defined from the outset and is not determined based on its benefit to participants. Furthermore, because virtual team members are employees, they can be expected to follow directions in ways that may not be appropriate with university students. So, while many of the developmental pathways of the two practices align remarkably well, their contexts are not identical. For this reason, while COIL-enhanced modules are a good introduction to online group work in virtual teams, their broader manifestations and anticipated outcomes must also be contextual to the educational institutions which support them.

Note

1. The course "Experience International Teamwork," was designed by instructor Eva Haug at Amsterdam University of the Applied Sciences. Summarised course description: "students work in COIL projects, organised into virtual teams, coached by their respective lecturers, thereby getting hands-on experience in virtual collaboration. The focus of the course and the learning outcomes is on developing the skills necessary to work in diverse (as in international) and remote teams. Her class COILed with Drexel University and Ulster Community College in the U.S. (2017–18).

Chapter 16

Employability skills as guiding principles for internationalising home curricula

Jos Beelen

The relevance of an internationalised home curriculum for all students is generally acknowledged. Other than study abroad, the home curriculum gives programs of study full control over the way students learn international, intercultural, and interdisciplinary perspectives. However, misconceptions, lack of strategies, lack of skills of academics, and lack of connection between stakeholders present major obstacles to internationalising teaching and learning "at home" (see Beelen, 2016, 2017a; Beelen & Jones, 2018).

The practical trajectory outlined in this chapter presents programs of study with the opportunity to focus on employability skills instead of on a semantic discussion on internationalisation. By linking this orientation on employability skills with the articulation of intended learning outcomes (ILOs), a pathway for developing employability skills in all students will be created. Within this pathway, international, intercultural, interdisciplinary, and future-focused dimensions serve to enhance students' acquiring employability skills.

The trajectory presented here evolved out of action research on internationalisation with academics. During the action research, taking employability skills as a starting point emerged as an enabler for the internationalisation process. It helped to overcome lengthy and semantic discussions on the meaning of internationalisation. After that, international and intercultural dimensions are included in these employability skills. These skills are then translated into ILOs.

Similar action research in Australia had resulted in the process model of internationalisation of the curriculum by Leask (2012, 2015). Action research in the Netherlands resulted in an adaptation by Beelen (2017a). The Dutch research took place in business studies at two universities of applied sciences. Subsequent action research in a range of disciplines at a third Dutch university of applied sciences and in Belgium and Norway suggests that this approach can be applied in other disciplines and other countries as well.

Early stages

In 2011, The Amsterdam University of Applied Sciences made internationalisation at home the focus of its internationalisation policies. After a few sessions in which we explained the concept of internationalisation at home to lecturers, we quickly concluded that such sessions were hardly effective. Lecturers grasped the concept well enough but struggled to implement internationalisation at home in their programs once they had returned to their departments.

We, therefore, initiated the practice of following up general internationalisation-at-home sessions with individual coaching sessions. The lecturers were approached as the specialists in the discipline and asked a range of questions by the facilitator, a disciplinary outsider. Because of this focus on questions, the title of the publication that grew out of this early stage was "Socrates in the Low Countries" (De Wit & Beelen, 2012).

The developments in Amsterdam ran parallel with those at Australian universities, where Betty Leask developed her framework and process model for internationalisation (Leask, 2012). During her National Teaching Fellowship, she facilitated workshops with lecturers in a range of disciplines and found that the disciplinary context was an essential element of internationalising curricula (see Leask & Bridge, 2013). Over the next few years the Dutch and Australian approaches developed in tandem. This process involved other researchers, notably Wendy Green and Craig Whitsed, who also followed a discipline-based approach for their publication on critical perspectives on internationalisation of the curriculum (2015) and attempted to bring to the fore the voices of academics as the key protagonists of curriculum internationalisation.

While the action research in Amsterdam bore similarities to the "imagination phase" described by Leask (2012, 2015) and the "disciplinary spaces" described by Green and Whitsed (2013, 2015), there were also differences. For example, the Questionnaire on Internationalisation of the Curriculum (QIC), that formed an element of the action research by Leask, was not effective in the Dutch context, also not when it was translated. One reason for this was that the QIC does not include the issue of English language proficiency, which emerged as a key topic for Dutch lecturers and for those teaching in Dutch medium programs.

Researching obstacles and enablers

The type of action research discussed above was further developed during a doctoral study that I undertook at the Centre of Higher Education Internationalisation (CHEI) in Milan between 2012 and 2016 (Beelen, 2017a). The study focused on international and domestic (i.e., delivered in Dutch) business programs at two Dutch universities of applied sciences. The aim of the study was to identify obstacles and enablers to the process of internationalising intended learning outcomes. While the primary research participants were lecturers, other stakeholders, such as international officers, were involved, too.

When I initiated the study in 2012, internationalisation of intended learning outcomes was gaining momentum. The 4th Global Survey concluded that internationalised learning outcomes were "booming" (Egron-Polak & Hudson, 2014, p. 106). However, this boom related mostly to institutional learning outcomes, rather than to learning outcomes at program and module levels, which can be assessed as part of student learning. In Europe, thinking about internationalised intended learning outcomes as indicators of the quality of internationalisation culminated in the introduction of the Certificate of Quality in Internationalisation (CeQuInt) in 2015 (see Aerden, 2015).

Employability studies

In addition to my own research on the implementation of internationalised learning outcomes, there has been a proliferation of other related studies on this topic. Some of these studies had been conducted in the European context, such as the study by Humburg, Van der Velden, and Verhagen (2013) and the Erasmus Impact Study (European Commission, 2014). Others focus on individual national contexts, such as Finland (Centre for International Mobility, 2014), Australia (Lilley, 2014) and the Netherlands (The Netherlands Association of Universities of Applied Sciences, 2014). Other studies examined how individual universities' approach to implementing internationalised learning outcomes (e.g., Funk, Den Heijer, Schuurmans-Brouwer, & Walenkamp, 2014) or focused on the distinct approaches adopted by six Dutch universities of applied sciences in the Netherlands when internationalising the same program (e.g., Kostelijk, Coelen, & de Wit, 2015).

Not only were the contexts of these employability studies quite diverse, their perspectives also differed considerably. The study by The Netherlands Association of Universities of Applied Sciences does not connect the acquisition of employability skills to internationalisation of teaching and learning. This may be attributed to the fact that the study was mainly conducted from the perspective of employers within the Dutch labour market.

On the other hand, the studies by the Centre for International Mobility (2014) and the Erasmus Impact Study (European Commission, 2014) focused on the perceptions of both employers and mobile students. These two studies establish a positive correlation between international student mobility and the acquisition of employability skills but do not address how the home curriculum can facilitate non-mobile students to learn the skills that the mobile minority may acquire abroad (Jones, 2011, pp. 22–23. This question remains valid, as up until now only a few and small-scale studies (e.g., Soria & Troisi, 2014; Watkins & Smith, 2018) have explored how students develop international skills at home.

How employability skills levered the internationalisation process

For action research into the internationalisation of learning outcomes in this study, the employability studies proved an important focal point. Introducing a range of employability skills into the early stages of action research with lecturers turned out to be a key enabler. Discussing employability skills proved a more productive starting point than discussing the concept, meaning, value, or semantics of internationalisation (at home) and trying to contextualise the concept to the program. However, the research led to the identification of other obstacles and enablers. Some of these had been known before, while others had not been identified yet, or had only been known in general terms. These obstacles and enablers are described below.

Obstacles and enablers to internationalising home curricula

The PhD study resulted in the identification of a range of obstacles and enablers to internationalising home curricula. These could be organised into four categories: external, disciplinary, internal, and personal. External obstacles are beyond the control of universities and can be related to global or national developments, educational systems, or legal restrictions. The discipline itself and its traditions in research, teaching, and learning constitute disciplinary obstacles and enablers. Internal obstacles are found within universities, faculties, and programs of study. Finally, personal obstacles are related to the skills of individual stakeholders in the process of internationalising learning outcomes.

Subsequent action research (see Beelen, 2017b) at other universities led to the identification of more obstacles and enablers. These are included in the discussion below, insofar as they are relevant to the articulation of internationalised learning outcomes that facilitate the development of employability skills.

External obstacles and enablers

Among the most persistent obstacles to internationalising the home curriculum are misconceptions about the character of internationalisation at home. Many participants in the action research remarked that the original definition of internationalisation at home (Crowther et al., 2001, p. 8) did not offer them much guidance. A key outcome of this study was the development of a new definition: "internationalisation at home is the purposeful integration of international and intercultural dimensions into the formal and informal curriculum for all students within domestic learning environments" (Beelen & Jones, 2015, p. 76; see also Beelen & Jones, 2018).

However, publishing a definition will not end misconceptions. The Swedish government published an Inquiry (Swedish Government Inquiries, 2018) as the basis for a new national policy for internationalisation. While the Inquiry acknowledges the importance of internationalisation at home, and even quotes the definition, it still considers it as an alternative for those students that do not study abroad. The same is true for the joint agenda on internationalisation of the Dutch university associations (Vereniging Hogescholen & Vereniging van Samenwerkende Nederlandse Universiteiten, 2018), which form an important component of the policies of the Ministry of Education, Science and Culture.

Considering internationalisation of the curriculum an alternative for mobility tends to limit internationalised teaching and learning to one semester, the standard period that some students spend abroad. Rather, the full duration of the curriculum for all students should be used as a vehicle to incorporate international and intercultural dimensions, which enhance the acquisition of employability skills.

Disciplinary obstacles and enablers

Business and management programs, both English and Dutch medium, focused more strongly on intercultural communication than on internationalisation. The tendency to consider internationalisation as equivalent to intercultural communication has been observed before in the business discipline (see Green & Whitsed, 2015, p. 13). In my study, English medium programs developed intercultural communication skills in stand-alone modules, while Dutch medium programs attempted to develop these skills in conjunction with training for foreign language proficiency. In both cases, intercultural communication skills tended to be developed outside the business discipline, and therefore more as personal than as professional skills. The research, therefore, confirmed Green & Whitsed's observation.

Internal obstacles and enablers

Internal obstacles and enablers can be distinguished at several levels: institution, faculty, and department/program. Misconceptions around internationalisation at home were encountered at all levels, but were most prevalent at program level, where teaching, learning, and assessment are designed.

Institutional level

At institutional level, strategies to support internationalisation-at-home policies were found lacking in most universities. In the Netherlands, Van Gaalen and Gielesen (2016, p. 54) found that few universities have strategies to support their institutional policy for internationalisation at home. There was also little evidence of universities monitoring internationalisation activities within programs of study. This is to some extent due to the particular nature of internationalisation at home, which can only be shaped in the disciplinary context of a program of study and, therefore, from the bottom up.

A key obstacle was the lack of institutional strategies for offering training or professional development in internationalisation of the home curriculum. While some universities offer training for teaching in an international classroom, there was generally no training for redesigning curricula with an aim to integrate international and intercultural dimensions.

A related obstacle was the lack of connection between key stakeholders in the internationalisation of teaching and learning, notably between specialists in didactics and educational developers on the one hand and in internationalisation experts on the other. Since the internationalisation of teaching and learning needs stakeholders in both fields, it is of paramount importance that expertise in both these fields is identified and combined. Action research brought to light that educational support of programs of study is organised very differently across universities, even within the same country. In some cases, educational developers were part of a teaching and learning centre at central level. In other cases, they were primarily assigned to faculties or to individual programs of study. In yet other cases no apparent infrastructure for educational development could be found at all. This confirms Carroll's view that institutions demonstrate a considerable variety in "curriculum design culture" (Carroll, 2015, pp. 102–103). This lack of connection between specialists in education and in internationalisation was found even when educational support was directly linked to a program of study.

The divide between the "silos" of education and internationalisation is demonstrated by critical voices on Dutch education's focus on employability skills; for example, Meester, Bergsen, and Kirschner (2017), who stress the importance of knowledge. They do this from an educational perspective without reference to the role of internationalisation in acquiring employability skills. This shows yet again that there are two parallel discourses on employability skills: one from the perspective of internationalisation and the other from the perspective of education.

The action research showed that faculties (as organisational units) presented an obstacle rather than an enabler to the process of curriculum internationalisation. They did not effectively transmit institutional views down to the programs of study, or operationalise them. The faculties' internationalisation plans did not offer much guidance since programs within faculties tend to be diverse enough to require very different contextualisations of internationalisation. Faculties did not offer opportunities for professional development for internationalisation either. In contrast, international officers in faculties were found to be key enablers since they understood the concept of internationalisation at home and had resources to work with lecturers in individual programs. However, their contributions were not systemic because they only had the opportunity to work with a few champions and the process was not supported by educational developers.

Program level

At program level, a key obstacle was the lack of specific and detailed input from employers, as members of a program advisory board, on employability skills. While competencies had been discussed in general terms with these boards, employability skills and learning outcomes had not. A systemic obstacle was that lecturers were, generally, not included in opportunities to meet the advisory boards.

Another obstacle within programs was the lack of consistent intended learning outcomes (ILOs) that related to the added value of study abroad. During the action research, we initially looked if intended learning outcomes for internationalisation abroad (i.e., study or internship) could serve as a starting point for the discussion on learning outcomes for internationalisation at home. After all, it can be argued that if study abroad is considered an additional experience for some students, the outcomes of the home curriculum constitute the standard that all students should achieve. However, when we tried to determine how the added value of study abroad was described, we found that the learning outcomes were hardly related to professional skills. Instead, such learning outcomes for study abroad as there were focused on the development of personal skills. This was maybe to be expected in programs with an optional study abroad component, but it applied equally to international programs with compulsory study abroad.

This obstacle also raises the question as to what extent mobile students acquire employability skills purposefully; that is, through a guided trajectory that includes intended learning outcomes and assessment of the added value (beyond credits for disciplinary content). In other words, to what extent is the acquisition of these skills planned and purposeful?

It has been previously demonstrated that mobile students belong to a "cultural elite" (Saarikallio-Torp, & Wiers-Jenssen, 2010; King, Findlay, & Arens, 2010) with a mind-set that encourages them to go abroad. While studies such as the Erasmus Impact Study indicate that students demonstrate a range of transversal skills after their return, it may be possible that they had these skills before they left.

Another reason why outgoing mobility is not the most effective tool to acquire employability skills is that it reaches only a minority of students. Statistics Netherlands (2018) published data on credit mobility of Dutch students which show that, on average, 22% of students go abroad for study or internship of at least 15 credits. The respondents' main reasons for not going abroad are "too expensive" and "other obligations."

It can be argued that the home curriculum is a far better vehicle for the development of employability skills than study abroad, since the home curriculum extends over several years (as opposed to the usual six months or less for study abroad) and the home institution has control over the educational process, including intended learning outcomes and their assessment. It also allows for employability skills to be developed in the framework of disciplinary competencies rather than as personal attributes that are detached from the content of the program.

Personal obstacles and enablers

The PhD research was conducted within universities of applied sciences in which internships are an important component of study programs. Even lecturers who were involved in the supervision of internships had not previously reflected on the outcomes of a program of study in terms of employability skills.

However, they were quite familiar with the concepts of graduate competencies (competence-based education was gradually introduced in Dutch universities of applied sciences from the mid-1990s). Lecturers were also familiar with the term "employability," as they were with the terms "soft skills" and "21st-century skills"; however, there was a tendency to equate these terms with intercultural communication skills. The term "employability skills" was valued quite differently by lecturers across disciplines in universities of applied sciences, with business programs having a more positive association with the term than, for example programs in social work.

Contextualising broader concepts to the program of studies

In all disciplines, lecturers struggled with contextualising broader concepts to the program of studies. This certainly applied to the concept of internationalisation. Lecturers frequently remarked that their managers should be involved in the work so that they would "also understand what internationalisation really means." Lecturers also expected that enhanced understanding of internationalisation would lead to managers being more involved and giving better direction to the process of curriculum internationalisation. The struggle with concepts was not limited to internationalisation but also occurred in relation to global citizenship, ethical responsibility, and other overarching concepts.

The action research on *internationalising* learning outcomes demonstrated a lack of experience in articulating learning outcomes in general. Even those lecturers who had followed the compulsory Basic Teaching Qualification Programme struggled to "craft" or rephrase intended learning outcomes and determine appropriate assessment.

It is here that we touch upon what actually constitutes the lack of skills and expertise that the Global Surveys consistently identify as one of the key obstacles to internationalisation (see Egron-Polak & Hudson, 2014, p. 68) but does not "unpack" beyond teaching in English. The action research demonstrated that this lack of skills has two components: "imagining" internationalisation and educational competencies for designing education. Both of these components are included in the conceptual model that is presented below.

Conceptual model

The PhD study led to an adaptation of the process model by Leask (2012). In the revised version (see Figure 16.1), the discussion on employability skills forms the beginning of the imagination phase, which concludes with the articulation of internationalised ILOs. This differs slightly from Leask's model, as this has been moved forward from "revise and plan" to "imagination." This adaptation establishes a direct alignment between employability skills and ILOs and makes lecturers the key actors in articulating ILOs, thus increasing their sense of ownership of learning outcomes.

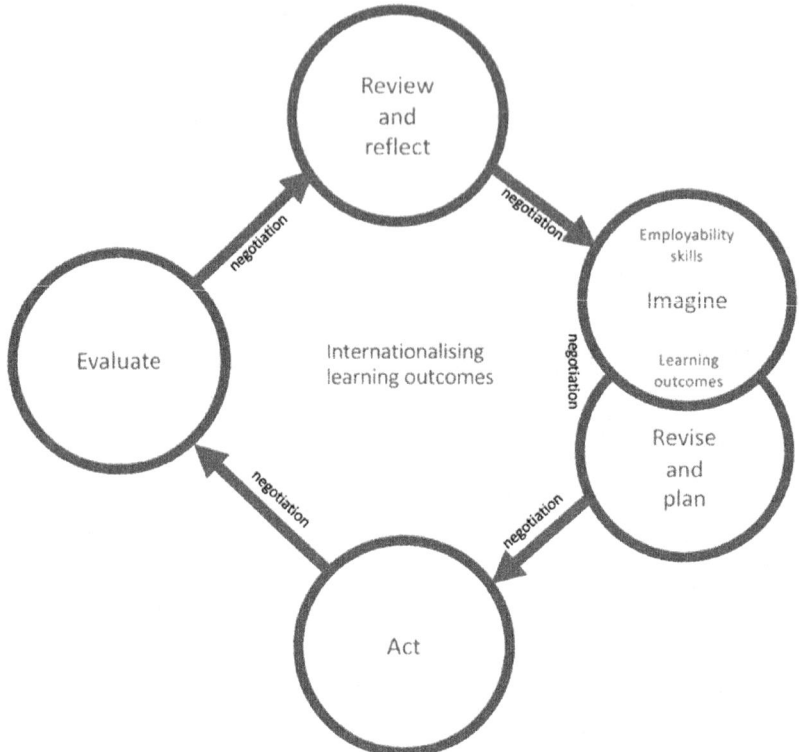

Figure 16.1 The process model by Leask (2012) adapted for Dutch universities of applied sciences (Beelen, 2017a, p. 229, Fig. 10.1).

Source: Adapted with permission Beelen (2017a, p. 229, Fig. 10.1).

This adaptation was made specifically for the context of business programs at Dutch universities of applied sciences but has since proved applicable in other contexts and disciplines.

Towards a guided trajectory for the implementation of employability skills

Building on the outcomes of the PhD study, the action research was subsequently extended to other universities of applied sciences in the Netherlands, Belgium, and Norway. In each of these universities, teams from a range of disciplines were involved, varying from engineering and information technology to social work. The trajectories were designed to last 8–10 months, with four to five full-day work sessions, alternating with Skype sessions in which the participants received feedback on learning outcomes, initially at program level and later at module level.

Going through the trajectories simultaneously with a number of teams (usually four to seven) from different disciplines was considered meaningful by the lecturers, who enjoyed comparing the work of the teams during the work sessions. Over time, teams developed different speeds, due to differences in resources, management engagement, and time and resources.

As in the PhD study, the continued action research filled the gap in professional development for internationalisation of home curricula. It also confirmed that universities of applied sciences have very different infrastructures to support educational development.

Overall, the initiative to internationalise the curricula of a number of pilot programs was taken by international officers, who felt responsible for giving internationalisation of teaching and learning an impulse. For international officers of continental European universities this is in itself not unusual, since they have a wide range of tasks with regard to internationalisation, ranging from management of mobility to policy development.

A trajectory in steps

Incorporating employability skills into the process of internationalising learning outcomes constituted a positive force in action research and was developed into the key aspect of the trajectory.

The principle was to reverse the traditional top-down approach to internationalising curricula, by which European, national, institutional, and faculty policies are all stacked on top of each other. Lecturers were generally not familiar with most of policies and felt pressured by the demands of all these policy levels. In the revised approach, postponing the discussion on institutional policies served to strengthen a bottom-up approach and challenge lecturers to assume responsibility for teaching and learning within their own program, and to consider themselves the "owners" of the internationalisation process.

On the basis of the outcomes of the action research, the following approach, in steps, was developed.

Step 1: Clarifying settings and processes

This step serves to determine the roles and positions of the participants. Key questions are, who to involve (management, international officers, and curriculum committees), how the process is resourced in terms of hours, whether the participants have volunteered, what information is available from alumni surveys or other external sources, and which relevant institutional documents should be taken into consideration at a later stage. A key issue is to what extent educational developers or quality assurance officers are involved to support lecturers.

In this step, lecturers consider Sinek's (2011) Golden Circle, an effective tool for focusing on the "why" discussion first and to later guide the discussion to the "what" and finally into the "how." In this adapted version from the original model, "what" represents the learning outcomes that include the international and intercultural dimensions that the program considers essential for its (future) graduates. The "how" represents the activities through which these learning outcomes are achieved.

Step 2: Introducing employability skills as a framework for imagination

This step focuses on external sources of information feeding into discussion on what the program wants to achieve, the type of graduates that it wants and needs to educate, and the external circumstances in which it operates.

As a point of orientation, drivers that reshape the workforce landscape (e.g., Davies, Fidler, & Gorbis, 2011) prove useful. This is because they are not very recent, and therefore provoke discussion on the extent to which they are still relevant for the program's context. Connected to the drivers are Work skills 2020, which outlines the skills required to deal with these drivers. Reviewing these skills opens a conversation on employability skills and the ways in which international perspectives could enhance these skills. At this point, several sets of employability skills effectively drive home the message that lecturers have a choice. Specifically, they should not just adopt a particular set of skills but rather adapt existing sets or define their own versions.

The purpose of introducing lists of employability skills from outside of both the national and European context serves to highlight that these are topics that are being discussed across the globe, and also to urge lecturers to make a choice on the basis of their discipline and local context. In addition to the lists of employability skills, lecturers are encouraged to integrate as much available external input as possible. This can be international, national, regional, and local policy documents and reports; surveys of alumni and employers; and views of advisory boards.

At this stage, lecturers frequently struggle with imagining the professional field of their graduates in the future, which drives home the need to include learning outcomes for dealing with uncertainty and ambiguity. Another point of discussion is notions of professional ethics and contextualising the concept of global citizenship to the program, so that these can be developed as an integrated professional dimension and not only a personal one.

Step 3: From employability skills to program learning outcomes (PLOs)

The next step is to merge employability skills into existing program learning outcomes (PLOs), as a step towards internationalising the module learning outcomes (MLOs) and their assessment.

Dutch programs at universities of applied sciences have national profiles with a jointly agreed-upon set of competencies. Although individual programs are free to modify these graduate competencies, lecturers (and managers) may feel reluctant to add international or intercultural dimensions to existing competencies. They may fear that this can lead to issues with accreditation and, therefore, may not be prepared to suggest changes to these competencies.

The focus on complying with nationally agreed-upon standards may lead to reluctance in choosing a profile that distinguishes the program from similar programs at other universities. Even when such national profiles do not exist, lecturers still find it difficult to pinpoint what sets their program apart from others.

Step 4: From PLOs to module learning outcomes (MLOs)

This step involves deriving learning outcomes for semesters and modules from the PLOs in a process of "reverse engineering." In some cases, it is helpful to first determine the learning outcomes per semester and sequence them in leading up to the PLOs. It can then be determined which of the modules within that semester would be the best learning environments for achieving the semester learning outcomes.

At this stage, it is important to get rid of meaningless phrasings such as "in an international context" or "(inter)national" as they make it difficult to assess achievement of MLOs. Another key point of attention is to discuss "awareness" versus "competence" and to make sure that skills are described as the application of knowledge rather than as just knowledge. ILOs that focus on knowledge, with "knows" as active verb could well be replaced by ILOs that specify "apply knowledge."

Step 5: Zero-assessment

This step involves a scan of current MLOs to determine to what extent these already meet the desired outcomes. This involves a comparison of the PLOs that were newly derived from the PLOs with the current MLOs.

This step also involves an analysis of current learning activities and the extent to which they actually contribute to achieving MLOs. The Program Logic Worksheet (see Deardorff, 2015, p. 121) is a meaningful tool in this step as it guides lecturers to distinguish input, activities, output, outcomes, and impact. Particularly, the distinction between output and outcomes is a key point of discussion. This represents the difference between the student's product (the output) and what they learn from making this product (the outcome).

Step 6: Plan of action

The final step involves drawing up a plan of action, which outlines which modules need to be (re)developed in order to achieve the rephrased MLOs. A key discussion point at this stage is how the action plan will be presented to the management of the program. The action plan provides managers with the opportunity to select lecturers to contribute to the development beyond the champions of internation- alisation and "usual suspects." Support of educational developers should be an integral part of the plan of action as assessment of internationalised ILOs can be considered the essence of the learning and the internationalisation process.

A point of consideration is whether the plan should include the articulation of session learning outcomes (SLOs) – that is, learning outcomes for each of the ses- sions that constitute a module. Some lecturers may resist SLOs as they feel these limit their flexibility in teaching and hold them accountable more than they feel comfortable with. Others may welcome them as providing clarity on the contri- bution of each session to achievement of the MLOs, particularly when a module is taught by several lecturers.

Conclusions

The trajectory described above is time consuming and requires intensive sup- port to guide the process. On the other hand, the added value is considerable. Working on internationalising learning outcomes for employability leads not only to fundamental discussions on the future of the profession, but also on the ambitions and current educational practices of the program. Rephrasing learn- ing outcomes, therefore, has a meaning beyond internationalisation and contrib- utes to the overall quality of education in the program.

Integrating employability skills into curriculum design and ensuring that they are included in PLOs and MLOs is a complicated process that involves many stakeholders. The contribution of educational developers is crucial for this pro- cess. Little is known about how educational developers engage with internation- alisation of curricula outside the Anglophone world (for the UK see Killick, 2018) and with the role of internationalisation in enhancing employability skills. More research is required to find out what knowledge and inspiration they need to be able to fulfil their role effectively.

Chapter 17

Cultural understanding as a key skill for employability

Nannette Ripmeester and Darla K. Deardorff

Introduction

Given an increase in the importance of employability for today's college graduates, international student recruitment has seen a growing emphasis on return on investment (ROI). "It is becoming more and more vital that universities also prepare graduates for the world of work. This means that the development of soft skills, like team-playing and resilience, often becomes as important as the technical skills and knowledge acquired during a degree," mentions Nunzio Quacquarelli, CEO of QS, in the report The Global Skills Gap in the 21st Century. With employers' desire to hire students well-prepared for diverse work environments (British Council, 2013a; Leppänen, Saarinen, & Airas 2014; Ripmeester, 2014), higher education institutions need to more closely examine the link between intercultural preparation and workplace success. Such preparation goes beyond student mobility, given the small percentages of students who actually study abroad (Institute of International Education, 2017).

This chapter examines data along with higher education institutional approaches to developing intercultural competence as a graduate outcome as institutions strive to enhance students' employability defined as "a holistic approach that takes into consideration both personal and external factors" (Ripmeester, 2018, p. 41). Further, "employability is more than just a job that makes good money in a students' early career days. It is about maximising the talents of each student and preparing students for the world that awaits them upon graduation – this is what (ideally) employability refers to" (Ripmeester, 2018, p. 41). In today's world, intercultural understanding is essential in being considered job-market ready given that our world has become more global than ever before as indicated by the Worldwide Educating for the Future Index (The Economist Intelligence Unit, 2017).

Importance of employability and employability skills as graduate outcome

There are several studies that explore employability as a student outcome (Nilsson & Ripmeester, 2016; European Commission, 2014; Jones, 2014). For example, the StudentPulse™ research in 2014 indicated the importance of career prospects for prospective international students,[1] making it the second most important reason to opt for a higher education degree abroad, after "broadening my horizon," followed by "improving my language skills." In further examining the link between student perspectives and employability, data from the International Student Barometer™ (ISB)[2] can be used to understand some trends across the globe from international students' perspectives. With 3.2 million student responses to date, the ISB (Ammigan & Jones, 2018) is the largest annual survey of international students' satisfaction, involving 1400 institutions in 33 countries. In the most recent available dataset on the ISB, students were asked in an online questionnaire to rate certain aspects of the student experience. Based on this ISB data for 2017–18, 89% of students indicated that the importance of the earning potential of the chosen degree is highly important. Overall, business, technology, and engineering students attach more importance to earning potential than do physical sciences, history, or linguistics students. Altogether, students' perceived earning potential as the third strongest reason to opt for a particular institution, closely followed by, respectively, institution reputation (94%) and research quality (90%). This means that higher education institutions can no longer ignore employability outcomes to remain successful in attracting students to their institution.

When looking at the learning satisfaction in the ISB in 2017–18 (see Figure 17.1), other items that received the highest scores include the quality of the lectures

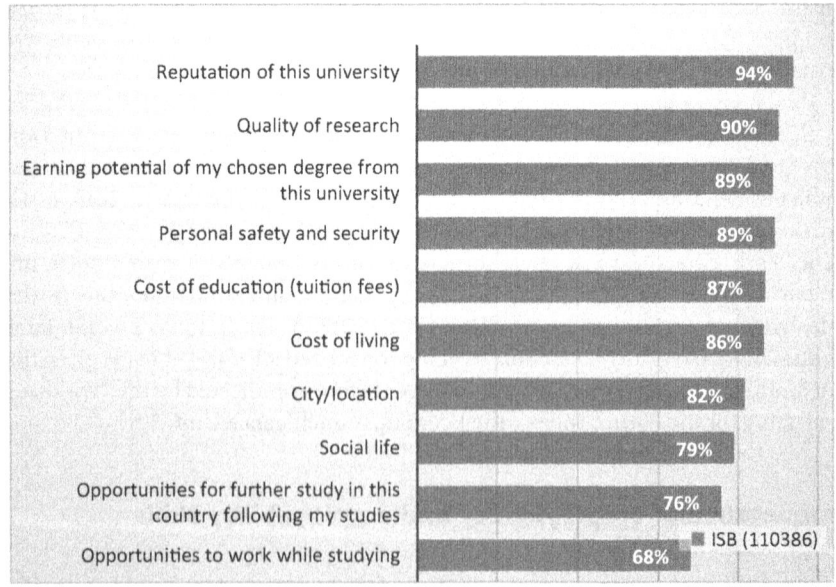

Figure 17.1 Global ISB data ©i-graduate.

(34%), course organisation (34%), learning that leads to employment (34%), and the academic content (34%). Again, the element associated with employability scored high, as the third most important reason for current international students to recommend their international study experience to their peers. Over one-third of international students (32%) indicated that establishing future contacts was by far the most important element to recommend the international study experience to fellow (prospective) students.

Employability outcomes are unquestionably an ROI for (international) students, as evidenced by the ISB results and supported by articles (West, 2017), policy documents (Gribble, 2015) and ranking surveys (QS World University Rankings, 2018) across the globe. Therefore, higher education institutions need to more explicitly state the employment outcomes when recruiting international students.

However, an academic degree is not "just" about the job upon graduation. An academic degree is also about expanding knowledge and perspectives, gaining an enhanced understanding of the world around us, and creating a better future for all, all of which are often stated as desired student outcomes. These outcomes complement employability outcomes quite well. If higher education institutions provide students with an education that ensures they will be able to maximise their talents and hone their intercultural skills, institutions then maximise students' employability (Ripmeester, 2017). Despite the academic debate around employability skills (Suleman, 2016), there seems to be agreement among employers about what they deem the most essential employability skills (British Council, 2013a; QS 2018). Kashif Tay, Early Professionals Manager at IBM, UK, noted that "there are many words which make better sense than soft skills, for instance interpersonal skills or transferable skills, but I think we should simply call them professional skills – if you do not get this right, it will be truly difficult to find a job" (Ripmeester, 2016a).

Why intercultural skills are an important part of employability in our global world

Professional skills, or intercultural skills, matter in today's diverse world, not only in the workplace but also in society. With the ever-increasing divides within society, intercultural skills are the bridge that can ensure more successful interactions across differences, whether those differences are related to generational, gender, religious, racial, ethnic, national or socio-economic differences, and whether those interactions are in the workplace or beyond. As stated by OECD leader Gabriela Ramos, these intercultural skills are "vital for individuals to thrive in a rapidly changing world and for societies to progress without leaving anyone behind.... Citizens need the skills to be competitive and ready for a new world of work...," and, "more importantly, they also need to develop the capacity to analyse and understand global and intercultural issues..." given the growing complexities found in today's societies around the world, particularly given the unprecedented flows of humanity coupled with fluid and dynamic identity affiliations (OECD, 2017). Developing these intercultural skills boosts employability while at the same time ensuring that employees can adapt and work successfully in diverse work teams (British Council, 2013a). Beyond the workplace, intercultural skills help support achievement of the United Nations' Sustainable Development Goals, ensure the effective and responsible use of media platforms, and helps promote the necessary skills to live harmoniously in diverse communities.

There has been much written about intercultural skills across different disciplines, with a wide range of terms used, including intercultural competence, cultural intelligence, intercultural communication, and intercultural sensitivity. Such a wide range of terms often generates confusion about specific skills needed. When reviewing the vast array of definitions of intercultural frameworks, one finds commonality in essential intercultural skills of respect, listening, adaptation, relationship building, multiple perspective taking, self-awareness, and cultural humility (UNESCO, 2013) as what are necessary to communicate and behave appropriately and effectively across differences, whatever those may be.

Various approaches for higher education institutions to incorporate intercultural employability training into curricula

Higher education institutions around the world implement different approaches for incorporating intercultural skills in order to graduate global-ready students. In a recent study conducted globally, Deardorff and Arasatanam-Smith (2017) found that while higher education institutions may have traditionally relied on student exchange and mobility programs as a key way to develop such intercultural skills, increasingly such skills are being developed through the curriculum, both formal and informal. For example, the University of British Columbia started an intercultural development program to bridge diverse groups on campus with the goal of developing intercultural skills for participants. The program included a series of workshops, an experiential learning component (to practice their skills in real-world contexts), and a community of practice. Other approaches at different post-secondary institutions for developing intercultural skills included the use of a technology platform for connecting learners who may not have the opportunity to study abroad, the infusion of community service into the curriculum (service learning), the internationalisation of the curriculum (especially through inclusion of missing voices/perspectives), and the intentional connecting of both domestic and international students on campus beyond "surface" programs. Institutions also recognise the importance of ensuring that both teaching and administrative staff receive adequate intercultural preparation since, at times, students' intercultural skills may already exceed those of university staff.

Through the careful examination of 29 case studies in this global study of how post-secondary institutions are addressing intercultural skill development, the following themes emerged:

1 The **importance of intentionality**, given that intercultural skills do not just happen in the process of a university education. This also means that intercultural skills development cannot simply be reduced to a one-time training or even to one course.

2 The **relevance of context**, given that intercultural skills are applied in very specific real-world settings, outside of the four walls of a classroom. These contexts, especially work settings, vary by audience, geography, and purpose, and by social, economic, historical, political, and cultural realities, all of which must be taken into account and addressed.

3 The **indispensability of active engagement**, which means intercultural skill development must go beyond a formal learning setting to actual interactions, whether face to face or online.

4 The **limitation of knowledge**, which means higher education must go beyond the long prevailing mantra that language and knowledge are sufficient for constituting intercultural skills. Knowledge and language are not sufficient for successful intercultural interactions, which highlights the importance of active engagement noted previously, and opportunities for applying such skills.

5 The **significance of multiple perspectives** cannot be emphasised enough when it comes to developing intercultural skills. Being able to see an issue or problem from multiple perspectives is essential for successful employees in today's diverse workforce.

6 The **need for customisation** emerged as another key theme, coupled with the recognition that a one-size-fits-all approach to "training" for intercultural skills will not work, given that learners are at different places in their own intercultural journeys.

These are six themes that emerged from the intercultural case studies from around the world. What are the implications for higher education institutions? These findings point to the importance of the curriculum – both in and out of the classroom – and the fact that institutions can no longer rely predominantly on education abroad and student mobility programs as the main mechanisms for developing intercultural skills. In turn, this means that there needs to be a focus on the core role of academics in developing intercultural skills in students through their content and delivery of the curriculum, which points to the importance of adequate intercultural preparation for academics. This also means that institutions need to do more in connecting with their local communities to provide opportunities for students to engage in real-world settings, such as through local companies, non-profits, civil society organisations, and so on.

How do employers view intercultural skills as part of employability skills?

With the realisation that intercultural skills need to be intentionally addressed in curricula, engaging real-world settings, the role for employers becomes apparent (Ripmeester, 2016b). Research from the British Council (2013a) shows that employers frequently define intercultural skills as "the ability to understand different cultural contexts and viewpoints." Another key skill mentioned is "demonstrating respect for others," followed by "accepting different cultural contexts and viewpoints," and "openness to new ideas and ways of thinking." The British Council survey, conducted together with Booz Allen Hamilton, also asked employers to prioritise intercultural skills, more general soft skills, and technical skills against each other, resulting in a similar outcome: demonstrating respect for others and being able to work in diverse teams score slightly above qualifications that are considered work-field or job-related expertise.

In a small-scale research project, another study set out to investigate what value employers attach to intercultural skills and how this impacts graduate's employability, according to them. A series of semi-focused interviews were conducted with eight global employers as part of the CareerChats project,[3] exploring the alignment between career needs, expectations, and motivations of students, HEIs, and global employers. The interviews with global employers were focused on trying to establish why intercultural skills are deemed important, according to them. CareerChats was ignited by a webinar exploring the importance of study abroad and its outcomes on employability. Stuart Jehan, Global Fund Strategic Development Manager of Robeco, mentioned during this webinar "With business becoming more global, employers are looking for candidates that are more adapt to different environments. There is the perception among many employers that graduates who have studied overseas tend to work more efficiently in an environment comprising more cultures, are more open to work in other parts of the world during their careers and are also more likely to be competent (or even fluent) in a foreign language". He then adds that "It is this intercultural competence and perhaps this greater willingness to be internationally mobile that potentially adds value to a candidate."[4]

During the series of interviews with employers (Ripmeester, 2014), it became apparent that employers attach great value to intercultural skills and international exposure. However, in an earlier study among corporate employers, those of varying size, sector, and scope were asked whether an international study experience in itself was considered an advantage for individual students to get hired. The answer was straight forward and clear: "If you are comparing apples with apples, you go for the one with the global experience. However, global experience is not required to get hired, but … without the global perspective, you lack the understanding of how different people and different perspectives can contribute." mentioned Kaleen Robinson, VP HR outsourcing at AON Hewitt, based in North America and responsible for 17,000 people globally. Anna Jezowska, Human Resources Management advisor for Croon in Poland, supports this view: "It is an asset." Or, as Nicole Bueters, Head of Talent Acquisition with Philips mentioned, "We are keen to recruit recent graduates able to work in an ever-changing environment, who strive for innovation and can handle change, because that will be the environment, they will be working in. Our world is on the move and we need those people who can handle that constant change … you need proof of your capability of stepping outside of your comfort zone." Similar findings came from a Finnish study carried out by CIMO. International mobility seems to produce the kind of skills employers are looking for, albeit these skills are not directly linked to the competencies and experiences required of the candidates in the recruitment process (Leppänen, Saarinen & Airas 2014). The employers interviewed for the CareerChats project did underline the importance and added value of intercultural skills, provided, however, that prospective job candidates are aware of what intercultural skills truly comprise. Study abroad experiences are seen as beneficial, but an international experience *per se* is not sufficient to signify the development of intercultural skills. Incorporating intercultural skills training into the curricula, therefore, is believed to be of more value as it ensures all students get the opportunity to sharpen their intercultural competence. According to Kashif Tay, Early Professionals Manager at IBM, UK, adaptability, language skills, and the ability to survive in a new country are important skills for recent graduates entering the labour market. Selene Siregar, recruiter at Michael Page in Singapore, mentions in the interview for the CareerChats project that "Universities, especially research universities, should provide more practical subjects, relevant to daily job life. Universities cannot just think about educating academics, they need to see that most graduates will go to the path of professionals." (CareerChats, 2017).

Conclusions

Given that international students and employers indicate the importance of employability skills, and in particular intercultural skills, as vital for success in the workplace, higher education institutions need to be more intentional and explicit about how they are addressing such skills as a student outcome – for all students, not just those who are privileged to study abroad. This means closely examining not only the curriculum but also the co-curriculum to ensure students have opportunities to work with others across difference – within and beyond the institution, including the local community. Technology and digital solutions may also help in supporting such intercultural training activities. Preparing students to be successful on the job market entails training them to truly understand the differences around them and this will be of value to all stakeholders involved, from the individual student to the broader society.

Notes

1. The StudentPulse surveyed prospective international students before embarking on a study abroad survey. The survey was conducted by i-graduate with 2366 students.
2. The International Student Barometer (ISB) is an indicator of how successful institutions are in meeting the hopes and ambitions of international students who decide to study at that institution.
3. CareerChats is a project for which global employers, international students, and higher education professionals have been interviewed to explore the alignment between career needs, employability expectations, and related motivations.
4. How does study abroad boost your employability? The employer perspective webinar by CareerProfessor.works, 14/03/16. https://youtu.be/qRKK5cM_hH0 (17m20s and 17m50s).

Conclusions

Cate Gribble and Robert Coelen

Why this book?

At the conclusion of this book, it is worth reflecting on the motivations for bringing together authors to write on the topic of internationalisation and employability. The intense interest in this important subject is largely the result of major developments in the global labour market. The employability advantages of an internationalised education span disciplines and national contexts. All students stand to benefit from developing key skills, knowledge, and attributes that will enhance their capacity to work in a range of contexts. Employers have been asking for well-developed transversal skills but are generally not aware that a range of internationalisation activities provide students with substantial opportunities to develop these skills. Companies also, increasingly, value employees who can straddle multiple cultures. As workplaces become increasingly diverse, the ability to successfully navigate cultural difference is prioritised. Technology, the internet and the emergence of "virtual teams" means that graduates may be required to operate across cultural contexts without leaving home. Central to this book is a critical examination of how internationalisation in its range of forms contributes to enhancing graduate employability via the acquisition of key skills, knowledge, and attributes.

This book is intended for diverse target audiences, all of which have a deep interest in the relationship between internationalisation in higher education and employability. We have been fortunate enough to attract expert authors from a range of academic and professional domains as well as geographical perspectives. The result is a significant array of perspectives examining the interface between higher education and the labour market in an increasingly globalised environment.

The authors in this collection demonstrate the enormous scope for internationalisation to contribute to the development of graduate employability. However, while the benefits of internationalisation and employability are often well understood by those intimately involved in internationalisation in higher education, there is an urgent need to further promote key messages to a broader audience. Proponents of internationalisation risk operating in an "echo chamber" and more work must be done to champion the broad employability benefits of internationalisation to a range of stakeholders, including higher education institutions, government, peak bodies, employers, and, not least, students themselves.

In the past decade, recognition of the personal and professional advantages of an internationalised higher education has grown. The following points highlight the core messages emerging from this book, as well as the scope of work still required to ensure the employability benefits of internationalisation are realised.

Key messages

Articulating the link between internationalisation and employability

Higher education institutions (HEIs) can play a significant role in reinforcing the link between internationalisation and the development of transversal skills now prioritised by employers. At an institutional level, academics and professional staff (e.g., careers and employability) can help students to better understand and articulate how their international education experience translates into critical employability skills and attributes. This is equally important for students who complete their entire degree abroad as for students engaged in transnational education (TNE) settings or participating in internationalisation at home (IaH) initiatives.

Communicating the benefits of internationalised higher education beyond the academy

The authors in this book present compelling arguments for HEIs to do more to counter lack of understanding and misinformation about international education that persists in the broader community. HEIs can look for ways to develop communication channels between industry and government in order to communicate these important messages to external stakeholders. HEIs can play an influential role in raising awareness of the added value of an internationalised education, not only in terms of developing intercultural competencies, international awareness, and an enhanced world view, but also for the development of transversal skills demanded by employers. These communication channels can also be used to dispel prevailing myths, including the idea that international students pose a flight risk, or that local knowledge and skills are more valuable than international experience.

Equity

Throughout this book, the issue of equity looms large. The massification of higher education means that more students than ever are participating in HE globally. In turn, this has resulted in a competitive labour market, with growing numbers of students vying for graduate positions. To avoid creating further stratification within higher education and across society more broadly, institutions must continually work towards ensuring that the advantages of internationalisation are available to as many students as possible.

While the growth in short-term mobility is a positive development opening up opportunities for students from a diversity of backgrounds to benefit from international experiences, the majority of students will remain on campus for their entire degrees. Internationalisation at home provides considerable opportunities to bring the benefits of an international and intercultural education to those students who may otherwise miss out. However, strong institutional leadership, rigorous curriculum design and evaluation, as well professional development opportunities for staff are required to ensure that IaH is recognised as a legitimate way of ensuring all students benefit from developing the critical employability skills associated with experiences abroad.

Immigration policy

Policy settings in host countries influence the extent to which nations benefit from the internationalisation of higher education. In part, the trend for international students to seek post-study employment has been driven by host nation immigration policy. Finding the right balance between providing post-study work opportunities without displacing local graduates in competitive labour markets has proved challenging for governments, particularly in the climate of anti-immigration populism in many counties. Australia and the UK have tightened post-study work rights while Canada, New Zealand, the Netherlands, and Germany have expanded those opportunities. Employability is one of the main drivers of student choice, suggesting that countries which fail to provide students with the opportunity to gain work experience will struggle to attract international students. Critical to achieving desirable policy settings is evidence-based research and the availability of robust data sets to fully understand student flows and the motivations underpinning a decision to study abroad.

While determining the right policy settings are imperative, governments can also take the lead in influencing public opinion by promoting the benefits of international education and the contribution internationally educated graduates make to the workplace.

Looking ahead

Over the past decade, we have seen greater emphasis on the learning outcomes of an internationalised education as well as recognition of the link between transversal skills acquisition and international learning. For many students, the decision to engage in international education is highly strategic – a way to find positional advantage in competitive global labour markets. Students now expect that international education will deliver an employability advantage in the job market.

To meet the needs and expectations of both students and employers, HEIs, governments and other stakeholders will need to invest in research in several critical areas. These include,

a   developing more rigorous methods for measuring and evaluating the development of employability skills in ways that go beyond self-reporting and perceptions;
b   understanding how, and to what extent, students can develop employability skills, such as intercultural competence, without physically crossing borders;
c   how to provide the enhancement in transversal skills, such as those enjoyed by internationally mobile students, on the home campus; and
d   the role of policy in promoting mobility and other forms of internationalisation in ways that deliver broad, individual, and national benefits.

Globally, there are growing social and economic pressures to prepare graduates who can negotiate rapidly transforming employment contexts. The authors in this collection present fresh insights into the potential for internationalisation in higher education to prepare graduates for a diversity of workplaces and contexts, thereby contributing to improved graduate outcomes, positive socio-cultural impacts, and greater economic prosperity.

References

Adams, T., Banks, M., Olsen, A. (2011). International education in Australia: From aid to trade to internationalization. In R. Bhandari & P. Blumenthal, P. (Eds.), *International students and global mobility in higher education. International and Development Education.* New York: Palgrave Macmillan.

Advisory Panel on Canada's International Education Strategy. (2012, August). International education: A key driver of Canada's future prosperity. Retrieved from website: http://www.international.gc.ca/education/advisory-consultation.aspx?view=d

Aerden, A., (2015). An introduction to international and intercultural learning outcomes. Brussels: European Consortium for Accreditation in Higher Education. Retrieved from ecahe.eu

Ahrens, J. (2010). International student mobility literature review. Report to HEFCE.

Al-Mahmood, R., & Gruba, P. (2007). Approaches to the implementation of generic graduate attributes in Australian ICT undergraduate education. *Computer Science Education, 17*(3), 171–185.

Aldrich, H., & Herker, D. (1977). Boundary spanning roles and organization structure. *Academy of Management Review, 2*(2), 217–230.

Allen R., (2017). Lessons from history for the future of work: Nature news & comment. Retrieved March 2, 2018 from https://www.nature.com/news/lessons-from-history-for-the-future-of-work-1.22825

Allotey, G. A. (2017). Unemployment rate more than GSS' 12% – Jobless graduates. http://citifmonline.com/2017/03/24/unemployment-rate-more-than-gss-12-jobless-graduates/

Alphin, H., Chan, R., & Lavine, J. (2017). *The future of accessibility in international higher education.* Hershey, PA: IGI Global.

Altbach, P. (2010). Why branch campuses may be unsustainable. *International Higher Education 58,* 2–3.

Altbach, P. G., & de Wit, H. (2018). The challenge to higher education internationalization. *University World News,* 27 February, Issue No. 00494.

Altbach, P. G., & Knight, J. (2007). The internationalization of higher education: Motivations and realities. *Journal of Studies in International Education, 11*(3–4), 290–305.

Altbach, P. G., Kelly, D. H., & Lulat, Y. G-M. (Eds.) (1985). *Research on foreign students and international study: An overview and international bibliography.* New York: Praeger Publishers.

Altbach, G., & Rumbley, L. E. (Eds.) *International faculty in higher education.* New York: Taylor and Francis.

Ammigan, R., & Jones, P. (2018). Improving the student experience: Learning from a comparative study of international student satisfaction, *Journal of Studies in International Education, 22* (4), 283–301.

Archer, W., & Davidson, J. (2008). *Graduate employability: The view of employers*. London: The Council for Industry and Higher Education.

Archer, W., & Davison, J. (2012). *Graduate employability: What do employers think and want?* London: The Council for Industry and Higher Education. Retrieved from http://aces.shu.ac.uk/employability/resources/0802Grademployability.pdf

Armstrong, D. & Cole, P. (2002). Managing distances and differences. In P. Hinds & S. Kiesler (Eds.), *Geographically distributed work*. Cambridge, Massachusetts. USA: MIT.

Asma, A., & Lim, L. (2000). Cultural dimensions of Anglos, Australians, and Malaysians. *Malaysian Management Review*, December 2000, 9–17.

Association of American Colleges & Universities. (2018). Erasmus impact study confirms EU student exchange scheme boosts employability and job mobility. Retrieved from https://www.aacu.org/resources/global-learning/erasmus

AUCC. (2014). Canada's universities in the world. AUCC Internationalization Survey. Retrieved from https://www.univcan.ca/wp-content/uploads/2015/07/internationalization-survey-2014.pdf

Australian Education International. (2010). *International graduate outcomes and employer perceptions*. Canberra: Commonwealth of Australia.

Australian Government Department of Education and Training. (2018). *Australian students studying overseas*. Retrieved from https://internationaleducation.gov.au/research/australianstudentsoverseas/pages/australians-students-overseas.aspx

Australian Government Department of Foreign Affairs and Trade. (n.d.). The New Colombo Plan. Retrieved from http://dfat.gov.au/people-to-people/new-colombo-plan/pages/new-colombo-plan.aspx

Bacchus, M. K. (2008). The education challenges facing small nation states in the increasingly competitive global economy of the twenty-first century. *Comparative Education, 44*(2), 127–145.

Bamber, M. (2013). What motivates Chinese women to study in the UK and how do they perceive their experience? *Higher Education 2014*, 68, 47–68.

Banks, M., & Olsen, A. (2008). *Outcomes and impacts from international education: From international student to Australian graduate, the journey of a lifetime*. Canberra: Commonwealth of Australia.

Barbaric, D. (2017). *Policy options for outbound student mobility: An inter-jurisdictional review of policy goals and initiatives*. Toronto: Centre for the Study of Canadian and International Higher Education, OISE-University of Toronto.

Barrie, S. (2006). Understanding what we mean by the generic attributes of graduates. *Higher Education, 51*(2), 215–241.

Barrie, S., Hughes, C., & Smith, C. (2009). *The national graduate attributes project: Integration and assessment of graduate attributes in curriculum*. Sydney: Australian Learning and Teaching Council.

Beelen, J. (2016). Developing employability skills at home: An emerging focus in internationalisation of universities of applied sciences. In S. Zotti (Ed.), *International lectures: 22 Beiträge zur Internationalisierung der Hochschulen*, (pp. 19–22). Vienna: OeAD.

Beelen, J. (2017a). Obstacles and enablers to internationalising learning outcomes in Dutch universities of applied sciences (Doctoral dissertation Università Cattolica del Sacro Cuore, Milan, Italy).

Beelen, J. (2017b). Internationalising learning outcomes at The Hague University of Applied Sciences. In J. Walenkamp & J. Beelen (Eds.), *The world's a stage* (pp. 190–211). Delft/The Hague: Eburon/The Hague University of Applied Sciences.

Beelen, J., & Jones, E. (2015). Redefining internationalization at home. In A. Curaj, L. Matei, R. Pricopie, J. Salmi & P. Scott (Eds.), *The European higher education area: Between critical reflections and future policies* (pp. 67–80). Dordrecht: Springer.

Beelen, J., & Jones, E. (2018). Internationalization at home. In P. Nuno Texeira & J. Sheol Shin (Eds.), *Encyclopedia of international higher education systems and institutions*. Dordrecht: Springer.

Bennett, D. (2016). Developing employability in higher education music. *Arts and Humanities in Higher Education, 15*(3–4), 386–413.

Berquist, B. (2017). *New Zealand's international PhD strategy: A holistic analysis 2005–2015*. University of Auckland. 2017. Retrieved from https://tinyurl.com/ya9fjn92

Bikson, T. K., & Law, S. A. (1994). *Global preparedness and human resources*. Santa Monica, CA: RAND Institute of Education and Training.

Billett, S. (2009). Realising the educational worth of integrating work experiences in higher education. *Studies in Higher Education, 34*(7), 827–843.

Bilsland, C., Nagy, H., & Smith, P. (2014). Planning the journey to best practice in developing employability skills: Transnational university internships in Vietnam. *Asia-Pacific Journal of Cooperative Education, 15*(2), 145–157.

Black, H. T., & Duhon, D. L. (2006). Assessing the impact of business study abroad programs on cultural awareness and personal development. *Journal of Education for Business, 81*(3), 140–144.

Black, K. (2004). A review of factors which contribute to the internationalisation of a programme of study. *Journal of Hospitality, Leisure, Sport and Tourism Education, 3*(1), 5–18.

Bloom, B. (1956). *Taxonomy of educational objectives: The classification of educational goals: Cognitive domain. Handbook 1: Cognitive domain*. Longmans, Green.

Bodycott, P., & Lai, A. (2017). China: The role of Chinese parents in decisions about overseas study. In G. Mihut, P. G. Altbach, & H. de Wit (Eds.), *Understanding higher education internationalization: Insights from key global publications* (pp. 197–201). Rotterdam: Sense Publishers.

Boe, L. (2018). *The scale of UK higher education transnational education 2015–16* (p2). London: Universities UK International.

Bosley, G. W. (2010). Beyond immersion: Global engagement and transformation through intervention via student reflection in long-term study abroad. In E. Jones (Ed.), *Internationalisation and the student voice: Higher education perspectives* (pp. 55–67). London: Routledge.

Bourn, D., & Neal, I. (2008). *The global engineer: Incorporating global skills within UK higher education*. London: Institute of Education and Engineers Against Poverty.

Bowden, J., Hart, G., King, B., Trigwell, K., & Watts, O. (2000). *Generic capabilities of ATN university graduates*. Canberra: Department of Education, Training and Youth Affairs.

Bowman, K. (2010). Background paper for the AQF Council on generic skills.

Boyle, E. A., Hainey, T., Connolly, T. M., Gray, G., Earp, J., Ott, M., & Pereira, J. (2016). An update to the systematic literature review of empirical evidence of the impacts and outcomes of computer games and serious games. *Computers & Education, 94*, 178–192.

Bradford, A. (2015). Changing trends in Japanese students studying abroad. *International Higher Education*, (83), 22–23.

Braun, V., & Clarke, V. (2006). Using thematic analysis in psychology. *Qualitative Research in Psychology*, 3(2), 77–101.

Brazil's Science Without Borders programme facing cuts in 2016. *ICEF Monitor* (2015, September 15).

Briggeman, B. C., & Norwood, F. B. (2011). Employer assessment of the college graduate: What advisors need to know. *Journal of Natural Resources and Life Sciences Education*, 40(1), 19–28.

Brink, R., Mearns, M., & Du Plessis, T. (2014). Managing information for work-integrated learning at higher education institutions. *Mousaion*, 32(3), 13–28.

British Academy, & University Council of Modern Languages. (2012). *Valuing the year abroad: The importance of the year abroad as part of a degree programme for UK students: A position statement*. London: British Academy.

British Council. (2013a). *Culture at Work: The Value of Intercultural Skills in the Workplace*. London: British Council.

British Council. (2013b). *The shape of things to come: The evolution of transnational education: Data, definitions, opportunities and impacts analysis*. London: British Council.

British Council. (2014). *Exploring the impacts of transnational education on host countries: A pilot study*. Going Global. London: British Council.

British Council. (2015). *Students in the driving seat: Young people's voices on higher education in Africa*. London: British Council.

British Council. (2016). *Repositioning higher education in Ghana, Kenya, Nigeria and South Africa*. London: British Council.

British Council. (2017). *Broadening Horizons: Addressing the needs of a new generation*. Retrieved from British Council Education Intelligence: https://www.britishcouncil.org/sites/default/files/mta-bh_2017.pdf

British Council. (2018). *Generation UK-China*. Retrieved from https://www.britishcouncil.cn/en/programmes/education/generation-uk

British Council/Harvard. (2010). Nigeria: The next generation report. Working Paper Series, October 2010, PGDA Working Paper No. 62. http://www.hsph.harvard.edu/pgda/working.htm

Broekhuizen, H. V. (2016). Graduate unemployment and higher education IIE, (2017). A world on the Move: Trends in global student mobility. https://www.iie.org/Research-and-Insights/Publications/A-World-on-the-Move Institutions in South Africa, Hendrik Van Broekhuizen Stellenbosch Economic Working Papers: 08/16. University of Stellenbosch.

Brookes, M., & Becket, N. (2009). An investigation of the internationalisation of UK hospitality management degrees. *Journal of Hospitality & Tourism Education*, 21(3), 17–24.

Brynjolfsson E., & McAfee, A., (2014). *The Second Machine Age: Work, Progress, and Prosperity in a Time of Brilliant Technologies*. USA: W. W. Norton & Company.

Cai, Y. (2013). Graduate employability: A conceptual framework. *Higher Education*, 65(4), 457–469.

Cam, K. T. H. (2016). Work-integrated learning process in tourism training programs in Vietnam: Voices of education and industry. *Asia Pacific Journal of Cooperative Education*, 17(2), 149–161.

Campus France. (2013). La mobilité des étudiants d'Afrique sub-saharienneet du Maghreb. https://ressources.campusfrance.org/publi_institu/etude_prospect/mobilite_continent/fr/note_07_hs_fr.pdf

CareerChats. (2017). Managing expectations, moving towards solutions. *CP Magazine*. Rotterdam, Expertise in Labour Mobility.

Carolyn Yang, Y. T., & Chang, C. H. (2013). Empowering students through digital game authorship: Enhancing concentration, critical thinking, and academic achievement. *Computers and Education, 68*, 334–344.

Carroll, J. (2015). *Tools for teaching in an educationally mobile world*. London: Routledge.

Cavanagh, J., Burston, M., Southcombe, A., & Bartram, T. (2015). Contributing to a graduate-centred understanding of work readiness: An exploratory study of Australian undergraduate students' perceptions of their employability. *International Journal of Management Education, 13*, 278–288.

Center for International Mobility. (2014). Hidden Competencies: Competencies that are hidden, competencies that are recognized. Retrieved from http://www.cimo.fi/instancedata/prime_product_julkaisu/cimo/embeds/cimowwwstructure/32427_Faktaa_1_2014_Hidden_Competences.pdf

Center for International Policy Studies. (CIPSP), University of Ottawa and Munk School of Global Affairs, University of Toronto. (2017, Nov.). Global Education for Canadians: Equipping young Canadians to succeed at home and abroad. Report of the Study Group on Global Education. Retrieved from http://goglobalcanada.ca/

Central Statistics Agency. (CSA). (2015). *Urban employment unemployment survey – Ethiopia*. Addis Ababa: CSA.

Centre for China & Globalisation. (2018). Studying abroad: Wise decision or not. Retrieved from http://en.ccg.org.cn/studying-abroad-wise-decision-or-not/

Chan, B. T.-Y. (2011). Postgraduate transnational education in nonbusiness subjects: Can it fit conceptualizations of curriculum internationalization? *Journal of Studies in International Education, 15*(3), 279–298.

Chapman, A., & Pyvis, D. (2005). Identity and social practice in higher education: Student experiences of postgraduate courses delivered 'offshore' in Singapore and Hong Kong by an Australian university. *International Journal of Educational Development, 25*(1), 39–52.

Chapuis, N., & S. Fortier. (2016). Student mobility is essential to Canada's global future. Retrieved from https://www.univcan.ca/media-room/media-releases/opinion-student-mobility-essential-canadas-global-future/

Cheong, K.-C., Hill, C., Fernandez-Chung, R., & Leong, Y.-C. (2016). Employing the 'unemployable': Employer perceptions of Malaysian graduates. *Studies in Higher Education, 41*(12), 2253–2270.

Chin, J., Dukes, R., & Gamson, W. (2009). Assessment in simulation and gaming: A review of the last 40 years. *Simulation & Gaming, 40*(4), 553–568.

China National Congress. (2010). Outline of national plan for medium and long-term education reform and development. Retrieved from https://internationaleducation.gov.au/News/newsarchive/2010/Documents/China_Education_Reform_pdf.pdf

Clifford, V. (2009). Engaging the disciplines in internationalising the curriculum. *International Journal for Academic Development, 14*(2), 133–143.

Clifford, V. (2010). The internationalised curriculum: (Dis)locating students. In E. Jones (Ed.), *Internationalisation and the student voice: Higher education perspectives* (pp. 169–180). London: Routledge.

Cole, D., & Tibby, M. (2013). *Defining and developing your approach to employability: A framework for higher education institutions*. York: Higher Education Academy.

Commission for Higher Education (CHE). (1978). *Higher education in Ethiopia: Facts and figures*. Addis Ababa: CHE.

Corbin, J., & Strauss, A. (2008). *Basics of qualitative research*, 3rd ed. Thousand Oaks, CA: SAGE Publications.

Cranmer, S. (2006). Enhancing graduate employability: Best intentions and mixed outcomes. *Studies in Higher Education, 31*(2), 169–184.

Crawford, P., Lang, S., Fink, W., Dalton, R., & Fielitz, L. (2011). *Comparative analysis of soft skills: Perceptions of employers, alum, faculty and students.* East Lansing, MI: Michigan State Univ.

Crawley, M. (2017). Universities growing more reliant on foreign student fees. Retrieved on February 15, 2018 from http://www.cbc.ca/news/canada/toronto/international-students-universities-ontario-tuition-1.4199489

Crosling, G., & Ward, I. (2002). Oral Communication: The needs and uses of business graduate employees. *English for Specific Purposes. 21*(1), 41–57.

Crossman, J. E., & Clarke, M. (2010). International experience and graduate employability: Stakeholder perceptions on the connection. *Higher Education, 59*(5), 599–613.

Crowther, P., Joris, M., Otten, M., Nilsson, B., Teekens, H., & Wächter, B. (2001). *Internationalization at home: A position paper.* Amsterdam: EAIE.

Cuthbert, D., Smith, W., & Boey, J. (2008). What do we really know about the outcomes of Australian international education? A critical review and prospectus for future research. *Journal of Studies in International Education, 12*(3), 255–275.

Daly, A. (2011). Determinants of participating in Australian university student exchange programs. *Journal of Research in International Education, 10*(1), 58–70.

Darling-Hammond, L. (2014). *Next generation assessment: Moving beyond the bubble test to support 21st century learning.* John Wiley & Sons.

Daud, S., Abidin, N., Mazuin Sapuan, N., & Rajadurai, J. (2011). Enhancing university business curriculum using an importance-performance approach: A case study of the business management faculty of a university in Malaysia. *International Journal of Educational Management, 25*(6), 545–569.

Davies, A., Fidler, D., & Gorbis, M. (2011). *Future work skills 2020.* Palo Alto, CA: Institute for the Future for the University of Phoenix Research Institute.

Davies, B., Gore, K., Shury, J., Vivian, D., Winterbotham, M., & Constable, S. (2012). *UK commission's employer skills survey 2011: UK Results.* London: UK Commission for Employment and Skills.

De Freitas, S., & Routledge, H. (2013). Designing leadership and soft skills in educational games: The e-leadership and soft skills educational games design model (ELESS). *British Journal of Educational Technology, 44*(6), 951–968.

De Wit, H., & Beelen, J. (2012). Socrates in the low countries: Designing, implementing, and facilitating internationalisation of the curriculum at the Amsterdam University of Applied Sciences (HvA). In J. Ryan (Ed.), *Cross-cultural teaching and learning for home and international students. Internationalisation of pedagogy and curriculum in higher education* (pp. 156–167). London: Routledge.

De Wit, H., & Jones, E. (2014, November 14). We need to change the language of internationalisation. *University World News.*

Deardorff, D. K. (2006). Identification and assessment of intercultural competence as a student outcome of internationalization. *Journal of Studies in International Education 10,* 241–266.

Deardorff, D. K. (2009). *The SAGE handbook of intercultural competence.* Thousand Oaks, CA: SAGE Publications.

Deardorff, D. K. (2015). *Demystifying outcomes assessment for international educators: A practical approach.* Sterling, VA: Stylus.

Deardorff, D. K., & Ararasatnam-Smith, L. (2017). *Intercultural competence in international higher education: International approaches, assessment, application.* Routledge.

Dearing. (1997): The Dearing Report. Higher education in the learning society. Her Majesty's Stationary Office, 1997.

Deloitte Access Economics. (2017). *Assessing returns on international collaboration.* (2017). Wellington: Universities New Zealand. Retrieved from https://www.universitiesnz. ac.nz/sites/default/files/Deloitte%20Access%20Economics_UNZ_International_ collaboration_FINAL_report.pdf

Delors, J. (1996): Education: The necessary Utopia. In *Learning: The treasure within.* Report to UNESCO of the International Commission on Education for the Twenty-first Century. The United Nations Educational, Scientific and Cultural Organization, 1996, (pp. 13–35).

Department of Education and Training, Australia. (2014). *Research snapshot: Transnational education in the higher education.* Retrieved from https://internationaleducation.gov.au/ research/Research-Snapshots/Documents/Transnational%20education_HE_2013.pdf

Department of Education and Training, Australia. (2015). *Research snapshot: Transnational education in the higher education sector.* Retrieved from https://internationaleducation. gov.au/research/Research-Snapshots/Documents/Transnational%20education_ HE_2016.pdf

Department of Statistics, Malaysia. (2016). Labour force survey report, Malaysia 2015. Retrieved from https://www.dosm.gov.my/v1/index.php?r=column/pdfPrev&id=TFV qZ2NtWW9iNlJBV0pTQnZUUzBEZz09

Dept. Foreign Affairs and Trade (DFAT). (2017). *New Colombo Plan.* Australian Government: Canberra.

Deterding, S., Dixon, D., Khaled, R., & Nacke, L. (2011). *From game design elements to gamefulness.* Proceedings of the 15th International Academic MindTrek Conference on Envisioning Future Media Environments - *MindTrek 2011, 9–11.*

Diamond, A., Walkley, L., Forbes, P., Hughes, T., & Sheen, J. (2011). Global graduates into global leaders. London: National Centre for Universities and Business. Retrieved from: http:// www.ncub.co.uk/index.php?option=com_docman&task=doc_download&gid=42&Itemid

Dingley, M. (2016, August 17). Brexit's impact on international education and student mobility. Retrieved from Go Abroad: https://www.goabroad.com/articles/study-abroad/ brexit-s-impact-on-international-education-student-mobility

Di Pietro, G. (2013). *Do study abroad programs enhance the employability of graduates.* Bonn, Germany: Discussion paper, No 7675. Retrieved from http://ftp.iza.org/dp7675.pdf

Djajadikerta, H. G., & Zhang, Z. (2015). *A new paradigm for international business.* Proceedings from the conference on free trade agreements and regional integration in East Asia. Singapore: Springer Proceedings in Business and Economics.

Doyle, J. (2016). *IEAA international employability guide: International students.* Melbourne: International Education Association of Australia.

Dwyer, M. M. (2004a). More is better: The impact of study abroad program duration. *Frontiers: The Interdisciplinary Journal of Study Abroad, 10,* 151–163.

Dwyer, M. M. (2004b). Charting the impact of studying abroad. *International Educator,* 14–20.

Dyer, S., & Lu, F. (2010). Chinese-born international students' transition experiences from study to work in New Zealand. *Australian Journal of Career Development, 19* (2), 23–30.

Edelstein, R. J., & Douglass, J. A. (2012). To judge international branch campuses, we need to know their goals. *Chronicle of Higher Education,* 27 February 2012.

Education New Zealand. (2011). *Leadership Statement for International Education.* Retrieved 2018 from https://enz.govt.nz/assets/Uploads/Leadership-Statement-for-International-Education.pdf

Education New Zealand. (2017). New Zealand international education snapshot 2016.

Education New Zealand. (2018). International education strategy, He Rautaki Matauranga A Ao 2018-30. Retrieved from https://enz.govt.nz/assets/Uploads/International-Education-Strategy-2018-2030.pdf

Egron-Polak, E., & Hudson, R. (2014). *Internationalization of higher education: Growing expectations, essential values.* IAU 4th Global Survey Report. Paris: International Association of Universities.

El Masri, A., Choubak, M., & Litchmore, R. (2015). *The global competition for international students as future immigrants: The role of Ontario universities in translating government policy into institutional practice.* Toronto: Higher Education Quality Council of Ontario. http://www.heqco.ca/en-ca/Research/ResPub/Pages/The-Global-Competition-for-International-Students-as-Future-Immigrants.aspx

Employment Ontario. (2015). Soft skills assessment tool feasibility study: A case for digital gaming. Retrieved from http://www.workforceplanningboard.org/wp-content/uploads/2016/04/soft_skills_feasability_study_final__en_.pdf

Erasmus for Young Entrepreneurs. (2017). Latest statistics. Retrieved from https://www.erasmus-entrepreneurs.eu/press/EYE_Programme_statistics_(January_2017)_58a61ff0b9417.pdf

Erasmus for Young Entrepreneurs. (n.d.). Retrieved from https://www.erasmus-entrepreneurs.eu/index.php?lan=en

Esbin, H. (2016). Virtual strangers no more: Serious games and creativity for effective remote teams. In C. Graham (Ed.), *Strategic management and leadership for systems development in virtual spaces.* Hershey, Pennsylvania, USA: IGI Global.

Esbin, H. (2017). Training industry: Turning virtual strangers into virtual teams: Best practices. Retrieved from: https://trainingindustry.com/articles/performance-management/turning-virtual-strangers-into-virtual-teams-best-practices/

EuroDesk. (2015, April). How can learning mobility of young people increase their employability. Retrieved from http://www.movit.si/fileadmin/movit/2ED/How_can_learning_mobility_of_young_people_increase_their_em.pdf

European Commission. (2014). Modernisation of higher education in Europe: Access, retention and employability 2014. *Eurydice Report.* Luxembourg: Publications Office of the European Commission.

European Commission, DG Education and Culture. (2018). Mid-term evaluation of 2018 of the Erasmus+ -programme - Report of the commission. Retrieved February 26, 2018 at http://eur-lex.europa.eu/legal-content/FR/TXT/?uri=COM:2018:50:FIN

European Commission. (2014). *The Erasmus Impact Study: Effects of mobility on the skills and employability of students and the internationalisation of higher education institutions.* Luxembourg: European Commission.

European Commission. (2017, January 26). From Erasmus to Erasmus+: A Story of 30 years. Retrieved from European Commission: http://europa.eu/rapid/press-release_MEMO-17-83_en.htm

European Commission. (n.d.). Erasmus for young entrepreneurs. Retrieved from http://ec.europa.eu/growth/smes/promoting-entrepreneurship/support/erasmus-young-entrepreneurs_en

Fabling, E. (2016 August). Moving places: Fostering the employability of international graduates. Paper presented at the New Zealand International Education Conference in Wellington, Auckland, New Zealand.

Farrugia, C., Sanger, J., (2017). *Gaining an employment edge: the impact of study abroad on 21st century skills & career prospects.* USA: IIE Center for Academic Mobility Research and Impact.

Fernandez-Chung, R. M., & Leong, Y. C. (2018). *TNE graduate employment study: An analysis of graduate employment trends in Malaysia, Phase III.* Retrieved from https://www.britishcouncil.org/education/ihe/knowledge-centre/developing-talent-employability/analysis-graduate-employment-trends-malaysia

Fernandez-Chung, R. M., Cheong, K. C., Ching, L. Y., & Hill, C. (2014). *TNE graduate employment study: An analysis of graduate employment trends in Malaysia, Phase I.* Retrieved from https://www.britishcouncil.org/education/ihe/knowledge-centre/developing-talent-employability/analysis-graduate-employment-trends-malaysia

Fernandez-Chung, R. M., Cheong, K. C., Ching, L. Y., & Hill, C. (2015). *TNE graduate employment study: An analysis of graduate employment trends in Malaysia, Phase II.* Retrieved from https://www.britishcouncil.org/education/ihe/knowledge-centre/developing-talent-employability/analysis-graduate-employment-trends-malaysia

Ferrazzi, K. (2012). How successful virtual teams collaborate. *Harvard Business Review.* Retrieved from: https://hbr.org/2012/10/how-to-collaborate-in-a-virtua

Fielden, J., Middlehurst, R., & Woodfield, S. (2007). *Global horizons for UK students.* London: The Council for Industry and Higher Education.

Filter Bubble. (n.d.). In Wikipedia. Retrieved from: https://en.wikipedia.org/wiki/Filter_bubble

Finch, D. J., Hamilton, L. K., Baldwin, R., & Zehner, M. (2013). An exploratory study of factors affecting undergraduate employability. *Education + Training, 55*(7), 681–704.

Finch, D. J., Peacock, M., Levallet, N., & Foster, W. (2016). A dynamic capabilities view of employability: Exploring the drivers of competitive advantage for university graduates. *Education + Training, 58*(7), 61–81.

Fitch, K., & Desai, R. (2012). Developing global practitioners. *Journal of International Communication, 18*(1), 63–78.

Fletcher, D., & Sakar, M. (2013). Psychological resilience: A review and critique of definitions, concepts, and theory. *European Psychologist, 18*, 12–23.

Foreign Affairs, Trade and Development Canada (DFATD). (2014, January 15). Canada's international education strategy: Harnessing our knowledge advantage to drive innovation and prosperity. Retrieved on January 15 from: http://international.gc.ca/global-markets-marches-mondiaux/assets/pdfs/overview-apercu-eng.pdf

Franklin, K. (2010). Long-term career impact and professional applicability of the study abroad experience. *Frontiers: The Interdisciplinary Journal of Study Abroad, 19*, 169–190.

Fry, G. W., & Paige, R. M. (2008, May 27). *Study abroad for global engagement: A preliminary report on the SAGE research project.* Proceedings from NAFSA conference 2008. Washington, DC: NAFSA.

Fugate, M., Kinicki, A. J., & Ashforth, B. E. (2004). Employability: A psycho-social construct, its dimensions, and applications. *Journal of Vocational Behavior, 65*(1), 14–38.

Funk, A., Den Heijer, J., Schuurmans-Brouwer, A., & Walenkamp, J. (2014). *Internationalizing curricula: Needs and wishes of alumni and employers with regard to international competences.* The Hague: The Hague University of Applied Sciences.

Gacel-Avila, J. (2018). Internationalization of higher education in Mexico: Progress and challenges. In R. Helms (Ed.), *Mapping internationalization globally: National profiles and perspectives* (pp. 24–27). American Council on Education: Washington, DC.

Galloway, T., Lippman, L., Burke, H., Diener, O., & Gates, S. (2017). *Measuring soft skills and life skills in international youth development programs: A review and inventory of tools.* Retrieved from https://static.globalinnovationexchange.org/s3fs-public/asset/document/YP_Action_Measuring_Soft_Skills_in_Youth_Dev_Programs_Final.pdf?kPg0blMupuZf3EPxWGt_or.RsldKDZie

Garam, I., & Andreotti, V., (2015). *Facts Express 1b/2015: Do mobility periods change students' attitudes?* Helsinki, Finland: Centre for International Mobility CIMO.

Garam, I. (2005). *Opiskelijoiden kansainvälinen liikkuvuus ja työelämä. Työnantajien näkemyksiä ulkomailla opiskelun ja harjoittelun merkityksestä.* Helsinki, Finland: Centre for International Mobility CIMO (in Finnish only).

Gardner, P., Gross, L., & Steglitz, I. (2008). *CERI research brief. Unpacking your study abroad experience: Critical reflection for workplace competencies* (CERI research brief 1–2008). East Lansing: Collegiate Employment Research Institute, Michigan State University.

Garton, C., & Wegryn, K. (2006). *Managing without walls: Maximize success with virtual, global and cross-cultural teams.* Lewisville, Texas, USA.

GATE, Global Alliances for Transnational Education. (1997). *Certification Manual.*

Gault, J., Leach, E., & Duey, M. (2010). Effects of business internships on job marketability: The employers' perspective. *Education + Training, 52*(1), 76–88.

Getnet, T. (2017). Over 100 recent graduates in Addis lack jobs. *Capital News*, April 2, 2017.

Go International. (2018). *Latest mobility facts and figures.* Retrieved from Go International, http://go.international.ac.uk/content/how-many-students-are-going-abroad-uk

Gothard, J., Gray, T., & Downey, G. (2012). *Bringing the learning home: Programs to enhance study abroad outcomes in Australian universities: Final Report.* Dept. of Education, Australian Government: Canberra.

Government, V. (2008). *Quyết định số 1505/QĐ-TTG của Thủ tướng Chính phủ: Phê duyệt Đề án "Đào tạo theo chương trình tiên tiến tại một số trường đại học Việt Nam giai đoạn 2008 - 2015"* (Prime Minister's Decision 1505/QĐ-TTg: Approval of implementing advanced programs in selected Vietnamese universities for the period 2008-2015. Ha Noi, Vietnam: Vietnamese Government.

Grapragasem, S., Krishnan, A., & Mansor, A. N. (2014). Current trends in Malaysian higher education and the effect on education policy and practice: An overview. *International Journal of Higher Education, 3*(1), 85–93.

Gray, J., Jerde, T., Prabhakaran, R., & Carroll, C. (2016). Knack science & data analytics report, (2) Sept 2016.

Green, W., Gallagher, J., Colbeck, D., Gothard, J. & King, E. (2016). "Putting your international experience to work". http://www.murdoch.edu.au/tlc/project/pisaew/the_team.html

Green, W., & Leggett, A. (2014). Beyond the numbers: Enhancing the quality of learning in study abroad programs. *HERDSA Conference*, July 2014: Hong Kong. http://conference.herdsa.org.au/2014/pdf/8d(i).pdf

Green, W., & Whitsed, C. (2013). Reflections on an alternative approach to continuing professional learning for internationalisation of the curriculum across disciplines. *Journal of Studies in International Education, 17*(2), 148–164.

Green, W., & Whitsed, C. (Eds.) (2015). *Critical perspectives on internationalising the curriculum in disciplines: Reflective narrative accounts from business, education and health.* Rotterdam: Sense Publishers.

Green, W., Gannaway, D., Sheppard, K., & Jamarani, M. (2015). What's in their baggage? The cultural and social capital of Australian students preparing to study abroad. *Higher Education Research & Development. 34*(3), 513–526.

Gribble, C. (2015). *Enhancing the employability of international graduates. A guide for Australian education providers.* Melbourne: IEAA.

Gribble, C. (2016). *Student mobility paramount to prosperity, but access remains a challenge - Report on key themes of APAIE 2016 Conference.* Retrieved from The Observatory on Borderless Higher Education: file:///C:/Users/cam716/Downloads/GA2%20APAIE%20 report%20FINAL%208Mar16%20(1).pdf

Gribble, C., & Tran, L. (2016). *International Trends in Learning Abroad; Information and Promotions Campaign for Student Mobility.* Universities Australia. Retrieved from https://www.universitiesaustralia.edu.au/uni-participation-quality/students/outbound-mobility/IEAA-Research-on-Learning-Abroad#.W8-rG1Uzaot

Grove, M. B., & Ham, C. (2017). "Assessment of the Iacocca International Internship Program." *3rd Annual Assessment Symposium.* Lehigh University, Bethlehem, PA.

Hadis, B. F. (2005). Gauging the impact of study abroad: How to overcome the limitations of a single-cell design. *Assessment and Evaluation in Higher Education, 30*(1), 3–19.

Hager, P., & Holland, S. (2006). *Graduate attributes, learning and employability* (Volume. 6). Dordrecht, Netherlands: Springer Science & Business Media.

Hanapi, Z., & Nordin, M. S. (2013). Unemployment among Malaysia graduates: Graduates' attributes, lecturers' competency and quality of education. *Procedia - Social and Behavioral Sciences, 112*, 1056–1063.

Hao, J., & Wen, W. (2016). When sojourners return: Employment opportunities and challenges facing high-skilled Chinese returnees. *Asian and Pacific Migration Journal, 25*, 22–40.

Hao, J., & Welch, A. (2012). A tale of sea turtles: Job seeking experiences of Hai Gui (high skilled returnees) in China. *Higher Education Policy, 25*, (2012), 243–260.

Harvey, L. (2001). Defining and measuring employability. *Quality in Higher Education, 7*(2), 97–109.

Harvey, L., Moon, S., Geall, V., & Bower, R. (1997). *Graduates' work: organisational change and students' attributes.* Birmingham: Centre for Research into Quality.

Haselberger, D., Oberhuemer, P., Perez, E., Cinque, M., & Capasso, F. (2012). Mediating soft skills at higher education institutions: Guidelines for the design of learning situations supporting soft skills achievement. Retrieved from: https://geacollege.si/wpcontent/ uploads/2015/12/MODES_handbook_en.pdf

Hautamäki, A., Leppänen, J., Mokka, R., & Neuvonen, A. (2017). *From pause to play.* Helsinki, Finland: Sitra Memorandum.

Havergal, C. (2016). Falling international student numbers "cost UK £8 billion." *Times Higher Education.* Retrieved from https://www.timeshighereducation.com/news/ falling-international-student-numbers-cost-uk-eight-billion-pounds

HE Global. (2016). *The scale and scope of UK higher education transnational education.* London: UK HE International Unit.

HE Research snipped #29. (2018). A degree is not enough: The universities that succeed and fail in 'selling' their story on future employability. https://blog.youthsight. com/a-degree-is-not-enough-the-universities-that-succeed-and-fail-in-selling-their-story-on-future-employability?utm_campaign=HE%20GDPR%20Save%20The%20 List&utm_source=hs_email&utm_medium=email&utm_content=62295003&_hsenc=p2AN-qtz-8CQw75B0TC-qn1_OX28BTLmiVpY2Tj2UkWSV6vHAH7TcmhvCbSqoxJ8 ZmHao6oekxqO_Q427zYXIoMwsRHd1JkI2YOgg&_hsmi=62295003

Helyer, R., & Lee, D. (2014). The role of work experience in the future employability of higher education graduates. *Higher Education Quarterly, 68*(3), 348–372.

Hemming Lou, K., & Weber Bosley, G. (2012). Facilitating intercultural learning abroad: The targeted intervention model. In M. Vande Berg, R.M. Paige, & K. Hemming Lou (Eds.), *Student Learning Abroad* (pp. 335–359). Virginia: Stylus.

Hickey, B. (2017). Newsroom Pro's 8 things at 8: Migration debate turns ugly after new record high. 27 April 2017. Retrieved from https://pro.newsroom.co.nz/articles/1652-newsroom-pro-s-8-things-at-8-migration-debate-turns-ugly-after-new-record-high

Hillage, J., &. Pollard, E. (1998). *Employability: Developing a framework for policy analysis.* London: Department for Education and Employment.

Hinchliffe, Geoffrey William and Adrienne Jolly (2010): Graduate identity and employability. In: *British Educational Research Journal* 2010, iFirst Article, (pp. 1–22).

History of Migration. (n.d). In Te Ara The Encyclopedia of New Zealand. Retrieved from https://teara.govt.nz/en/history-of-immigration/page-15

Hoare, L. (2012). Transnational student voices. *Journal of Studies in International Education,* 16(3), 271–286.

Hodges, D., & Burchell, N. (2003). Business graduate competencies: Employers' views on importance and performance. *Asia-Pacific Journal of Cooperative Education,* 4(2), 16–22.

Holmes, L. (2001). Reconsidering graduate employability: The "graduate identity" approach. *Quality in Higher Education,* 7(2), 111–119.

Holmes, L. (2013). Competing perspectives on graduate employability: Possession, position or process? *Studies in Higher Education,* 38(4), 538–554.

Horio, T. (2017). *Internationalization of Japanese higher education.* Tokyo: MEXT. Retrieved from http://injapan.no/wp-content/uploads/2017/11/Horio-MEXT.pdf

Hsieh, H.-F., & Shannon, S. E. (2005). Three approaches to qualitative content analysis. *Qualitative Health Research,* 15(9), 1277–1288.

Huang, R. (2013). International experience and graduate employability: Perceptions of Chinese international students in the UK. *Journal of Hospitality, Leisure, Sport & Tourism,* 13, 87–96.

Hubbard, A., Manginelli, A., Kaltved, D., & Durham, A. (2017) *Marketing your international experience - A self-directed workbook for students preparing for the job interview process.* Stamford, CT: American Institute for Foreign Study Retrieved from https://abroad.du.edu/_customtags/ct_FileRetrieve.cfm?File_ID=13002

Huckel, D., & Ramirez, K. (2016). *New Zealand international education benchmark 2016.* Sydney, Australia: Studymove.

Huckel, D., & Ramirez, K. (2018). *New Zealand international education benchmark 2017.* Sydney, Australia: Studymove.

Humburg, M., Van der Velden, R., & Verhagen, A. (2013). *The employability of higher education graduates: The employers' perspective.* Brussels: European Union.

Hunter, W. D., White, G. P., & Godbey, G. C. (2006). What does it mean to be globally competent? *Journal of Studies in International Education,* 10(3), 267–285.

Iacocca International Internship Program. (n.d.). Retrieved from Office of International Affairs, Lehigh University: https://global.lehigh.edu/internships

Ifenthaler, D., Eseryel, D., & Ge, X. (2012). Assessment for game-based learning. In *Assessment in game-based learning* (pp. 1–8). New York: Springer.

Immigration New Zealand. (2018, 8 August). Changes to post-study work rights for international students. Retrieved from https://www.immigration.govt.nz/about-us/media-centre/news-notifications/changes-to-post-study-work-rights-for-international-students

Institute of International Education. (2015). *Open doors: Report on international education.* New York: Institute of International Education (IIE).

Institute of International Education. (2017). *Open doors: Report on international education.* New York: Institute of International Education (IIE).

Institute of International Education. (n.d., a). *Generation study abroad.* Retrieved from Institute of International Education: https://www.iie.org/Programs/Generation-Study-Abroad/About

Institute of International Education. (n.d., b). *Benjamin Gilman study abroad scholarship.* Retrieved from https://www.gilmanscholarship.org/

Institute of International Education. (n.d.,c). *Brazil scientific mobility program.* Retrieved from https://www.iie.org/Programs/Brazil-Scientific-Mobility

Institute of International Education. (2018). *Open doors: Report on international education.* New York: Institute of International Education.

International Education Association of Australia. (2016). *International students: A guide for Australian employers.* Melbourne: IEAA.

Jackson, D. (2015). Employability skill development in work-integrated learning: Barriers and best practice. *Studies in Higher Education, 40*(2), 350–367.

Jackson, D. (2016). Re-conceptualising graduate employability: The importance of pre-professional identity. *Higher Education Research & Development, 35*(5), 925–939.

James-MacEachern, M., & Dongkoo, Y. (2016). Exploring factors influencing international students' decision to choose a higher education institution. A comparison between Chinese and other students. *International Journal of Educational Management, 31*(3), 343–363.

JASSO. (2012). *Tracking survey on Japanese people studied abroad.* Tokyo: Author. (Published in Japanese). Retrieved from http://ryugaku.jasso.go.jp/link/link_statistics/link_statistics_2012/

JASSO. (2018). *Job hunting guide for international students.* Tokyo: Author. Retrieved from https://www.jasso.go.jp/en/study_j/job/guide.html

Johnstone, B. (2003). The shape of research in the field of higher education and graduate employment: some issues. *Studies in Higher Education, 28*(4), 414–426

Jones, E. (2010). "Don't worry about the worries": Transforming lives through international volunteering. In E. Jones (Ed.), *Internationalisation and the student voice: Higher education perspectives.* London: Routledge.

Jones, E. (2011). Internationalisation, multiculturalism, a global outlook and employability. *Assessment, Teaching and Learning Journal* (Leeds Metropolitan University), *11*, 21–49.

Jones, E. (2012). Challenging received wisdom. In J. Beelen & H. De Wit (Eds.), *Internationalisation revisited: New dimensions in the internationalisation of higher education* (pp. 35–45). Amsterdam: CAREM.

Jones, E. (2012). Internationalisation and employability: Are we missing a trick? *FORUM EAIE Magazine.*

Jones, E. (2013). Internationalization and employability: The role of intercultural experiences in the development of transferable skills. *Public Money & Management, 33*(2), 95–104.

Jones, E. (2013a). Internationalisation and student learning outcomes. In H. de Wit (Ed.), *An Introduction to Higher Education Internationalisation.* Milan: Vita e Pensiero.

Jones, E. (2013b). Internationalization and employability: The role of intercultural experiences in the development of transferable skills. *Public Money & Management, 33*(2), 95–104.

Jones, E. (2014). Graduate employability and internationalization of the curriculum at home. *International Higher Education, 78*, Special Issue, 6–8.

Jones, E. (2016). Mobility, graduate employability and local internationalization. In E. Jones, R. Coelen, J. Beelen, & H. de Wit (Eds.), *Global and local internationalization* (pp. 107–116). Rotterdam, The Netherlands: Sense.

Jones, F. (2008). Managing virtual work teams. Society for human resource management. PowerPoint. Retrieved from https://www.shrm.org/academicinitiatives/universities/teachingresources/Documents/ManagingVirtualTeams.ppt

Kajanus, A. (2015). Overthrowing the first mountain: Chinese student-migrants and the geography of power. *Journal of Current Chinese Affairs, 44*(3), 79–102.

Kalafatelis, E., de Bonnaire, C., & Alliston, L. (2018). *Beyond the economic – How international education delivers broad value for New Zealand.* Wellington: Education New Zealand. Retrieved from https://intellilab.enz.govt.nz/document/414-beyond-the-economic-how-international-education-delivers-broad-value-for-new-zealand-pdf

Karmel, T., & Carroll, D. (2016). Has the graduate job market been swamped? NILS Working Paper Series No. 228. *National Institute of Labour Studies,* Finders University: Adelaide, Australia.

Kavanagh, M. H., & Drennan, L. (2008). What skills and attributes does an accounting graduate need? Evidence from student perceptions and employer expectations. *Accounting & Finance, 48*(2), 279–300.

Kehl, K., & Morris, J. (2008). Differences in global-mindedness between short-term and semester-long study abroad participants at selected private universities. *Frontiers: The Interdisciplinary Journal of Study Abroad, 15,* 67–79.

Keller, J. M. (1987). Development and use of the ARCS model of instructional design. *Journal of Instructional Development, 10*(3), 2–10.

Kelley, C., & Meyers J. (1995). *Cross-cultural adaptability inventory* (rev. ed.). Minneapolis: National Computer Systems.

Kelly, K. (2000). The higher education system in Vietnam. *World Education News and Reviews, 13*(3), 5–6.

Kelly, L. (2018). How China is winning back more graduates from foreign universities than ever before. Forbes. https://www.forbes.com/sites/ljkelly/2018/01/25/how-china-is-winning-back-more-graduates-from-foreign-universities-than-ever-before/#717809585c1e

Kemmis, S. 2007. Action research. In M. Hammersley (Ed.), *Educational research and evidence-base practice* (pp. 167–180). London: SAGE Publications.

Killick, D. (2018). *Developing intercultural practice: Academic development in a multicultural and globalizing world.* London: Routledge.

Kinash, S., Crane, L., Judd, M. M., & Knight, C. (2016). Discrepant stakeholder perspectives on graduate employability strategies. *Higher Education Research and Development, 35*(5), 951–967.

King, M. (2003). *The Penguin history of New Zealand.* Auckland, NZ: Penguin Group.

King, R., Findlay, A., & Arens, J. (2010). *International student mobility Literature Review.* Report to HEFCE, and co-funded by the British Council, UK National Agency for Erasmus. London: Higher Education Funding Council for England.

Knight, J. (2003). Updated definition of internationalization. *International Higher Education 33,* 2–3.

Knight, J. (2016). Transnational education remodelled: Toward a common TNE framework and definitions. *Journal of Studies in International Education, 20*(1), 34–47.

Knight, J., & McNamara, J. (2017). *Transnational education: A classification framework and data collection guidelines for international programme and provider mobility (IPPM).* London: British Council and DAAD.

Knight, P. T., & Yorke, M. (2003). *Assessment, learning and employability.* Maidenhead: SRHE and Open University Press.

Knight, P. T. & Yorke, M. (2004) *Learning, curriculum and employability in Higher education*. London: RoutledgeFarmer.

Knight, P., & Yorke, M. (2006). *Employability: Judging and communicating achievements*. No. 2 of the ESECT "Learning and Employability" series. York: Higher Education Academy.

Knowles, C. (2012). *Young Chinese migrants in London*. In Goldsmiths, University of London and Runnymede Trust, London.

Kok, W. (2004). *Facing the Challenge: The Lisbon Strategy for Growth and Employment*. High Level Group: Lisbon.

Kopp, R. (2012, July 26). Rotation fatigue in Japanese companies. *Japan Intercultural Consulting*. Retrieved from https://japanintercultural.com/en/news/default.aspx?news ID=194

Kormos, C., & Gifford, R. (2014). The validity of self-report measures of proenvironmental behavior: A meta-analytic review. *Journal of Environmental Psychology, 40*, 359–371.

Kosmützky, A., & Putty, R. (2016). Transcending borders and traversing boundaries: A systematic review of the literature on transnational, offshore, cross-border, and borderless higher education. *Journal of Studies in International Education, 20*(1), 8–33.

Kostelijk, E., Coelen, R., & De Wit, H. (Eds.) (2015). *The development of international competences by IBMS alumni; An examination of the match between education and professional needs*. Amsterdam: Centre for Applied Research on Economics and Management.

Kuh, G., O'Donnell, K., & Reed. S. (2013). *Ensuring quality and taking high-impact practices to scale*. Washington, DC: American Association of Colleges & Universities.

Labi, A. (2010). What do international students want? Jobs. *Chronicle of Higher Education, 56*(28), 32–34.

Lai, E., (2011). *Metacognition: A literature review*. Pearson Research Report. Retrieved June 30, 2018 from http://images.pearsonassessments.com/images/tmrs/metacognition_literature_review_final.pdf

Laurillard, D. (1997). *Applying systems thinking to higher education*. Position paper, Milton Keynes: Open University.

Leask, B. (2012). *Internationalisation of the curriculum in action; A guide*. Adelaide: University of South Australia.

Leask, B. (2015). *Internationalizing the curriculum*. London: Routledge.

Leask, B., & Bridge, C. (2013). Comparing internationalisation of the curriculum in action across disciplines: Theoretical and practical perspectives. *Compare, 43* (1), 79–101.

Leggott, D., & Stapleford, J. (2007). Internationalisation and employability. In E. Jones & S. Brown (Eds.), *Internationalising higher education* (pp. 120–134). London: Routledge.

Leitch, Lord S. (2006). *Leitch review of skills: Prosperity for all in the global economy – world class skills*. HM Treasury. London.

Leo, M. (2016). What you didn't know about fresh graduate unemployment in Malaysia. *EduAdvisor*. Retrieved from https://eduadvisor.my/articles/what-you-didnt-know-fresh-graduate-unemployment-malaysia-infographic/

Leppänen, J., Lähdemäki, J., Mokka, R., Neuvonen, A., Orjasniemi, M., & Ritola, M. (2013). *Piilotettu osaaminen*. Helsinki, Finland: Demos Helsinki.

Leppänen, J., Saarinen, M., Nupponen, M., & Airas, M. (2014). *Hidden competences, Faktaa - Facts and Figures 1/2014*. Helsinki, Finland: Centre for International Mobility CIMO.

Leung, A. K. Y., & Cohen, D. (2011). Within, and between-culture variation: Individual differences and the cultural logics of honor, face, and dignity cultures. *Journal of Personality and Social Psychology, 100*(3), 507–526.

Li, C. (2007). Foreign-educated returnees in the People's Republic of China: Increasing political influence with limited official power. *JIMI/RIMI 7*(4), 493–516.

Lilley, K. (2014). *Educating global citizens: Translating the 'idea' into university organisational practice.* Melbourne: International Education Association of Australia.

Lim, Y. M., Lee, T. H., Yap, C. S., & Ling, C. C. (2016). Employability skills, personal qualities, and early employment problems of entry-level auditors: Perspectives from employers, lecturers, auditors, and students. *Journal of Education for Business, 91*(4), 185–192.

Lin, H.-W., & Lin, Y.-L. (2014). Digital educational game value hierarchy from a learners' perspective. *Computers in Human Behavior, 30*, 1–12.

Lowry, D., Molloy, S., & McGlennon, S. (2008). Future skill needs: projections and employers' views. *Australian Bulletin of Labour, 34*(2), 192–247.

Luo, Y. Huang, Y. & Wang, S. L. (2011). Guanxi and organisational performance: A meta-analysis. *Management and Organization Review, 8*(1), 139–172.

Maddux, W., Bivolaru, E., Hafenbrack, A., Tadmor, C. & Galinsky, A. (2013). *Expanding Opportunities by Opening Your Mind: Multicultural Engagement Predicts Job Market Success Through Longitudinal Increases in Integrative Complexity.* Social Psychological and Personality Science, Sage Publications. Retrieved from http://spp.sagepub.com/content/early/2013/12/10/1948550613515005

Madison, D. S. (2011). *Critical ethnography: Method, ethics, and performance.* Thousand Oaks: SAGE Publications.

Maharason, M. & Hay, D. (2001). Higher Education and Graduate Employment in South Africa. *Quality in Higher Education, 7*: 2, 139–147.

Maher, A., & Graves, S. (2008). *Graduate Employability. Can higher education deliver?* Newbury Berks: Threshold Press.

Malerich, J. (2009). *The Value of international internships in global workforce development.* Tempe, AZ: Arizona State University. Retrieved from http://www.aieaworld.org/assets/docs/Issue_Briefs/thevalueofinternationalinternshipsinglobalworkforcedevelopment_malerich.pdf

Malicki, S., & Potts, D. (2013). *The outcomes of outbound student mobility: A summary of academic literature.* Retrieved from http://aimoverseas.com.au/wp-content/uploads/2013/08/UAAsiaBoundOutcomesResearch-Final.pdf

Matherly, C. A., & Tillman, M. J. (2015). Higher education and the employability agenda. In J. Huisman, H. de Boer, D. Dill, & M. Souto-Otero (Eds.), *The Palgrave international handbook of higher education policy and governance* (pp. 281–299). London: Palgrave Macmillan.

Matherly, C., Phillips, S., & Ragusa, G. (2015). International v. domestic research experiences for undergraduates (REU): A three year assessment of the preparation of students for global workforces. *American Society of Engineering Education.* New Orleans: ASEE.

Matross Helms, R., Rumbley, L. E., Brajkovic, L., & Miut, G. (2015). *Internationalizing higher education worldwide: National policies and programs.* Washington: American Council on Education.

Maud, J., Blum, N., Short, N., & Goode, N. (2012). *Veterinary students as global citizens: Exploring opportunities for embedding the global dimension in the undergraduate veterinary curriculum.* London: Royal Veterinary College and Development Education Research Centre, Institute of Education.

McBurnie, G., & Ziguras, C. (2006). *Transnational education. Issues and trends in offshore higher education,* London: Routledge.

McCrostie, J. (2017, August 9). More Japanese may be studying abroad, but not for long. *Japan Times.* Retrieved from https://www.japantimes.co.jp/community/2017/08/09/issues/japanese-may-studying-abroad-not-long/#.WieCWTdx2Ul

McKinsey Quarterly. (2013): Mapping China's middle class. URL: https://www.mckinsey.com/industries/retail/our-insights/mapping-chinas-middle-class

McMahon, M. (2006). Career development: A project for the 21st century. *Australian Journal of Career Development, 15*(3), 12–15.

McNamara, J., & Knight, J. (2014). *Impacts of transnational education on host countries: Academic, cultural, economic and skills impacts and implications of programme and provider mobility.* London: British Council.

McNamee, S., & Faulkner, G. (2001). The International exchange experience and the social construction of meaning. *Journal of Studies in International Education, 5*(1), 64–78.

McQuaid, R., & Lindsay, C. (2005). The concept of employability. *Urban Studies, 42*(2), 197–219.

Meester, E., Bergsen, S., & Kirschner, P. (2017, 22 December). *De holle retoriek van 21st century skills; Why would knowledge be less important?* [The empty rhetoric of 21st century skills; why would knowledge be less important?] Retrieved from https://www.scienceguide.nl/2017/12/holle-retoriek-21st-century-skills/

Mellors-Bourne, R., Jones, E., & Woodfield, S. (2015). *Transnational education and employability development.* York: Higher Education Academy.

Mernard-Warwick, J., & Palmer, D. (2012). Eight versions of the visit to La Barranca: Critical discourse analysis of a study-abroad narrative from Mexico. *Teacher Education Quarterly*, Winter, 121–138.

MEXT-Tobitate Office. (2017). *Survey on recruitment and study abroad.* Tokyo: Author. (Published in Japanese). Retrieved from https://mext.s3.amazonaws.com/2017/06/20170629.pdf

MEXT. (2017). *Current status of Japanese studying abroad.* Tokyo: Author. (Published in Japanese). Retrieved from http://www.mext.go.jp/a_menu/koutou/ryugaku/__icsFiles/afieldfile/2017/12/27/1345878_02.pdf

MEXT. (2018). *Current state and policy measures for international educational exchange.* Tokyo: Author. (Published in Japanese). Retrieved from http://www.mext.go.jp/b_menu/shingi/chukyo/chukyo4/043/siryo/__icsFiles/afieldfile/2019/01/21/1396556_6.pdf

Minami, T. (2018). *Japanese higher education policy for internationalization.* Tokyo: MEXT. Retrieved from http://www.jafsa.org/archives/001/201807/JAFSA%20Session_Tetsuhito%20Minami%20(NAFSA2018).pdf

Ministry of Business Innovation and Employment. (2016). Migration trends 2015/16. Retrieved from https://www.mbie.govt.nz/publications-research/research/migrants—monitoring/migration-trends-and-outlook-2015-16.pdf

Ministry of Business Innovation and Employment. (2018). Immigration and labour market outcomes of international tertiary students. Retrieved from https://www.mbie.govt.nz/publications-research/research/migrants—economic-impacts/immigration-and-labour-market-outcomes-march-2018.pdf

Ministry of Education, Federal Democratic Republic of Ethiopia. (2017). Education statistics annual abstract 2008 E.C. (2015/16). Report retrieved from http://www.moe.gov.et/statistics/-/asset_publisher/mlyNlPkHf57h/document/id/56803?inheritRedirect=false&redirect=http%3A%2F%2Fwww.moe.gov.et%2Fstatistics%3Fp_p_id%3D101_INSTANCE_mlyNlPkHf57h%26p_p_lifecycle%3D0%26p_p_state%3Dnormal%26p_p_mode%3Dview%26p_p_col_id%3Dcolumn-1%26p_p_col_count%3D2

Ministry of Education, Malaysia. (2015). Executive summary. Malaysia Education Blueprint 2015–2025 (Higher Education). Retrieved from Malaysia: http://www.moe.gov.my/images/dasar-kpm/articlefile_file_003108.pdf

Ministry of Education. (2017). Destinations and employment outcomes of young, international graduates. Factsheets and data tables retrieved from https://www. educationcounts.govt.nz/publications/tertiary_education/education-outcomes/ destinations-and-employment-outcomes-of-young,-international-graduates

Ministry of Higher Education. (2012a). *The national graduate employability blueprint 2012–2017*. Putrajaya: Ministry of Higher Education Malaysia.

Ministry of Higher Education. (2012b). Preliminary report: Malaysia education blueprint 2013–2025. Retrieved from http://www.moe.gov.my/en/pelan-pembangunan-pendidikan-malaysia-2013-2025

Ministry of Internal Affairs and Communications. (2017). *Policy evaluation of the promotion of global human resources development*. Tokyo: Author. (Published in Japanese). Retrieved from http://www.soumu.go.jp/main_content/000496468.pdf

Ministry of Training, Colleges and Universities (MTCU). (2016). Developing global opportunities: Creating a postsecondary international education strategy for Ontario. Discussion Paper. Retrieved on April 15, 2016 from https://www.tcu.gov.on.ca/pepg/consultations/international_education_strategy.html

MOET. (2016). *Hội nghị tổng kết đề án "Đào tạo theo chương trình tiên tiến tại một số trường đại học Việt Nam, giai đoạn* 2008–2015 (Implementing advanced university programs in some Vietnamese universities between 2008–2015). Summative conference. Hanoi, Vietnam: Ministry of Education and Training.

Mohajeri Norris, E., & Gillespie, J. (2009). How study abroad shapes global careers: Evidence from the United States. *Journal of Studies in International Education, 13*(3), 382–397.

Molony, J., Sowter, B., & Potts, D. (2011). *QS global employer survey report*. London: QS Intelligence.

Momani, B., & Stirk, J. (2017). International education opens doors to the world. *Montreal Gazette*, December 1, 2016. Retrieved from https://www.univcan.ca/media-room/media-releases/opinion-student-mobility-essential-canadas-global-future/

Moore, A., Moore, K., Stephens, C., & Roberts, C. (2018). Government, university and internship provider: When three is not a crowd. Presentation at the Global Internship Conference, Detroit.

Moreau, M-P. & Leathwood, C. (2006). Graduates' employment and the discourse of employability: a critical analysis. *Journal of education and work, 19*:4, 305–324.

Morris-Lange, S., & Brands, F. (2015). *Train and retain: Career support for international students in Canada, Germany, the Netherlands and Sweden*. The Expert Council's Research Unit. Berlin, Germany.

Mtebula, C. T. (2014) Employers and graduates perception survey on employability and graduateness: Products of the School of Construction Economics and Management at the University of Witwatersrand. Research Report. Retrieved from https://core.ac.uk/download/pdf/39676322.pdf

Murdan, S., Blum, N., Francis, S.-A., Slater, E., Alem, N., Munday, M., & Smith, F. (2014). *The global pharmacist*. Institute of Education - London. London: UCL School of Pharmacy & Development Education Research Centre, Institute of Education, University of London.

Murrell, A., & Schultz, B. (2017). Moving from study abroad to career integration: Destigmatizing the goal of employability. In J. Christian & M. Johnson (Eds.), *Career Integration: Reviewing the impact of experiences abroad on employment*. Retrieved from https://www.usg.edu/assets/international_education/documents/2017_CareerIntegration_Book.pdf

NAFSA. (2003). *In America's interest: Welcoming international students*. Report on the Strategic Task Force on International Student Access. January 2003. Retrieved on April 5, 2018 from https://www.nafsa.org/uploadedFiles/NAFSA_Home/Resource_Library_Assets/Public_Policy/in_america_s_interest.pdf

NAFSA. (2018). *Trends in US study abroad*. Retrieved from https://www.nafsa.org/Policy_and_Advocacy/Policy_Resources/Policy_Trends_and_Data/Trends_in_U_S__Study_Abroad/

National Center for Education Statistics. (2018). Table 303.40. Total fall enrolment in degree-granting postsecondary institutions, by attendance status, sex, and age: Selected years, 1970 through 2026. Retrieved from https://nces.ed.gov/programs/digest/d16/tables/dt16_303.40.asp?current=yes

Naylor, S., Bhati, A., & Kidd, P. (2010). *Multiple campus operation-challenges and opportunities in implementing work integrated learning (WIL)*. Paper presented at the Australian Collaborative Education Network Conference, September. Perth Australia. http://researchonline.jcu.edu.au/17009/1/Pages_from_Conf_Proc.ACEN_Article_pdf.pdf

New Oxford Dictionary of English. (2001). Oxford: Oxford University Press.

Ng, C. (2014). Highest and lowest paid fresh graduates, *Free Malaysia Today*. Retrieved from http://www.freemalaysiatoday.com/category/money/2014/05/13/highest-and-lowest-paid-fresh-graduates/

Ngoo, Y. T., Tiong, K. M., & Pok, W. F. (2015). Bridging the gap of perceived skills between employers and accounting graduates in Malaysia. *American Journal of Economics*, 5(2), 98–104.

Nguyen, H. T., Hamid, M. O., & Moni, K. (2016). English-medium instruction and self-governance in higher education: The journey of a Vietnamese university through the institutional autonomy regime. *Higher Education*, 72(5), 669–683.

Nguyen, H. T., Walkinshaw, I., & Pham, H. H. (2017). EMI programs in a Vietnamese university: Language, pedagogy and policy issues. In B. Fenton-Smith, P. Humphreys, & I. Walkinshaw (Eds.), *English medium instruction in higher education in Asia-Pacific* (pp. 37–52). New York: Springer.

Nguyen, T. A. (2009). *The internationalization of higher education in Vietnam: National policies and institutional implementation at Vietnam National University, Hanoi*. Tokyo: Waseda University Global COE Program, Global Institute for Asian Regional Integration (GIARI).

Nilsson, P. A., & Ripmeester, N. (2016). International student expectations: Career opportunities and employability. *Journal of International Students*, 6(2), 614–631.

Nolting, W., Donohue, D., Matherly, C., & Tillman, M. (2013). *Internships, service learning and volunteering abroad*. NAFSA: Association of International Educators: Washington, DC.

Norris, E. M., & Gillespie, J. (2009). How study abroad shapes global careers: Evidence from the United States. *Journal of studies in International Education*, 13(3), 382–397.

Norris, E. M., & Norris, J. G. (2005). Study abroad: Stepping stone to a successful international career. *NACE Journal*, 65(3), 30–36.

Nunn, A., Bickerstaffe, T., Jassi, S., Halliday, S.-A., Mitchell, B., Doyle, J., & Shindler, D. (2008). *UK Commission for Employment and Skills-Employability skills project. Review of evidence on best practice in teaching and assessing employability skills*. Leeds: Policy Research Institute, Leeds Metropolitan University.

O'Mahony, J. (2014). *Enhancing student learning and teacher development in transnational education*. York: Higher Education Academy.

O'Reilly, K., Paper, D., & Marx, S. (2012). Demystifying grounded theory for business research. *Organizational Research Methods, 15*(2), 247–262.

OECD. (2017). *Preparing our youth for an inclusive and sustainable world: The OECD PISA global competence framework*. Paris: OECD Publishing.

OECD and Asia Society. (2018). *Teaching for global competence in a rapidly changing world*. Retrieved March 2, 2018 from https://asiasociety.org/education/teaching-global-competence-rapidly-changing-world

OECD PISA. (n.d.). Retrieved January 3, 2018 from http://www.oecd.org/pisa/pisa-2018-global-competence.htm

OECD. (1996). *Employment and the growth of the knowledge economy*. Paris: OECD Publishing.

OECD. (2011). How many international students stay on in the host country? In *Education at a glance 2011: Highlights*. Paris: OECD Publishing.

OECD. (2013). *The state of higher education 2013*. Paris: OECD Publishing.

OECD. (2016). *Getting skills right: Assessing and anticipating changing skills needs*. Paris: OECD Publishing. Retrieved March 2, 2018 from http://www.oecd-ilibrary.org/employment/getting-skills-right_25206125

OECD. (2017). *Education at a glance 2017: OECD indicators*. Paris: OECD Publishing.

Oliver, P. (2011). Purposive sampling. In V. Jupp (Ed.), *The SAGE dictionary of social research methods*. London: SAGE Publications.

100,000 Strong in the Americas. (n.d.). Retrieved from U.S. Department of State: https://www.state.gov/p/wha/rt/100k/

Ontario Immigration. (2015). *OINP: International student category - Who can apply?* Retrieved April 19, 2016 from http://www.ontarioimmigration.ca/en/pnp/OI_PNPSTUDENTS.html

Ontario Ministry of Citizenship and Immigration. (2014). *A new direction: Ontario's immigration strategy*. Retrieved on October 1, 2018 from https://www.ontario.ca/page/new-direction-ontarios-immigration-strategy

Ota, H. (2018). Internationalization of higher education: Global trends and Japan's challenges. *Educational Studies in Japan: International Yearbook 12*, 91–105.

Ota, H., & Watabe, Y. (2018). Mapping internationalization of Japanese Universities: Goals, strategies and indicators. In H. Ward (Ed.), *Mapping internationalization globally: National profiles and perspectives* (pp. 21–24). Washington, DC: American Council on Education.

Panadero, E., Brown, G. T. L., & Strijbos, J. W. (2016). The future of student self-assessment: A review of known unknowns and potential directions. *Educational Psychology Review, 28*(4), 803–830.

Papademetriou, D., & Sumption, M. (2011). Rethinking points systems and employer – selected immigration. Migration Policy Institute. Washington, DC: USA. Retrieved from http://www.migrationpolicy.org/research/rethinking-points-systems-and-employer-selected-immigration

Park, Z. (2014). *What young graduates do when they leave study. New data on the destination of young graduates*. Wellington: New Zealand Ministry of Education.

Park, Z. (2017). *Moving places – Destinations and earnings of international graduates*. Wellington: New Zealand Ministry of Education.

Patrick, C.-J., Peach, D., Pocknee, C., Webb, F., Fletcher, M., & Pretto, G. (2008). *The WIL (work integrated learning) report: A national scoping study [Final Report]*. Brisbane: Queensland University of Technology.

Patton, M. Q. (2002). *Qualitative research & evaluation methods.* Thousand Oaks CA, USA: SAGE Publications.

Peach, D., Cates, C., Jones, J., Lechleiter, H., & Ilg, B. (2011). Responding to rapid change in higher education: Enabling university departments responsible for work related programs through boundary spanning. *Journal of Cooperative Education and Internships, 45*(1), 94–106.

Pence, H. M., & Macgillivray, I. K. (2008). The impact of an international field experience on preservice teachers. *Teaching and Teacher Education, 24,* 14–25.

Petzold, K. (2017). Studying abroad as a sorting criterion in the recruitment process. *Journal of Studies in International Education.* DOI: 102831531769754.

Playfoot, J., & Hall, R. (2009, April). *Effective education for employment: A global perspective.* Retrieved from http://eee-edexcel.com/xstandard/docs/effective_education_for_employment_web_version.pdf

Pool, L. D., & Sewell, P. (2007). The key to employability: Developing a practical model of graduate employability. *Education and Training, 49*(4), 277–289.

Pop, C., & Barkhuizen, N. (2010). The relationship between skills training and retention of graduate interns in a South Africa information, communication and technology company. *Literacy Information and Computer Education Journal, 1*(2), 75–83.

Potts, D. (2013). *Graduate perceptions of the early career value of international learning mobility: An exploratory study.* AUIDF. Retrieved from http://aiec.idp.com/uploads/pdf/2013-c-041-1-potts-thursday-3.05pm-%20nicholls.pdf

Potts, D. (2015). Understanding the early career benefits of learning abroad programs. *Journal of Studies in International Education, 19*(5), 441–459.

Potts, D. (2016, December 20). *Leading the way for learning abroad.* Retrieved from International Education Association of Australia: https://www.ieaa.org.au/blog/leading-the-way-for-learning-abroad

Potts, D. (2016). *Outcomes of learning abroad programs.* International Education Association of Australia. Retrieved from https://www.universitiesaustralia.edu.au/uni-participation-quality/students/outbound-mobility/IEAA-Research-on-Learning-Abroad#.W4xFz84zbDA

Potts, D. (2018). *Learning abroad and employability: Researching the connections.* International Education Association of Australia. Retrieved from http://ieaa.org.au/documents/item/1267

Prime Minister of Japan and His Cabinet. (2013). *Japan revitalization strategy – Japan is Back.* Tokyo: Author. Retrieved from https://www.kantei.go.jp/jp/singi/keizaisaisei/pdf/en_saikou_jpn_hon.pdf

Prospect Marketing. (2006). *The attitudes and perceptions of Australian employers towards an overseas study experience.* Brisbane: Queensland Education and Training International (QETI) & International Education Association of Australia (IEAA).

Proyecta 100,000. (n.d.). Retrieved from Consulado de Carrera de Mexico en Little Rock: https://consulmex.sre.gob.mx/littlerock/index.php/asuntos-comunitarios/educacion/proyecta-100-000

Prysor, D., & Henley, A. (2017). Boundary spanning in higher education leadership: Identifying boundaries and practices in a British university. *Studies in Higher Education (online),* 1–16.

Pyvis, D., & Chapman, A. (2007). Why university students choose an international education: A case study in Malaysia. *International Journal of Educational Development, 27*(2), 235–246.

QS Intelligence Unit. (2018). *The global skills gap in the 21st century*. London: QS.

QS World University Rankings. (2018). *Graduate employability rankings 2018*. London: QS.

Quek, A. H. (2005). Learning for the workplace: A case study in graduate employees' generic competencies. *Journal of Workplace Learning*, *17*(4), 231–242.

Rafikul, I., Hamid, M., Manaf, N. (n.d.). *Enhancing graduates' employability skills: A Malaysian case*. Retrieved from http://irep.iium.edu.my/28680/1/Rafikul_Malaysia.pdf

Ramón, J., & Cristóbal, S. (2015). The use of game theory to solve conflicts in the project management and construction industry. *International Journal of Information Systems and Project Management*, *3*(2), 43–58.

Ranjit, S. M. (2009). *Make yourself employable: How graduates can hit the ground running!* TQM Consultants Sdn. Bhd. Kuala Lumpur: Malaysia

Rao, T. V., Saxena, S., Chand, V. S., Narendran, R., Bharathan, K., & Jajoo, B. H. (2014). Responding to industry needs: Reorienting management education. *Vikalpa: The Journal for Decision Makers*, *39*(4), 1–10.

Reid, J. (2016). Redefining "Employability" as something to be achieved. *Higher Education, Skills and Work-Based Learning*, *6*(1), 55–68.

Reinders, H. (2014). Can I say something? The effects of digital game play on willingness to communicate. *Language Learning & Technology*, *18*(182), 101–123.

Ripmeester, N. (2014). International businesses: Consumers of global talent? In *Handbook of Internationalisation of Higher Education*. DUZ Academic Publishers, 2014, article, A 2.2–6.

Ripmeester, N. (2016a). *Employer insights: What gets your students hired?* EAIE blog.

Ripmeester, N. (2016b). Internationalisation and employability: Making the connection between degree and the world of work. In E. Jones, R. Coelen, J. Beelen, & H. De Wit (Eds.), *Global and local internationalization* (pp. 121–127). Rotterdam: Sense Publishers.

Ripmeester, N. (2017). Leveraging data to improve your AIR Circle. *CP Magazine*. Rotterdam: Expertise in Labour Mobility.

Ripmeester, N. (2018). When being book-smart is not smart enough. Skills graduates need to succeed in the future workplace. In *Internationalisation of higher education handbook* (pp. 39–48). DUZ Academic Publishers, Issue 1, 2018, E 1.10.

Rizvi, F. (2005). International education and the production of cosmopolitan identities. In A. Arimato, F. Huang, K. Yokoyama, & D. Hiroshima (Eds.), *Globalization and higher education*. Hiroshima: Research Institute of Higher Education.

Robertson, S., Hoare, L., & Harwood, A. (2011). Returnees, student-migrants and second chance learners: Case studies of positional and transformative outcomes of Australian international education. *Compare: A Journal of Comparative and International Education*, *41*(5), 685–698.

Romero, M., Usart, M., & Ott, M. (2015). Can serious games contribute to developing and sustaining 21st century skills? *Games and Culture*, *10*(2), 148–177.

Rose, P. (2013). Internships: Tapping into China's next generation of talent background and internships in China. *Asia-Pacific Journal of Cooperative Education*, *14*(2), 89–98.

Rospigliosi, A., Greener, S., & Bourner, T. (2011). Graduate employability and the propensity to learn in employment: A new vocationalism. *Higher Education Review*, *43*(3), 5–30.

Rowan-Kenyon, H. T., & Niehaus, E. K. (2011). One year later: The influence of short-term study abroad experiences on students. *Journal of Student Affairs Research and Practice*, *48*(2), 213–228.

Rowe, P. (2017). Toward a model of work experience in work integrated learning. In T. Bowen & M. Drysdale (Eds.), *Work-integrated learning in the 21st century (International perspectives on education and society)* (pp. 3–17). West Yorkshire, UK: Emerald Publishing.

Rubin, J., & Tippett, S. (2018, Spring). The SUNY U.S. - Mexico COIL Project: Expanding exchange where travel is limited. *IIE Networker*, 26–27.

Rubin, J. (2017). Embedding collaborative online international learning (COIL) at higher education institutions. In E. Egron-Polak, H. Teekens, L. Purser, & M. Greene (Eds.), *Internationalisation of higher education - A handbook. Volume 2*, 2017., Berlin: Dr Josef Raabe Verlag

Rubin, J., & Guth, S. (2015) Collaborative online international learning, an emerging format for internationalizing curricula. In A. Schultheis-Moore & S. Simon (Eds.), *Globally networked teaching in the humanities*. New York, USA: Routledge.

Saarikallio-Torp, M., & Wiers-Jenssen, J. (Eds.). (2010). *Nordic students abroad. Student mobility patterns, student support systems and labour market outcomes*. Helsinki: The Social Insurance Institution of Finland.

Salina, D., Nurazariah, A., Noraina, M. S., & Rajadurai, J. (2011). Enhancing university business curriculum using an importance-performance approach: A case study of the business management faculty of a university in Malaysia. *International Journal of Educational Management, 25*(6), 545–569.

Salmi, J., Sursock, A., & Olefir, A. (2017). *Improving the performance of Ethiopian universities in science and technology*. Washington: World Bank.

Saunders, V., & Zuzel, K. (2010). Evaluating employability skills: Employer and student perceptions. *Bioscience Education, 15*(1), 1–15.

Savard, A. (2015). Making decisions about gambling: The influence of risk on children's arguments. *The Mathematics Enthusiast, 12*(1), 226–245.

Schech, S., Kelton, M., Carati, C., & Kingsmill, V. (2017). Simulating the global workplace for graduate employability. *Higher Education Research and Development, 36*(7), 1476–1489.

Shah, A., Pell, K. and Brooke, P. (2004). Beyond first destinations: Graduate employability survey. *Active Learning in Higher Education, 5*(9), 9–26.

Shams, F., & Huisman, J. (2012). Managing offshore branch campuses: An analytical framework for institutional strategies. *Journal of Studies in International Education, 16*(2), 106–127.

Shatté, A., Perlman, A., Smith, B., & Lynch, W. (2017). The positive effect of resilience on stress and business outcomes in difficult work environments. *Journal of Occupational and Environmental Medicine, 59*(2), 135–140.

Shen, W. (2005). *A study on Chinese student migration in the United Kingdom*. Berlin: Springer Verlag.

Shimmi, Y., Ota, H., Watabe, Y., & Akiba, H. (2016). Study on the development of global human resource and the long-term impact of study abroad experiences: Results from an online survey for those who studied abroad and who did not. *Journal of Asian Culture Society International, 23*, 3–25. (Published in Japanese).

Shimmi, Y., Akiba, H., Ota, H., & Yokota, M. (2017). Long-term impact of undergraduate study abroad experiences on career: Comparative survey results among degree-seeking study abroad, credit-bearing study abroad, and non-study abroad groups. *Ryugakukoryu (Student Exchanges), 74*, 14–26. (Published in Japanese). Retrieved from https://www.jasso.go.jp/ryugaku/related/kouryu/2017/__icsFiles/afieldfile/2017/05/10/201705ryugakukoryu.pdf

Shimmi, Y., Yonezawa, A., & Akiba, H. (2018). Effect of study abroad experiences on income and career. In M. Yokota, H. Ota, & Y. Shimmi (Eds.), *Impact of study abroad on career development and life* (pp. 156–178). Tokyo: Gakukbunsha. (Published in Japanese).

Sin, I. L. (2013). Cultural capital and distinction: Aspirations of the 'other' foreign student. *British Journal of Sociology of Education, 34*(5–6), 848–867.

Sinek, S. (2011). *Start with why: How great leaders inspire everyone to take action.* London: Penguin.

Singh, P., Thambusamy, R., Ramly, A., Abdullah, I. H., & Mahmud, Z. (2013). Perception differential between employers and instructors on the importance of employability skills. *Procedia- Social and Behavioral Sciences, 90*, 616–625.

Singh, R., Thambusamy, R. X., & Ramly, M. A. (2014). Fit or unfit? Perspectives of employers and university instructors of graduates' generic skills. *Procedia- Social and Behavioral Sciences, 123*, 315–324.

Šlaus, I., & Jacobs, G. (2011). Human capital and sustainability. *Sustainability, 3*(1), 97–154.

Smart, J. (2017). *JW Thomson research on the University of Auckland's 360 Abroad brand.* Presented at the University of Auckland, July 2017.

Smith, A. L. (2013). *Mentoring in the moment: Influences of online cultural mentoring on in-country learning and intercultural competencies* (Order No. 3607938). Available from Dissertations & Theses @ CIC Institutions; ProQuest Dissertations & Theses A&I. (1496774468).

Smith, C., & Worsfold, K. (2015). Unpacking the learning–work nexus: 'Priming' as lever for high-quality learning outcomes in work-integrated learning curricula. *Studies in Higher Education, 40*(1), 22–42.

Smith, J. (2013). The 20 people skills you need to succeed at work. *Forbes.com.* Retrieved from http://www.forbes.com/sites/jacquelynsmith/2013/11/15/the-20-people-skills-you-need-to-succeed-at-work/#1d7f6adc64b5

Smith, M., Brooks, S., Lichtenberg, A., McIlveen, P., Torjul, P., & Tyler, J. (2009). *Career development learning: Maximising the contribution of work-integrated learning to the student experience.* Final project report. June 2009. Wollongong: University of Wollongong.

Soria, K. M., & Troisi, J. (2014). Internationalization at home alternatives to study abroad: Implications for students' development of global, intercultural and international competencies. *Journal of Studies in International Education, 18*(3), 261–280.

Spitzberg, B., & Changnon, P. (2009). Conceptualizing intercultural competence. In D. Deardorff (Ed.), *The SAGE handbook of intercultural competence.* San Francisco: SAGE Publications.

Staff, R. (2010). Agenda for new skills and jobs: EU sets out actions to boost employability and drive reform. Retrieved from http://europa.eu/rapid/press-release_IP-10-1541_en.htm

Standley, H. (2015) International mobility placements enable students and staff in higher education to enhance transversal and employability-related skills. *FEMS Microbiology Letters, 362*(19). Oxford Academic. Retrieved from https://academic.oup.com/femsle/article/362/19/fnv157/496364

Statements by the U.S. President and New Zealand Prime Minister on the TPP signing. (2016, February 5). Retrieved from https://nz.usembassy.gov/statements-by-the-u-s-president-and-new-zealand-prime-minister-on-the-tpp-signing/

Statistics Netherlands. (2018, 23 January). *Studiepuntmobiliteit hoger onderwijs 2015/16* [Credit mobility higher education 2015/16]. Retrieved from https://www.cbs.nl/nl-nl/maatwerk/2018/04/studiepuntmobiliteit-hoger-onderwijs-2015-16

Statistics New Zealand. (2016). *The kiwi factor in record net migration.* Retrieved from http://www.stats.govt.nz/browse_for_stats/population/Migration/international-travel-and-migration-articles/kiwi-factor-migration

Statistics New Zealand. (2018). *Migration drives high population growth.* Retrieved from https://www.stats.govt.nz/news/migration-drives-high-population-growth

Statistics New Zealand. (n.d.). *Census quick stats about a place: Auckland Region.* Retrieved from http://archive.stats.govt.nz/Census/2013-census/profile-and-summary-reports/quickstats-about-a-place.aspx?request_value=13170&tabname=Culturaldiversity

Stuart, G. R., Rios-Aguilar, C., & Deil-Amen, R. (2014). How much economic value does my credential have?: Reformulating Tinto's model to study students' persistence in community colleges. *Community College Review, 42*(4), 327–341.

Sugahara, S., & Coman, R. (2010). perceived importance of cpa's generic skills: A Japanese study. *Asian Journal of Finance & Accounting, 2*(1), 1–23.

Suleman, F. (2016). Employability skills of higher education graduates: Little consensus on a much-discussed subject. Elsevier. *Procedia – Social and Behavioral Sciences, 228,* 169–174.

Sung, H.-Y., Hwang, G.-J., & Yen, Y.-F. (2015). Development of a contextual decision-making game for improving students' learning performance in a health education course. *Computers & Education, 82,* 179–190.

Sutton, R. C., & Rubin, D. L. (2010). *Documenting the academic impact of study abroad: Final report of the GLOSSARI project.* Annual conference of NAFSA: Association of International Educators, Kansas City, MO.

Sutton, R. C., & Rubin, D. L. (2004). The GLOSSARI Project: Initial findings from a system-wide research initiative on study abroad learning outcomes. *Frontiers: The Interdisciplinary Journal of Study Abroad, 10,* 65–82.

Swedish Government Inquiries. (2018). *Internationalisation of Swedish higher education and research; A strategic agenda, summary of the report of the inquiry on increased internationalisation of higher education institutions* (Swedish Government Official Reports, SOU 2018:3). Stockholm: Author.

Tabuchi, H. (2012, May 29). Young and global need not apply in Japan. *The New York Times.* Retrieved from https://www.nytimes.com/2012/05/30/business/global/as-global-rivals-gain-ground-corporate-japan-clings-to-cautious-ways.html

Tamrat, W. (2018a). Graduate employability - whose responsibility? *University World News,* 09 Feb, Issue no 492.

Tamrat, W. (2018b). The importance of understanding inward student mobility. *University World News,* 20 April, Issue no 502.

Taylor, J. (1986). The employability of graduates: Differences between universities. *Studies in Higher Education, 11*(1), 17–27.

Teferra, D. (2014) Charting African higher education – Perspectives at a glance. *International Journal of African Higher Education 1*(1), 9–21.

Teferra, D. (2017a). *Flagship universities in Africa.* Basingstoke, UK: Palgrave Macmillan.

Teferra, D. (2017b). International academics in Africa: The South African experience. In M. Yudekevich, P. G. Altbach, and L. E. Rumbley (Eds.) *International Faculty in Higher Education.* New York: Taylor and Francis.

Teichler, U. (2012). Student mobility in Europe: The informational value of official statistics and graduate surveys. *European Higher Education at the Crossroads, 2012,* 485–509.

Teichler, U. (2015). The impact of temporary study abroad. In R. Mitchell, N. Tracy-Ventury, & K. McManus (Eds.), *Social interaction, identity, and language learning during residence abroad* (pp. 15–32). Amsterdam: Eurosla Monographs Series(4).

Teichler, U., & Janson, K. (2007). The professional value of temporary study in another European country: Employment and work of former ERASMUS students. *Journal of Studies in International Education, 11,* 486–495.

The Economist Intelligence Unit. (2017). *Worldwide educating for the future index*. London: The Economist.

The Netherlands Association of Universities of Applied Sciences. (2014). *Wendbaar in een duurzame economie; Een externe analyse van het economisch domein ten behoeve van de verkenning hoger economisch onderwijs* [Flexible in a sustainable economy; An external analysis of the economic domain for the 'verkenning hoger economisch onderwijs']. The Hague: Author.

The Star Online. (2012 March 4). Education system not producing thinking graduates, say experts. Retrieved from http://www.thestar.com.my/news/nation/2012/03/04/education-system-not-producing-thinking-graduates-say-experts/

The Value of Education. (2014). *Springboard for success*. London: HSBC Holdings plc.

The Value of Education. (2015). *Learning for life*. London: HSBC Holdings plc.

Thiru, S., & Ang, K. (2012). The bar council's employability survey: How employable are the new entrants to the bar? *Praxis, Oct.–Dec.*, 16–19.

Tibby, M. (2012, May 16–17). Learning for life and work: Re-configuring employability for the 21st century. *Report on Teaching and Learning Summit*, Manchester.

Tillman, M. (2012). Employer perspectives on international education. In D. Deardorff, H. de Wit, J. Heyl, & T. Adams (Eds.), *The SAGE handbook of international higher education*. San Francisco: SAGE Publications.

Tomlinson, M. (2007). Graduate employability and student attitudes and orientations to the labour market. *Journal of Education and Work, 20*(4), 285–304.

TOMODACHI *Initiative 2016 Annual Report*. (2016). Tokyo: Tomodachi.

TOMODACHI. (n.d.). Retrieved from http://usjapantomodachi.org/

Tran, L. T., Le, T. T. T., & Nguyen, N. T. (2014). Curriculum and pedagogy. In *Higher education in Vietnam: Flexibility, mobility and practicality in the global knowledge economy* (pp. 86–107). London: Palgrave Macmillan UK.

Tran, T. T. (2014). Is graduate employability the 'whole-of-higher-education-issue'? *Journal of Education and Work, 28* (3), 207–227.

Trilokekar, R., & El Masri, A. (2016, Sept). Canada's international education strategy: Implications of a new policy landscape for synergy between government policy and institutional strategy. *Higher Education Policy, 29*(4), 539–563.

Trines, S. (2017, September 2017). *Going north: The student mobility outlook from Brazil, Columbia, Mexico and Venezuela*. Retrieved from World Education News & Reviews: https://wenr.wes.org/2017/09/going-north-the-student-mobility-outlook-from-latin-america

Trooboff, S., Vande Berg, M., & Rayman, J. (2008). Employer attitudes towards studying abroad. *Frontiers: The Interdisciplinary Journal of Study Abroad, 15*, 17–33.

Tustin, K., Chee, K. S., Taylor, N., Gollop, M., Taumoepeau, M., Hunter, Poulton, R. (2012). *Extended baseline report: Graduate longitudinal study New Zealand. (2012)*. Wellington: Universities New Zealand.

2017 Foreign Policy White Paper. (2017). Retrieved from www.fpwhitepaper.gov.au

Tymon, A. (2013). The student perspective on employability. *Studies in Higher Education, 38*(6), 841–856.

UNESCO. (2013). *Intercultural competences*. Paris: UNESCO.

UNESCO. (n.d.). *Global flow of tertiary-level students*. Retrieved from http://www.uis.unesco.org/Education/Pages/international-student-flow-viz.aspx

Universities Australia. (2012). Offshore programs of Australian universities. Retrieved from file:///C:/Users/e5105772/Downloads/LINKS%202012%20offshore%20programs%20final.pdf

Universities Australia. (2014). *Offshore programs of Australian universities*. Australia.

Universities Australia. (2015). *National strategy on work integrated learning in university education*. Australia: Universities Australia.

Universities Canada. (2017). Canada's global moment: Students from around the world choose Canada. Retrieved from https://www.univcan.ca/media-room/media-releases/canadas-global-moment-students-around-world-choose-canada/

Universities UK International. (2018). *Gone International: Expanding opportunities: Report on the 2015–16 graduating cohort*. London: Author. Retrieved from https://www.universitiesuk.ac.uk/International/Documents/Gone%20International_expanding%20opportunities_digital.pdf

University of Glasgow. (2011). *Employers' perceptions of the employability skills of new graduates*. London: Edge Foundation.

Van Gaalen, A., & Gielesen, R. (2016). Internationalisation at home: Dutch higher education policies. In E. Jones, R. Coelen, J. Beelen, & H. de Wit (Eds.), *Global and local internationalization* (pp. 149–154). Rotterdam: Sense Publishers.

Van Hoof, H. B., & Verbeeten, M. J. (2005). Wine is for drinking, water is for washing: Student opinions about international exchange programs. *Journal of Studies in International Education, 9*(1), 42–61.

Van Mol, C. (2017). Do employers value international study and internships? A comparative analysis of 31 countries. *Geoforum, 78*, 52–60.

Vande Berg, M., Connor-Linton, J., & Paige, R. M. (2009). The Georgetown Consortium Project: Intervening for student learning abroad. *Frontiers: The Interdisciplinary Journal of Study Abroad, 18*, 1–75.

Vande Berg, M. (2007). Intervening in the learning of US students abroad. *Journal of studies in international education, 11*(3–4), 392–399.

Vereniging Hogescholen & Vereniging van Samenwerkende Nederlandse Universiteiten. (2018, 14 May). *Internationaliseringsagenda hoger onderwijs* [Internationalisation agenda for higher education]. The Hague: Authors.

Vu, T., Rigby, B., Wood, L. N., & Daly, A. (2011). Graduate skills in business learning. *Asian Social Science, 7*(4), 2–11.

Wächter, B. (2017). Europe: Questioning the student mobility imperative. In G. Mihut, P. G. Altbach, & H. de Wit, H. (Eds.), *Understanding higher education internationalization: Insights from key global publications* (pp. 223–226). Rotterdam: Sense Publishers.

Wang, Y. (2012): *Education in a changing world: Flexibility, skills and employability*. The World Bank. Washington DC.

Ward, C. (2001). The A, B, Cs of acculturation. In D. Matsumoto (Ed.), *Handbook of culture and psychology* (pp. 411–446). New York: Oxford University Press.

Watkins, H., & Smith, R. (2018). Thinking globally, working locally: Employability and internationalization at home. *Journal of Studies in International Education, 22*(3), 210–224.

Watts, A. G. (2006). *Career Development Learning and Employability*. York, England, Higher Education Academy.

Webb, G. (2005). Internationalisation of curriculum: An institutional approach. In J. Carroll & J. Ryan (Eds.), *Teaching international students, improving learning for all* (pp. 109–118). London: Routledge.

Welch, B., Vo-Tran, H., Pittayachawan, S., & Reynolds, S. (2012). Crossing borders: Evaluating a work integrated learning project involving Australian and Vietnamese students. *Australian Academic & Research Libraries, 43*(2), 120–134.

West, C. (2017). Leveraging global experiences in the job market. *International Educator*. Washington DC, NAFSA.

Wickramasinghe, V., & Perera, L. (2010). Graduates', university lecturers' and employers' perceptions towards employability skills. *Education + Training, 52*(3), 226–244.

Wiers-Jenssen, J. (2011). Background and employability of mobile vs. non-mobile students. *Tertiary Education and Management, 17*(2), 79–100.

Wilkinson, G. (2017). Access and New Employability Skills. In G. Crosling & G. Atherton (Eds.) *Current and emerging themes in global access to post-secondary education*. Bingley: Emerald Publishing.

Willott, C., Blum, N., Burch, W., Page, B., & Rowson, M. (2012). *The global doctor*. London: UCL Institute for Global Health & Development Education Research Centre, Institute of Education.

Wolf, K., & Yong, K. H. (2009). Industry ready graduates for a global job market–a reflection on transnational education. Paper presented at the Curtin International Business Conference, Miri, Malaysia.

World Bank. (2013). *Skills module survey of Ethiopia*. Washington: World Bank.

World Bank. (2015). *Enterprise Survey Ethiopia*. Retrieved from http://www.enterprisesurveys.org/data/exploreeconomies/2015/ethiopia.

World Bank. (2015). *Ethiopia economic update IV: Overcoming constraints in the manufacturing sector. Africa region*. Washington: World Bank.

World Bank. (2016). *5th Ethiopia economic update. Why so idle? Wages and employment in a crowded labor market*. Washington: World Bank.

World Economic Forum. (2015). *New Vision for education: Unlocking the potential of technology*. Retrieved March 2, 2018 from http://www3.weforum.org/docs/WEFUSA_NewVisionforEducation_Report2015.pdf

Wright, T., Jones, E., & Welland, S. (2018). Learning & employability gains from international experience. In B. Berquist, K. Moore, & J. Milano (Eds.), *International internships: mission, methods & model, a collection of papers from the Global Internship Conference* (pp. 247–262). Boston: Academic Internship Council.

Yokota, M. (2016). *Survey of global personnel development and long-term impact of study abroad*. Tokyo: School of Global Japanese Studies, Meiji University. Retrieved from http://recsie.or.jp/wp-content/uploads/2016/04/Survey-on-study-abroad-impact_EN.pdf

Yonezawa, A. (2010). Japanese corporate society and English with study abroad. *IDE Contemporary Higher Education, 526*, 38–43. (Published in Japanese).

Yorke, M. (2006). Employability in higher education: What it is - what it is not. *Learning and Employability, Series 1*. York: Higher Education Academy. Retrieved from http://www.heacademy.ac.uk/resources/detail/employability/employability336

Zacher, H. (2014). Career adaptability predicts subjective career success above and beyond personality traits and core self-evaluations. *Journal of Vocational Behavior, 84*(1), 21–30.

Zenebe, W. (2018 Feb 28). Thirteen thousand apply for 95 positions at Water and Sewerage Authority. *Ethiopian Reporter* (Amharic News Paper). https://www.ethiopianreporter.com/article/7969. Accessed on 3 March 2018.

Zewde, B. (2002). *Pioneers of Change in Ethiopia: The reformist intellectuals of the early twentieth century*. Addis Ababa: Addis Ababa University.

Ziguras, C. (2018). Australia's cosmopolitan campuses count their blessings. In R. Helms (Ed.), *Mapping internationalization globally: National profiles and perspectives* (pp. 6–9). Washington, DC: American Council on Education.

Ziguras, C., & McBurnie, G. (2011). Higher education in the Asia-Pacific Region: From distance education to the branch campus. In S. Marginson, S. Kaur, & E. Sawir (Eds.), *Higher education in the Asia–Pacific: Strategic responses to globalization* (pp. 105–122). Dordrecht, Netherlands: Springer.

Zimmerman J., & Meyer F. (2013). Do we become a different person when hitting the road? Personality development of sojourners. *Journal of Personality and Social Psychology*, *105*(3), 515–530. American Psychological Association.

Index

Italic and bold page numbers indicate figure and table, respectively.